THE VICTIMS' RIGHTS MOVEMENT

The Victims' Rights Movement

What It Gets Right, What It Gets Wrong

Michael Vitiello

NEW YORK UNIVERSITY PRESS

New York

NEW YORK UNIVERSITY PRESS
New York
www.nyupress.org

© 2023 by New York University
All rights reserved

Please contact the Library of Congress for Cataloging-in-Publication data.
ISBN: 9781479820726 (hardback)
ISBN: 9781479820757 (library ebook)
ISBN: 9781479820740 (consumer ebook)

New York University Press books are printed on acid-free paper, and their binding materials are chosen for strength and durability. We strive to use environmentally responsible suppliers and materials to the greatest extent possible in publishing our books.

Manufactured in the United States of America

10 9 8 7 6 5 4 3 2 1

Also available as an ebook

*To my friend and former Criminal Law Professor Stephen Schulhofer
and to my friend and former colleague Joshua Dressler,
with special recognition for their influence on my
development as a criminal law scholar*

CONTENTS

Introduction: The View from 30,000 Feet   1

1. A Brief History of the Victims' Rights Movement   9

2. What the Victims' Rights Movement Gets Right   23

3. Victimhood, Demagoguery, and Mental Health   32

4. The Warren Court's Criminal Procedure Revolution and
   Its Inspiration for the Victims' Rights Movement   49

5. Eliminating and Extending Statutes of Limitations   65

6. Victim Impact Statements and an Assessment of the
   Value of a Human Life   82

7. California's Three Strikes and You're Out Legislation:
   A Case Study in the VRM's Excesses   122

8. What Should We Do if We Really Want to Help Victims?   145

Acknowledgments   165

Notes   167

Index   237

About the Author   248

Introduction

The View from 30,000 Feet

The Victims' Rights Movement (VRM) has been one of the most consequential political forces in the United States over the past fifty-plus years. It has scored major legislative victories across the country. Every state and the federal government have adopted major VRM laws. Indeed, many states have added VRM policies to their constitutions.[1]

For most of the past fifty-plus years, the VRM drew support from a broad coalition across the U.S. political divide. Some of the VRM's strength came from the fact that organizations with widely different agendas coalesced within the movement. Diverse groups, like Mothers Against Drunk Driving, feminist groups working to expand enforcement of sex offenses and to redefine sexual assault and rape, law-and-order conservatives, and prosecutors and prison guard union organizations, among others, have come together under the VRM's banner.[2]

Politicians of all stripes jumped on board to support various laws to protect victims and to increase criminal sanctions. One branch of the movement traces its roots to the 1960s. Prominent law-and-order advocate Frank Carrington blamed the Warren Court and its criminal procedure revolution for the hike in crime rates.[3] Candidate and then president Richard Nixon used those issues as part of his strategy that led to his victory in 1968. And many of Ronald Reagan's policies originated in the VRM.[4] But politicians from all spots on the spectrum participated in expanding the movement's influence. For example, after Michael Dukakis lost to the first president Bush in 1988, in part because he had no effective counterpunch to Bush's Willie Horton ad, Democrats jumped on the bandwagon.[5] As Professor Aya Gruber has written, "In the wake of that defeat, Democratic senators Joe Biden and Chuck Schumer feared the 'Hortonizing' of the entire Democratic Party."[6] Their strategy included support for various crime control measures that succeeded in reestablishing Democrats as being tough on crime.[7]

Bill Clinton's success in co-opting much of the Republican agenda is widely recognized. That included tough-on-crime legislation. Even Bernie Sanders signed on to the Violence Against Women Act in 1994. While he objected to the reality that the law increased punishment and shifted priorities from education to incarceration, Sanders voted for the bill because it included provisions protecting women.[8]

At least during the decades when the movement gained traction, supporting it seemed like a no-brainer for many politicians.[9] Yet the criminal justice system did little to help crime victims and often left them feeling ignored or worse. Rape victims often felt demeaned by police officers who seemed to accuse them of being complicit in their victimization.[10] More generally, victims had little notice of criminal proceedings, including the resolution of cases in which they were victims.[11]

Beyond basic fairness, like notice to victims, the VRM was able to get far more sweeping legislation passed. Focusing on victims' rights is emotionally appealing. Criminal defendants are often singularly unattractive: someone who has raped and murdered seldom invokes much sympathy. Advocates for expanding victims' rights often are able to portray a victim in a positive light. The battle for the minds and hearts of voters is easy: seemingly a choice between good and evil.[12]

Ironically, the VRM got a foothold shortly after the American Law Institute's (ALI) major project to reform substantive criminal law and the Warren Court's efforts to make meaningful procedural rights for indigent criminal defendants. The ALI's project, drafting the Model Penal Code (MPC), was an effort to bring coherence to the criminal law and to tap into modern social science and psychology. The MPC, even with its blemishes, remains a remarkable effort to professionalize criminal law.[13]

The Warren Court's efforts to expand procedural rights, especially for indigent defendants, were grounded in concerns about racial injustice and the need to limit excessive police misconduct. While its efforts earned criticism from many policy makers and scholars, the Court brought attention to many injustices within the system. Some of its goals, like the requirement that states provide indigent defendants competent counsel, still earn the Court respect. Sadly, the Court's promise has not been fulfilled.[14]

Many supporters of the VRM attacked the Warren Court. The movement's appeal was emotional and tapped into national panic about rising crime rates and backlash against the expansion of minority rights.[15] Similarly, by contrast to the ALI's efforts to rationalize criminal law based on science and a coherent philosophy, the VRM reflects a rejection of expertise; instead, it taps into human emotions, often some of our worst sentiments, such as the desire for vengeance.[16]

Given the breadth of interest groups coming together to advance victims' rights, one should not be surprised that, looking back at the movement's history, some participants have recognized that they advanced regrettable policies. After years of an unsuccessful and wasteful war on drugs, a broad political consensus has begun unraveling some of the draconian criminal sentences for drug offenses. Many Americans now realize that generations of punitive policies have resulted in "mass incarceration" or, as some commentators describe it, the "carceral state."[17] Recent developments have awakened many Americans to the special burden on minority communities resulting from the expansion of the prison system.[18]

In the 1980s, California was a leader in adopting protections for crime victims. It has enshrined several protections in its constitution.[19] After years of prison construction and punitive provisions, the state adopted legislation creating a commission assigned with several tasks, many of which target excessive prison sentences. California is late to the game: many other states have been addressing overuse of prisons for several years.[20]

Despite these trends, the VRM remains an important force in the criminal justice arena. Proponents have succeeded in getting states to adopt a host of bills supporting their agenda. Energized by various sex and child sex abuse scandals, movement members are pushing to eliminate or extend statutes of limitations to allow the prosecution of sex offenders long after the commission of their crimes.[21] The movement retains influence despite countertrends. The #MeToo Movement demonstrates such an example. Many progressives, including many feminists, have joined the call for dismantling the "carceral state." They recognize racial unfairness in the criminal justice system. At the same time, many call for abandoning various protections (typically) for men charged with sex offenses. Consciously or unconsciously, they do so even though such measures will have disparate impacts on poor, often minority, defendants.[22]

The VRM still hopes to secure a victims' rights amendment to the U.S. Constitution.[23] The recognition that the United States has created a massive prison-industrial complex, unnecessary to protect public safety, has eroded some of the VRM's momentum, temporarily.[24] The VRM remains active in trying to get its constitutional amendment passed. The recent increase in crime rates, after years of declines, may give the VRM the boost that it needs to push the constitutional amendment across the finish line.[25] That would be unfortunate.

Writing in 2020, professors Paul Cassell and Meg Garvin, two of the most prominent VRM advocates, stated that "a comprehensive history of crime victims' rights in the criminal justice process remains to be written."[26] This book does not take on that task. Instead, it focuses on broad outlines on the VRM, highlighting some of its early history and self-proclaimed successes.

The VRM has accomplished some changes that are universally applauded, including rules requiring notice to victims and, in some instances, funding to help victims receive needed care. Some states have improved the handling of sexual assault cases as well.[27] But many VRM policies come with a significant cost, including adding to mass incarceration. This book is about the VRM, both its accomplishments and its excesses.

Chapter 1 provides a brief history of the movement, focusing on the broad consensus that it has achieved. As has occurred with other significant movements in the United States, groups with different agendas have joined together to advance their common goals.

Chapter 2 explores some of the VRM's most important accomplishments. Among the widely acknowledged achievements are expanded resources to help victims deal with trauma, greater sensitivity to sexual assault victims, and increased chances of receiving restitution from perpetrators of harm.

Chapter 3 begins a frontal critique of the VRM. Initially, it explores how "victimhood" has entered the nation's political dialogue. It then questions whether emphasizing one's status as a victim is psychologically helpful. As argued there, "victimhood" may have deleterious effects on one's need to heal from trauma. The chapter concludes that, along with promises that victims will experience closure by making victim impact statements, the VRM does not serve crime victims well by focusing on their status as victims.

Chapter 4 focuses on the early attack on the Warren Court. Frank Carrington, among others, accused the Court of favoring defendants over victims and urged a leveling of the playing field. The chapter also discusses the reality of Warren Court criminal procedure reforms: critics like Carrington not only overstated the impact of the Court's criminal procedure revolution but also failed to anticipate the Courts' erosion of those protections post-Warren. Today, one can hardly claim that the criminal justice system mollycoddles criminals.

Chapter 5 examines VRM efforts to eliminate or extend dramatically statutes of limitations in sexual assault and child sexual assault cases. It helps put in context the enormous public appeal of many VRM policy positions: how can one argue for the likes of Harvey Weinstein or Bill Cosby in opposing extending statutes of limitations to allow victims to come forward after years of suffering in silence? Or worse, how can one oppose such laws when the elimination of statutes of limitations would allow the state to proceed against pedophilic priests and Boy Scout leaders? Passion aside, such changes in the law, as chapter 5 argues, increase the risk of convicting innocent defendants, a cost that is real and worth avoiding.

Chapter 6 focuses on one of the VRM's major innovations in the criminal justice system: victims' impact evidence and statements. Among other arguments in support of such evidence, many VRM supporters tout victims' participation as needed to make the criminal justice system fair. They also contend that such participation helps victims achieve "closure," some form of healing from the trauma resulting from being crime victims. Chapter 6 explores the claims in favor of such evidence with a skeptical eye. It raises several points, including the constitutional arguments about victim impact evidence as well as a detailed discussion of the harm created by such evidence. The chapter also explores the myth of "closure," a term with no accepted psychological meaning. As argued in chapter 6, victims' rights advocates falsely promise victims a benefit that is not likely to occur through mere participation in the criminal justice system. Further, victims' participation at the criminal justice sentencing phase introduces racial bias into sentencing and increases punishment, especially in death penalty cases.

Chapter 7 picks up on the theme of mass incarceration and the role of the VRM in leading to excessive sentences. The chapter uses California's Three Strikes Law as a case study of the power of the VRM and the ultimate cost of its efforts. Among those costs are destroyed lives of offenders sentenced to prison for terms far longer than needed for social protection, sentences that are often criminogenic, and massive prison construction leading to billions of wasted dollars yielding little in the way of social good. Chapter 7 also turns to a newly emerging recognition that the United States' reliance on prison as a first resort has resulted in mass incarceration. It identifies some of the efforts to reverse that state of affairs, with efforts at changing drug laws and exploring alternatives to prison and expanding rehabilitative measures. But the chapter also identifies countertrends: thus, at a time when many Americans see the need for reform, headline cases often result in knee-jerk legislative reactions, leading to longer prison sentences. The chapter uses an example of California's legislative efforts to reduce drug enhancement while at the same moment increasing penalties for fentanyl drug crimes. Importantly, progress can easily be unraveled depending on the next headline case.

Chapter 8 asks what the nation should do if it really wants to help victims. This book argues that victims' advocates should work for universal health care. Victims need more than what is provided in the criminal justice system. In addition to helping victims, providing first class health care would reduce the number of victimizers. Often lost in the good-victim-bad-offender narrative is the reality that many victimizers were victims at some point in their lives. Chapter 8 also explores efforts to enact meaningful gun control measures. Gun rights advocates like the National Rifle Association (NRA) have developed a powerful narrative to counter inevitable calls for reform following mass murders. According to the NRA, expanded mental health care, not gun control legislation, is the proper remedy. Chapter 8 argues that the NRA has it partially right: a robust health care system is part of the solution. But it also concludes that the NRA's call for health care reform is all talk. More importantly, the chapter discusses the debate about the role of firearms in creating more or fewer victims. Meaningful gun control legislation would reduce harm to victims in two ways. One, fewer crime victims would be killed or experience serious bodily injuries. Two, fewer individuals would become suicides if guns were harder to come by.

The final chapter ends on a sour note. In 2008, the Supreme Court narrowly found that the Second Amendment creates a personal right to bear arms for purposes of self-defense. Since the Court's decision, which contained dicta suggesting many possible limitations that could be imposed on gun ownership, the Court's hard turn to the right has put many gun control measures enacted by blue states at risk of being struck down as violative of the Second Amendment. During the 2021 term, the Court demonstrated its willingness to overturn long-standing gun regulations. Its continued expansion of gun rights promises a sad future for the United States.

1

A Brief History of the Victims' Rights Movement

All fifty states and the federal government have enacted reforms advanced by the Victims' Rights Movement. Many states have incorporated victims' rights protections into their constitutions as well as into their penal codes.[1] The VRM has proposed a federal constitutional amendment to enshrine victims' rights into the Constitution, although the push has slowed in recent years.[2] As two prominent victims' rights advocates have pointed out, even if the federal constitutional amendment does not become law, most states have already adopted the proposed protections into state law.[3]

As indicated in the introduction, this book does not give a comprehensive history of the VRM. Instead, this chapter provides a broad overview of the VRM and explores some of its appeal. At times, for example, states have passed VRM legislation with overwhelming majority support.[4] Voter initiatives have also received similar popular support.[5] VRM reforms have often followed headline cases, highlighting truly innocent victims and their families with whom anyone can empathize.[6] The broad support for many VRM initiatives masks fault lines within the movement. Like other instances where major change has occurred in the United States, the success of the VRM resulted from a broad coalition of political groups with diverse interests at stake.

Today, the VRM may be losing some of its power; the consensus that led to some of its most important reforms has begun to fray. That should not be a surprise. The consensus has frayed, in part, because that accord always masked different strains within the movement. While one might ask, "who can be against victims?," the coalition creating the VRM has included single-issue groups, feminists, tough-on-crime conservatives, and various opportunistic politicians.

Other examples of such diverse coalitions working together abound. For example, the Eighteenth Amendment, which ushered in Prohibition, resulted from a broad coalition. Suffragettes saw saloons as evil

places where husbands squandered their wages on booze and prosti-
tutes.[7] They supported the amendment because they viewed alcohol as
contributing to domestic violence and marital rape. Progressives joined
the movement out of concern for poverty, often associated with drunk-
enness. Anti-German sentiment during the First World War contributed
to the suffragettes' efforts. More generally, so too did anti-immigrant,
anti-Catholic sentiment.[8]

Indeed, women's rights groups joined forces with the Ku Klux Klan.
The Klan's role in the passage of the Eighteenth Amendment helped expand its influence across the United States. Members supported Prohibition because they claimed that Black men were drunkards. The Klan also
focused on Catholic immigrants who drank wine and beer. The group's
anti-Catholic, anti-Semitic, anti-immigrant, and anti-alcohol position
made the Klan attractive to white Protestants, especially evangelicals.[9]
That, in turn, increased Klan membership. But by the end of Prohibition, the coalition that ushered in Prohibition had unraveled.[10]

By comparison, the coalition forming the VRM has been more enduring.[11] Despite that, the VRM's coalition may be unraveling. But I am
getting ahead of the story. This chapter begins with the early moments
of the VRM during the Warren Court years, when the Court's efforts to
address racial discrimination in society generally, and throughout the
criminal justice system specifically, produced a backlash from law-and-
order conservatives. As argued by Frank Carrington, acknowledged as
the father of the VRM, the Court's emphasis on criminal defendants
tipped the balance too far in their favor and ignored crime victims. This
chapter also examines how other actors joined the coalition. Notably,
feminist activists demanded better treatment for rape victims and more
severe punishment for rapists.

Along the way, other groups, often single-issue coalitions, have joined
the movement, adding to the VRM's political influence. Some of those
groups include Mothers Against Drunk Driving, an organization formed
after a drunk driver killed MADD's prime mover's child. Other groups
have sprung up after similar tragedies, including abductions of children
by sexual predators. As developed more fully in chapter 7, other powerful organizations like the National Rifle Association[12] and the California
Correctional Peace Officers Association (CCPOA) have given the VRM
a boost.[13]

This chapter also discusses the role that feminists have played in advancing the VRM's agenda. That discussion relies heavily on Professor Aya Gruber's book *The Feminist War on Crime*. She not only discusses how the feminist movement and the right-wing VRM united during the 1960s and beyond but also explores how, even in an era when many feminists oppose the carceral state, they continue to align with the VRM when it calls for longer punishments for sex offenders.[14]

Finally, this chapter offers some examples of where the VRM's agenda seems to be frayed and asks whether that represents a long-term trend.

Frank Carrington, the Warren Court, and the Early Days

Placing a precise moment when the VRM was born may be impossible. Yet almost certainly, the moment of conception occurred during the Warren Court years, notably between 1961 and 1968 or 1969. As developed in chapter 4, during those years the Court held that protections in the Bill of Rights, historically seen only as limitations on federal power, applied equally as limitations on state power. For example, in *Mapp v. Ohio*, the Court held that state courts had to exclude evidence seized in violation of a defendant's Fourth Amendment right to be free from unreasonable searches and seizures. Even more controversial was the Court's 1966 *Miranda v. Arizona* decision, which required police to provide suspects interrogated while in custody a series of warnings about their rights.

Miranda inspired right-wing law-and-order advocate Carrington to form Americans for Effective Law Enforcement. The organization's goals included working against the Warren Court's due process revolution. Conservative politicians like California governor Ronald Reagan shared Carrington's view that the Supreme Court, liberal judges, and academics were soft on crime. Politicians like 1968 presidential candidate Richard Nixon were listening. "Law and order" would advance his successful bid for the White House in 1968.[15]

Carrington and other victims' rights advocates were aided by the perception that crime was out of control in America's cities. During his campaign, Nixon pointed to smoke and fire engulfing major cities, often caused by riots in impoverished neighborhoods or by police violence against community members. Nixon played upon many Americans' fears when he said, "We hear sirens in the night."[16]

That message overlapped with the message of groups like Carrington's, which claimed to speak for forgotten Americans. Stereotypically, members of the Silent Majority were not college educated. They were not experts in criminal justice policy; they were hardworking Americans who "drive the spirit of America."[17]

Nixon's first vice president, Spiro Agnew, was at least as adept as Nixon in tapping into the working-class, largely white disaffection with the Warren Court and liberal "elites." His rhetoric was worth studying and included famous lines, including dismissing experts as "nattering nabobs of negativism" and as "an effete corps of impudent snobs." Notably, he joined the chorus criticizing the courts for abandoning crime victims: the "rights of the accused have become more important than the rights of victims in our courtrooms."[18] Thus, politicians like Nixon and Agnew were not only playing on economic insecurity of members of the Silent Majority but were starting to focus on crime victims as a subset within society in need of protection.

Justice Lewis Powell's preappointment career and early years on the Court are remembered more for his confidential memorandum "The Attack on the American Free Enterprise System," prepared for the U.S. Chamber of Commerce, and his generally conservative rulings in criminal procedure cases than for his special interest in victims' rights. But as reported in the *Los Angeles Times* in 1971, according to Powell "the time has come for concern for the rights of citizens to be free from criminal molestation of their persons. In many respects, the victims of crime have become the forgotten men of our society."[19]

Furman v. Georgia, the Supreme Court's 1972 decision overruling the death penalty as then implemented across the nation, may have cemented the role of crime victims in the right-wing movement. Technically, not a Warren Court decision—by then Warren Burger served as the chief justice—it pitted five justices who had served during the Warren Court against the four Nixon judicial appointees, all of whom dissented.[20]

Cases like *Miranda* and *Furman* and the success of politicians like Nixon in using crime as a wedge issue were gelling into the VRM. With financial support from the right-wing Heritage Foundation, Carrington published *The Victims* in 1975. As reflected in his testimony before Congress and in the book, he advanced several important policy positions.

Members of the emerging movement called for a rebalancing of the criminal justice system. "[P]erhaps the rights of potential victims and actual victims should be weighed much more heavily in the balance, than the rights of the convicted killers."[21] *The Victims* expanded on that claim. It urged providing a greater role to victims in the criminal justice system, cutting back on defendants' due process rights, increasing punishment, and expanding the use of the death penalty.

In 1979, Carrington founded the Crime Victims' Legal Advocacy Institute, Inc. Its goal was to protect crime victims in the civil and criminal justice systems.[22] Carrington's role as spokesman for the VRM propelled him and the movement into the limelight. Early in Reagan's presidency, Attorney General French created the Attorney General's Task Force on Violent Crime and appointed Carrington as a member.[23]

The commission's report advanced many of Carrington's organization's policy positions. It called for bail "reform" to make pretrial release more difficult and for the end of the Fourth Amendment exclusionary rule. It urged narrowing defendants' due process rights.[24] As developed in chapter 4, it implicitly rejected the modern view of criminal prosecutions as a dispute between the state and the defendant. Instead, it wanted to revert to a much earlier system that pitted the victim, as the private prosecutor, against the defendant. Like the movement's distrust of judges and criminal law experts, commission members seemed to distrust career prosecutors as well as experts not sufficiently responsive to the voice of the silent members of society.[25]

One important piece of legislation emerged from the commission's report. The 1982 Victim and Witness Protection Act established victims' rights to participate at the sentencing stage of a criminal trial. It also required prosecutors to consult with victims when they negotiate plea deals with defendants. The federal model eventually spawned a national trend, with all states providing some form of victim participation in the criminal justice system.[26] The victim impact statement has become such an important and controversial topic that it requires its own chapter in this book.[27]

Other Groups Joining the Movement, Including Single-Issue Groups

Despite Carrington's central role, his organization was not alone in advancing victims' rights during the 1960s, 1970s, and 1980s. A resource guide, "Landmarks in Victims' Rights and Services," lists the first important development in the VRM as California's 1965 legislation establishing a victims' compensation fund.[28] "Landmarks" cites the establishment of victim (notably rape victim) programs in 1972 as a seminal moment in the VRM.

The website of the National Organization for Victim Assistance (NOVA), which formed in 1975, states that it was the first group advancing victims' rights in the United States.[29] Among its goals are direct victim assistance, including helping victims get access to available aid and legislative advocacy.[30]

Often, family members of crime victims spearheaded organizations with focused agendas, often aimed at the kind of offender who killed their loved one. Family and Friends of Missing Persons began in 1974 in Washington State. Its organizers intended the advocacy group as a vehicle to provide support for families whose loved ones were missing or dead.[31] Charlotte and Bob Hullinger formed Parents of Murdered Children in 1978 to urge reforms after their daughter's ex-boyfriend murdered her. Like other VRM advocates, these organizations opposed parole and urged expansion of the death penalty.[32] Among the many other groups formed as a result of a personal tragedy was Mothers Against Drunk Driving. Candace Lightner formed the group in 1980 after a drunk driver killed her thirteen-year-old daughter.[33]

Similar examples to Lightner abound. The brutal rape and murder of Stephanie Roper in 1982 led her mother, Roberta Roper, along with her supporters to form the Stephanie Roper Family Assistance Committee. That organization eventually became the Maryland Crime Victims' Resource Center. Like many other victims' organizations, it provides a host of services, from support to advocacy for victims and their families.[34]

Perhaps the most famous crime and subsequent VRM activities involved six-year-old Adam Walsh's abduction and brutal murder. Following his murder, Adam's parents, John and Reve Walsh, became active in advancing child protection legislation, including the 1984 Missing Children's Assistance Act.[35] That act set up the National Center for Missing and Exploited Children. In 2006, President Bush signed into law the Adam Walsh Child Protection and Safety Act, creating a database of convicted child molesters and increasing prison sentences for offenders who commit sexual and violent crimes against children.[36]

Congress (and eventually many states) enacted the Jacob Wetterling Crimes Against Children and Sexually Violent Offender Registration Act in 1994. Included in that act was Megan's Law, named for Megan Kanka, a seven-year-old child killed by a known sex offender who moved across the street from the girl's family.[37] One provision of the law, now widely adopted, requires that a convicted sex offender notify the local police when moving into a community. Megan's Law, a subsection of the Wetterling Act, requires the establishment of a public sex offender registry.[38]

Different laws have created and expanded limitations on sex offenders who are not incarcerated. A few victims' rights laws provide for the publication of information about sex offenders, including their addresses.[39] Such information has led to vigilante activity by community members in some publicized cases. Another provision in registration laws limits where sex offenders may live. For example, a law may provide that a sex offender may not live within a specified distance from schools, playgrounds, or other places where children may congregate. Some of those restrictions are so severe that sex offenders cannot find suitable housing within their communities. An occasional news account describes how such offenders end up living under highway overpasses.[40]

States have adopted a wide variety of laws involving similarly horrific crimes. For example, in 2005 Florida adopted Jessica's Law in response to another kidnapping, rape, and murder of a young girl. The law increased punishments for several sexual offenses involving children, including a twenty-five-year mandatory minimum prison sentence for a first-time child sex offender, with a possible maximum term of life in prison. It increased the monitoring of sex offenders upon their release from prison. The law included a sexual predator registry, identifying where convicted offenders reside. Other states followed suit, including California, which adopted it through the initiative process.[41]

Marsy's Law provides yet another example of legislation adopted in reaction to a brutal crime. Marsy Nicholas's ex-boyfriend murdered her in 1983. Her brother, Henry Nicholas, the president of Broadcom Corporation, provided funding to push California to adopt Proposition 9 in November 2008. Although Marsy's killer received a life sentence and died in prison without release on parole, her brother became frustrated with having to attend parole hearings over the several years between his incarceration and death. Beginning in 2007, Nicholas was the driving force to get Proposition 9 adopted as an amendment to California's constitution. Subsequently, several other states adopted similar laws, either by constitutional amendments or by legislation.[42] The law provides for a panoply of rights for victims. Marsy's Law strengthened several rights provided by other laws. In explaining how Florida's version of Marsy's Law works, prominent victims' rights supporters Cassell and Garvin have written, "The provisions in the recently enacted victims' rights amendments are more comprehensive than the Florida provision adopted nearly thirty years ago. Typically, these newer amendments contain fifteen or more specific rights for crime victims, along with detailed provisions concerning the enforcement of rights and a definition of the 'victims' who can avail themselves of the rights. The combination of a robust set of rights and explicit standing and enforcement provisions is the common thread in this new wave of state-constitutional amendments known as 'Marsy's Laws.'"[43] Notably, the law includes a provision, akin to *Miranda* rights read to criminal suspects: district attorneys must provide victims and their family members with a card explaining the particular rights created and expanded by Marsy's Law. The website of the California Attorney General's Office includes a description of those rights.[44] Some are general protections, like the command that victims and their families have their rights to dignity and privacy treated with respect. The state should ensure their safety, including assessment by courts in determining bail for criminal suspects. The law allows victims and their families to refuse to be interviewed by defense counsel or, if discovery is allowed, to set conditions on that discovery process. Other provisions include the requirement of notice of various proceedings, including trial, sentencing, parole, and other proceedings. The law also creates a right to a speedy trial and to prompt resolution of postjudgment proceedings. Marsy's Law gives victims the right to a presentence report, subject only to redaction of information made confidential by other laws. The state must also notify victims of defendants' release dates from prison or the fact that a prisoner has escaped. The law also provides that victims are entitled to restitution from defendants.[45]

No doubt, many provisions in these laws are reasonable. Some reflect the need to treat victims and their families with respect. Later chapters deal with the many excesses of these kinds of laws. One issue not fully explored in later chapters is the controversy surrounding sexual predator registration laws. Human Rights Watch has created a website where it discusses some of the excesses of these kinds of law.[46] A primary concern is that they are overly broad and last far too long. The laws' breadth includes many offenders who are not the type of dangerous criminals who inspired such laws.[47] The registration requirements are overly long, often requiring offenders who were involved in improper conduct in their youth to remain registered well beyond a time when they continue to be a threat. The laws are based on inaccurate stereotypes about sex offenders, particularly that they are not capable of rehabilitation, a contention rebutted by empirical evidence. Such laws have led to harassment of and violence toward such offenders.[48] As observed above, some laws are so restrictive that offenders cannot find housing within their communities because virtually any home or apartment is located too close to a school or other place off-limits to registered offenders.[49]

The laws discussed above share common denominators: a crime victim's family becomes energized by the loss of a loved one. These laws are often aimed at a set of offenders and victims. Single-issue advocates may not have been involved with the VRM prior to their personal loss but may be embraced by the movement.[50] But the broader VRM most often joins their efforts and expands its often-severe punitive efforts.

Other groups, whose interest in the VRM is less obvious, have become involved with the movement as well. Chapter 7 explores the VRM's role in the passage of California's Three Strikes Law. It also discusses the role that the National Rifle Association played in passage of that draconian law, even though there is no obvious overlap between gun rights and victims' rights.[51] That chapter also examines the role of the California Correctional Peace Officers Association (CCPOA) in securing passage of Three Strikes and in funding victims' rights organizations in that state.[52] The connection between the CCPOA's interests and those of the VRM is clear enough, if somewhat troubling: the association has advanced numerous expensive laws that have cost Californians dearly, while benefiting the CCPOA's narrow economic interests.[53]

This chapter does not present an exhaustive list of participants in the VRM. But the next section explores the feminist movement's role in advancing the VRM's goals. Feminist groups were active early in the VRM and were essential to the passage of many of its reforms.

Women's Liberation and the Law-and-Order Wing of the VRM

The Women's Movement has focused on victims' rights at least since the mid-nineteenth century. Its early involvement in efforts to ban alcohol illustrates that point. Suffragettes' struggle to enfranchise women was, in effect, a victims' rights movement.[54]

As summarized by Daniel Okrent, author of *Last Call: The Rise and Fall of Prohibition*, "Men would go to the tavern, drink away mortgage money, drink so much they couldn't go to work the next day, beat their wives, abuse their children. That's what launched the beginning of the temperance movement."[55] Involvement in efforts to ban alcohol brought women's issues into the public discourse. Writing in *Time* magazine, Olivia Waxman argued that the most important legacy of women's involvement in passing the Eighteenth Amendment was making women part of the national political conversation.[56]

In the modern era, women became involved in the VRM indirectly. Initially, the Women's Movement[57] advanced policies to protect children from abuse.[58] The movement became more involved in criminal justice policy in the 1970s when members began to focus on rape and sexual assault. Some early efforts to address sexual assault were met with resistance, including from law-and-order groups. Male-dominated police forces often treated rape victims with skepticism, especially in cases involving acquaintance rape, but also in cases of violent stranger rape.[59]

Grassroots feminist groups organized events like Take Back the Night, aimed at women's safety. Similarly, and controversially, some feminists targeted pornography as a source of implicit violence against women.[60] Yet another target was domestic violence, an area where police were notoriously lax in enforcement of the law.[61]

In many states, feminists succeeded in getting legislatures to reform definitions of rape and sexual assault. They challenged long-held views of rape as a protection of husbands' rights to their property and as a crime focusing on women's purity and chastity.[62] Instead, they urged that sexual assault violated a woman's autonomy, a position that has led to the expansion of definitions of sexual assault. For example, some states' penal codes now include definitions of sexual crimes that are essentially aimed at intercourse to which a victim has not consented, without any reference to violence. Feminists also urged changes to sexual assault laws to increase the focus on male aggression and to decrease the emphasis on female resistance.[63]

In urging expanded definitions of sex offenses, feminists argued that the burden of proving the absence of consent ended up unfairly on the victim. That in turn created a credibility battle, often resulting in humiliating questions about a woman's prior sexual activity. As explained by the New Jersey Supreme Court, "Courts and commentators historically distrusted the testimony of victims, 'assuming that women lie about their lack of consent for various reasons: to blackmail men, to explain the discovery of a consensual affair, or because of psychological illness.'"[64] That concern was part of the impetus to adopt "rape shield" laws, limiting the defendant's ability to inquire into the victim's prior sexual conduct.

Feminists also targeted other evidentiary rules that made convictions unduly difficult. For example, some states did not allow a conviction based on a victim's uncorroborated testimony.[65] Some courts gave cautionary instructions indicating the difficulty of proving rape. Failure to report the crime promptly often led to the rejection of the charges or an instruction to the jury to view the victim's testimony skeptically.[66] Although debated in the literature, many reform efforts proceeded on the view that a woman risked her safety by resisting; but without adequate resistance, the state could not prove that the defendant committed rape.[67]

Feminists did not uniformly gain support of law-and-order conservatives. Indeed, some of the early feminists opposing domestic violence, for example, were antiauthoritarian, antigovernment activists.[68] But by the 1980s, many feminists had become pro-police, pro-prosecution. At that point, feminists' efforts to increase punishment for sex offenses overlapped with the VRM generally.[69]

Over the next several decades, the Women's Movement and the VRM joined forces in advancing the needs of victims in many areas. Rape victims are an important subset of victims in need of support. Many VRM advocates are trained in rape counseling as a specialty. Often, VRM supporters focus on sexual assault victims when they are advancing the expansion of victims' rights, not limited to sexual assault victims.[70] As Professor Gruber has noted, in some contexts feminists have welcomed strict law-and-order approaches to criminal justice, "despite the strange bedfellows."[71]

As Gruber has developed, by the 1980s and 1990s, media coverage of child kidnappings, rapes, and murders drove criminal justice policy.[72] As described above, cases like Adam Walsh, Megan Kanka, and Marsy Nicholas provided powerful headlines, generating incentives for politicians to act. During that period, feminists joined the broader VRM's demands for severe sanctions: "During predator panic, legislatures passed laws tacking on more years to already exorbitant sex offender sentences."[73] For example, as discussed in chapter 5, many laws, including those increasing punishment and disabilities for sex offenders, are often based on inaccurate information about sex offenders. While a small number of offenders are violent, repeat offenders, difficult to rehabilitate, VRM advocates and legislators have acted on inaccurate information about percentages of sex offenders who are incapable of rehabilitation. In addition, broadly written prohibitions have often swept young offenders into the criminal justice system.[74]

In recent years, stories have emerged in the press revealing the excesses of such laws. Noted earlier are stories about registered sex offenders who cannot find any place to live within their communities because of laws limiting them from living within a specified distance from places where children congregate.[75] Indiscretions by young people, conduct more indicative of sexual curiosity than criminality, have led to them remaining on sex offender registries.[76] Once identified as registered offenders, their outraged neighbors have made their lives miserable.

Gruber's *The Feminist War on Crime* examines how many contemporary feminists have distanced themselves from such extreme laws. Despite that, she recounts how some feminist activists were more influential than law-and-order conservatives in advancing some of the more draconian sex offender laws.[77] She also faults current feminists who generally opposed mass incarceration for their willingness to demand longer sentences for some sex offenders.[78]

Also as discussed throughout this book, tension exists between reform efforts and the VRM. Anyone listening to national media senses a different tone about racial injustice and mass incarceration. Some media outlets now question the fairness of long prison sentences, for example, for young adults who are convicted of felony murder, despite having minor roles in such crimes.[79] But as Gruber makes clear, even the liberal community often finds itself divided over such issues.

The Movement's Staying Power

The next chapter discusses some of the unquestionable accomplishments of the VRM. But most of the book develops the unwarranted costs it imposes. Depending on where one looks, one can see evidence that the VRM's coalition is unraveling. But undoing the movement's excesses is challenging.

As mentioned above, several aggrieved parents and family members have joined forces with the VRM to advance single-issue laws. In some instances, they have withdrawn from the movement. Often, that has been a result of the excessive zeal of VRM members.

Two examples suggest the pattern. The first involves Candy Lightner, who formed Mothers Against Drunk Driving after an intoxicated driver killed her daughter in 1980. Five years later, she withdrew from the organization because, according to Lightner, the organization was headed in the wrong direction. It was dominated by neo-prohibitionists. Later she would even represent the American Beverage Institute in opposing the reduction of the blood alcohol level standard.[80]

Even more dramatic is the case of Patty Wetterling. After the abduction of her eleven-year-old son, she successfully lobbied the Minnesota legislature to adopt the nation's first sex offender registry. Three years later, in 1994, President Clinton signed the Jacob Wetterling Crimes Against Children and Sexually Violent Offender Registration Act, which required states to create their own registries. More recently, she stated that she has "turned 180 degrees from where [she] was."[81]

Various sources have described Wetterling's journey. A 2016 New Yorker article, for example, described how she began corresponding with a nineteen-year-old named Ricky. Ricky was a registered sex offender who was prosecuted for third-degree sexual abuse when he was sixteen years old, after having consensual sex with a girl he believed to also be sixteen. In reality, she was only thirteen.[82]

Wetterling also met a ten-year-old child in a juvenile sex offender treatment facility that also seemed to have a profound impact on her. "He was nine when he first went into treatment. I was overwhelmed by that. I kept thinking about this kid, who goes away, gets sex-offender treatment, then goes back to his junior high school, and is on the public registry—this young person who really wants to return to school, to learn, to make friends, but can't have a second chance. That's a life sentence for this kid."[83]

Registration laws are so broad that offenders may come within their provisions based on conduct no rational person would believe justifies continued registration with its ongoing disabilities. Offenders can be registered for offenses such as "public urination, sexting, and conducting so-called 'Romeo and Juliet' relationships between teenagers." Wetterling, though largely responsible for the enactment of the initial registries, believes that the lists have gone too far.[84]

As is the case with Wetterling, some individuals who part company with the VRM do so because of a fundamentally different perception about the goals of the criminal justice system. Often, VRM advocates maintain a one-size-fits-all punitive attitude, whereas former allies urge greater emphasis on the causes of crime. Gruber has summarized that point: "As director of Minnesota's Sexual Violence Prevention Program, [Wetterling] oversaw a 2015 report that called for deprioritizing punitive responses in favor of 'taking on the root causes like alcohol and drug use, emotionally unsupportive family environments, and societal norms.'"[85]

Examples like these suggest how some members of the VRM coalition abandon the movement when its excesses become obvious. But as explored throughout this book, the VRM has staying power even in an age when many Americans have become aware of our overreliance on prisons and of racial inequities within our system. In part, as explored in the next chapter, the VRM can claim successes that we should all applaud. But the VRM often relies on headline cases to push excessively punitive measures. The problem for the movement's critics is to acknowledge legitimate criminal justice goals while explaining the need for nuanced handling of such issues. That is the hope of the remainder of this book.

2

What the Victims' Rights Movement Gets Right

Anyone who has read chapter 1 knows that this book focuses on the Victims' Rights Movement's excesses. However, failing to acknowledge some of the VRM's successes would be unfair to the many individuals who have contributed positively to the criminal justice system. Often, they have been family members of crime victims or victims themselves, deserving of empathy.[1] This chapter reviews some of those successes.

No one has written a definitive history of the VRM. This book does not pretend to do so. Whether the VRM deserves credit or blame for specific reforms presents its own set of problems, in part because there is no definitive history of the movement. As described in chapter 1, the VRM has consisted of a loose coalition of groups, often spanning a broad political spectrum. In a chapter prepared for a National Victim Assistance Academy, three authors listed groups as diverse as the early and more modern Women's Movement, the Civil Rights Movement, the Antiwar Movement, and the Law-and-Order Movement as part of the larger Victims' Rights Movement.[2] That suggests a large tent or, perhaps, a fluid collaboration among diverse groups.

As developed in chapter 7, some legislation, like California's Three Strikes Law, received backing by the law-and-order wing of the VRM. Some VRM groups stayed on the sidelines. In some instances, the feminist wing of the VRM backed legislation, like the Violence Against Women Act, while law-and-order supporters of the VRM did not.[3] Likewise, some VRM organizations consider the Brady Bill a major accomplishment, despite criticism from the law-and-order wing of the VRM.[4] Some members of the law-and-order wing are fierce gun rights advocates. They reject efforts to limit access to guns despite victimization that results from easy access to weapons, as discussed in chapter 8. Also, as developed in chapter 1, some legislation supported by the VRM results from the efforts of single-issue supporters, like Mothers Against Drunk

Driving. Single-issue campaigns may not represent core concerns of the VRM, even if many VRM groups coalesce around such issues.

To account for the divergence of views among some VRM groups, this chapter focuses on reforms that most VRM members would consider foundational to their movement. As developed below, often those reforms are aspirational but still have not achieved the highest ambitions of movement members.

The first section begins with an examination of the VRM's complaint that the criminal justice system ignores victims. Basic fairness demanded greater respect for crime victims. As reviewed there, the VRM has secured greater rights for victims. This chapter then turns to a powerful example of systematic mistreatment of rape victims and efforts at reform. The second section discusses the treatment of rape victims and describes some improvements in that area. The discussion focuses on then-professor Susan Estrich's dramatic retelling of her rape and its impact on reforming police and prosecutors' engagement with rape victims. The third section examines efforts at providing crime victims with financial support through one of two mechanisms. States and the federal government have developed compensation funds for some crime victims. State and federal statutes also typically allow judges to order restitution from defendants. Along the way, this chapter focuses on work yet to be done to achieve worthwhile goals of the movement.[5]

Basic Fairness

Prominent victims' rights advocates remind readers that early in history, including in colonial America, victims played a prominent role in the administration of justice.[6] Victims conducted investigations, brought charges, and prosecuted wrongdoers before the development of professional police departments and prosecutors. That changed during the Enlightenment, marked in part by a change in ideas about the harm caused by crime. No longer viewed narrowly as a harm against a fellow citizen, crime was seen as a crime against society.[7] An individual might pursue damages in what developed into a modern-day tort system, but an offender who committed crimes against the king's peace in England or against society generally in the United States needed to be punished for retributive and deterrent purposes.[8]

While acknowledging this history, victims' rights advocates argue that the criminal justice system unfairly relegated crime victims to serving as witnesses and leaving them only with the civil justice system to address their harm.[9] This is not the place to debate the importance of public prosecutors, who serve the interests of justice, rather than those of crime victims. Much can be said in support of that evolution. Importantly, especially when civil litigation might not provide a crime victim with much in the way of compensation, expanding the role of victims in the criminal justice system might be the best hope for relief.

Concern about the lack of a voice in criminal justice issues was part of the push for recognizing victims' rights throughout the United States. Groups backing expanded services for victims spanned a broad political spectrum. For example, the women's liberation movement joined with the law-and-order victims' movement to expand protections for victims, despite their political differences.[10]

Some victims' complaints were and are compelling. Often victims need medical care and financial assistance related to their injuries not available from other sources. Prosecutors were under no obligation to inform victims about the progress of the case against the defendants accused of harming them. Victims often did not receive notice of a pretrial release of the accused individuals. Victims might be required to attend judicial proceedings, forced to leave work, without being informed that the case in which they were involved had been resolved by a guilty plea or otherwise dismissed.[11]

While victims' rights advocates advanced other ways in which the system was unfair, many of those claimed rights are more controversial. For example, chapter 6 examines the complex question about victim impact statements and argues that such evidence is often inappropriate. Also, Frank Carrington, one of the prime movers of the VRM, argued that the Warren Court had tipped the scale unfairly in favor of criminal defendants at a cost to victims. Chapter 4 questions that claim. But for the purposes of this chapter, anyone with a modicum of empathy can see victims' real needs and can applaud efforts to address those needs.[12]

California was one of the first states to adopt a Victims' Bill of Rights.[13] Among other rights, California's law includes a right to restitution from the defendant. It also requires that the state provide the victim with notifications of sentencing and parole hearings.[14] Other laws in

California have expanded notifications and other rights for victims. All states provide some protections, either in their state constitution or in legislation.[15]

Congress has created a similar set of victims' rights. The Crime Victims' Rights Act of 2004 provides several rights to victims of federal offenses or of offenses in the District of Columbia. That law includes notice requirements, a right to protection, and a right to restitution.[16]

Some laws include rather broad statements that seem entirely appropriate. For example, California's Marsy's Law, which amended the state's constitution, includes a provision that requires that a victim be "treated with fairness and respect for his or her privacy and dignity" throughout criminal justice processes.[17] While such "rights" as fair treatment and respect seem noncontroversial, determining whether the system validates such generalized rights seems virtually impossible.

One website hosted by a victims' rights organization lists "key federal victims' rights legislation,"[18] which included over thirty statutes as of 2016. Many of them were the product of specific crimes and were advanced by aggrieved family members.[19] Similar examples can be found at the state level as well. Mothers Against Drunk Driving is such an organization. In 1980, a drunk driver killed Cindy Lightner's thirteen-year-old daughter. MADD's first mission statement was "to aid the victims of crimes performed by individuals driving under the influence of alcohol or drugs, to aid the families of such victims, and to increase public awareness of the problem of drinking and drugged driving."[20] According to MADD's website, its efforts contributed to cutting drunk driving deaths in half.[21]

Often, victims and their advocates have identified serious problems with the criminal justice system. Other chapters focus on why some of those provisions are bad policy, often sweeping far too broadly.[22] As described in chapter 1, MADD offers such an example.[23] For now, this section describes some noteworthy successes of the VRM.

Rape Reform

In 1974, a man held an ice pick to Susan Estrich's throat and raped her in her own car. Afterward, she told her story first to two officers, then to four more. She reviewed mugshots into the night. Later, she received a call from a clerk who told her that her car had been found without any tires and that she needed to sign for it and get it towed.

Several years later, as a professor at Harvard Law School, she published an article and then a book, *Real Rape*, recounting her experience as a rape victim. Despite the traumatic experience, she described herself as a "very lucky rape victim." Her book described less lucky victims. Typical of the way the system responded, especially to acquaintance rape, was a story about a woman who was raped by her ex-boyfriend. The district attorney explained that he was not prosecuting the boyfriend because the victim "was trying to use the system to harass her ex-boyfriend."[24]

Apart from rape-specific procedural hurdles, Estrich focused on the typical law enforcement response to rape victims' claims. Large percentages of rape cases did not move through the system. Police often found cases unfounded; even if founded, prosecutors often dismissed the cases as well. While the percentage of acquaintance rape cases that were dismissed was far greater than that of stranger rape cases, even stranger rape victims often did not have their cases proceed through the criminal justice system. Police and prosecutors, mostly male, not only failed to prosecute but often showed a lack of decency toward rape victims.[25]

A lot has changed since Estrich wrote her book, even though the system has a long way to go. Many reform measures are welcome, including the development of rape crisis centers, greater recognition that rape can occur between acquaintances or within a marriage, and laws limiting the inappropriate use of a woman's prior sexual history to discredit her in court.[26] Many police departments have specialized units to deal with sexual assault victims.[27] Organizations have created training programs to sensitize police officers who deal with sexual assault cases.[28]

To be clear, reforms have not gone far enough, as many critics observe. For example, Professor Margo Kaplan has summarized how rape reform has failed to address ongoing concerns:

> This failure [of the criminal justice reforms] is in part attributable to the enduring influence of rape myths at every level of the criminal justice system. While sexual assault most commonly occurs when the defendant knows the victim, police are less likely to investigate such cases and much more likely to find allegations of stranger rape credible. Prosecutors are

also less likely to pursue cases where the victim knows the perpetrator; when they do, juries are less likely to convict the defendant. Police and prosecutors remain reluctant to take on cases that rely primarily or solely on the victim's testimony. Yet the expectation of corroboration is unrealistic for an offense that usually occurs in a private setting with no witnesses beside the perpetrator and victim, and which often lacks expected indicators of force and struggle (such as bruises and lacerations).[29]

But various organizations continue to push for reforms. Efforts, for example, by the American Law Institute (ALI) to advance further reforms were finalized at the organization's 2022 annual meeting.[30]

One might question whether the VRM can take credit for these progressive changes. For example, the website of the Washington Coalition of Sexual Assault Programs credits reforms protective of victims of sexual assault to the Anti–Sexual Assault Movement and other women-based movements, not the VRM.[31] Despite that, the collaboration between women's advocacy groups and the larger VRM has advanced many core protections now available for victims of sexual violence.[32]

Also, as with the discussion of rights extended to victims generally, one ought to be cautious about endorsing the entirety of the agenda designed to protect sexual assault victims. For example, chapter 5 deals with efforts to repeal statutes of limitations in sexual assault cases. As argued there, such provisions often come at the expense of fundamental principles of the criminal law, including the need to protect innocent defendants from conviction. So too, some of the more extreme efforts to limit a defendant's ability to introduce evidence of the complaining witness's prior sexual conduct may run afoul of basic principles of criminal law and procedure, including, in some cases, a defendant's Sixth Amendment right to defend himself.[33] Finally, some VRM members push for longer prison terms for offenders. That is troubling considering increasing recognition that the United States incarcerates offenders far too often and for far too long.

Despite reservations about some reforms advanced by the VRM, no one should doubt the importance of increased protection for rape victims.

Victim Compensation Funds and Restitution

Estimating the financial impact of crime is challenging. One prominent book about the VRM cites a now somewhat dated study claiming that the burden of crime on society was $1.705 trillion annually.[34] While such estimates are open to criticism, one fact is indisputable: crime carries financial and emotional costs for victims. Given the fact that low-income victims bear a disproportionate share of those losses, one can applaud efforts to provide funds to help victims get necessary medical and psychological care. Legislatures have created two funding sources to help victims. States and Congress have created victim compensation funds and have given judges authority to order defendants to pay victims restitution.

Even before the "official" beginning of the VRM, California created the first victim compensation program. Since 1965, every state has developed a program that can grant financial assistance to help pay for crime-related expenses.[35] Such laws include various limitations. For example, the California Victim Compensation Board (CalVCB) can give compensation only to victims who have suffered physical injuries or emotional injuries related to a threat of physical injuries.[36] Expenses can include the cost of medical care, counseling, and funerals.[37] The CalVCB now funds nineteen trauma recovery centers statewide. Those centers have expanded services, including to individuals who might not be willing to participate in the criminal justice system.[38]

The federal Victims of Crime Act of 1984 (VOCA) created a source of funding to provide financial relief to victims. That legislation allows states to qualify for funding, and all do participate.[39] To date, VOCA has resulted in billions of dollars being distributed to crime victims.[40]

A closer look at the administration of some compensation programs suggests that they do not go far enough. California's Committee on Reform of the Penal Code February 2022 report suggests that too few qualifying individuals apply for available services because of lack of adequate notice of existing resources. At least one grand jury investigation found that Black applicants for compensation were denied far more frequently than white applicants because of a requirement that the victim "reasonably cooperate" with law enforcement efforts. The committee also questions whether funding for restitution is adequate, especially because the amount available in the fund may vary widely from year to year.[41]

Today, victim compensation funds exist across the country and in the federal system. As a general matter, providing aid to victims is worthwhile. But as is the case in California, questions about the administration of such programs, including adequacy of funding, sufficient notice to victims, and racial disparities, erode confidence in such programs.[42]

The other innovation advanced by the VRM was restitution. Restitution differs from compensation funds because it comes directly from the criminal, paid to the victim. Judges' ability to award restitution varies greatly. Even within a jurisdiction, as is the case with federal legislation, the law may require the judge to order restitution in some cases, while making it optional for others.[43] Laws vary significantly from state to state.[44] Nonetheless, when it works restitution provides victims with relief without forcing them to pursue tort damages.

One obvious problem with restitution is that most defendants are unable to pay it. Often, offenders committing property crimes are doing so because they lack financial resources. For example, drug addicts who commit property crimes are not likely to be able to pay restitution. As such, restitution may have more symbolic than tangible value.[45]

Beyond the likelihood that an offender may lack resources to pay restitution, the availability of restitution may pose complex sentencing questions for judges. Most sentencing schemes provide multiple, sometimes competing goals for the sentencing judge. What happens when, for example, a judge believes that an offender may be more easily rehabilitated if she does not have to pay restitution but the victim wants restitution?[46] One example suggests how this tension may arise. Often, impoverished offenders become trapped in the system when they have to pay a fine. An inability to pay may result in increased fines and interest penalties, resulting in a downward spiral. Not ordering restitution may result in an offender's ability to develop economic security, which often correlates with reduced likelihood of recidivism.[47] That may pose a clear conflict between the core goals of the criminal law, including the reduction of recidivism, and the VRM's goals. At least insofar as a sentencing judge can advance both goals, efforts to expand laws allowing for restitution are worthy of support.

Chapter 8 explores how much more the nation might do for victims. Among other things discussed there is the need for a national affordable health care system. By comparison to measures in place now, medical and psychological care would not turn on technical niceties of state laws. At this juncture, however, victims' rights advocates deserve praise for the many services that are available, even if they are less than ideal.

Conclusion

This chapter has focused on reforms that deserve support. Some reforms are incomplete; for example, critics can point to lack of sufficient funding or training in some police departments. They can also contest some reforms that victims' rights advocates have achieved or still hope to achieve. This book deals with some of the more controversial policies elsewhere. For now, however, critics ought to applaud the coalition of VRM groups that have pushed the reforms described above. Even where room for improvement remains, for example, in making health care available to crime victims, the VRM has advanced some important policy goals.

3

Victimhood, Demagoguery, and Mental Health

This chapter explores a fundamental question: does the criminal justice system's approach to victims serve them well? Reframed, is it psychologically helpful to see oneself as a victim? For example, feminists disagree among themselves whether to characterize a woman who has been raped as a victim or as a survivor.[1] Psychological literature suggests that the difference is not academic: as argued below, overcoming one's perception as a victim advances psychological healing.

Today, many Americans have become obsessed with victimhood. For example, during a December 2020 political rally, former president Trump declared that he and his followers were victims: "We are all victims. Everybody here. All these thousands of people tonight. They're all victims. Every one of you."[2] Claiming victimhood presumably gives a person a political advantage or a special moral status. But often, claims of victimhood, such as Trump's, seem outrageous.

Before turning to the central question, the chapter discusses some threshold questions. Why would a person want to claim victim status? In Trump's case, the claim is implausible and made for political gain. But what about claims of victimhood within the criminal justice system? States and the federal government have had to define the term because benefits may be available based on that status. Given that reality, one ought to ask what policies should determine the meaning of the term "victim."

After discussing these threshold questions, the chapter examines the psychological literature about victimhood. That literature suggests that much of the message given to crime victims by the Victims' Rights Movement is not therapeutic and may be contraindicated. The chapter then turns to the Brock Turner sexual assault case that made international headlines. It uses that case to examine competing messages given to crime victims or survivors.

The first section addresses the American obsession, especially among right-wingers, with victimhood. The second section briefly discusses some statutory definitions of the term "victim." It introduces an idea developed more fully in chapter 8 that the nation would serve victims well by creating a universal health care system. The third section examines the psychological literature. Finally, the fourth section discusses the treatment of Turner's sexual assault victim as a case study in victimhood.

The National Obsession with Victimhood

Trump's claim to victimhood, quoted above, was presumably based on the mistaken belief that the election was stolen from him. Even multiple legal defeats and a lack of credible evidence of voter fraud have not stopped Trump and many supporters from advancing the cause. While the claim seems like madness, it taps into a broader debate about victimhood.

While the phenomenon is not limited to the Conservative Movement, victimhood as a mentality has become increasingly central to the movement in recent years.[3] Some political commentators have attributed the Conservative Movement's more fervent embrace of victimhood as stemming from Trump's personal victim ideology.[4] Other notable political figures have expressed similar sentiments of victimhood in recent months: Senator Josh Hawley accused the media of "muzzling" him after his actions on January 6, 2021, led publishing company Simon & Schuster to cancel publication of his book.[5] After being called out for her behavior toward other representatives, Representative Marjorie Taylor Greene claimed on Newsmax that *she* was the victim of bullying. Greene's behavior was called into question after a video of her taunting Representative Alexandria Ocasio-Cortez, calling Ocasio-Cortez a supporter of terrorism, went viral.[6]

Recently, right-wing politicians have begun opposing the teaching of critical race theory even when school districts have no plans to do so. Mississippi governor Tate Reeves summed up that view when he signed a bill preventing critical race theory from being taught in Mississippi public schools and community colleges: "Critical race theory is running amok" in the United States. Summing up, he suggested that whites are victimized by discussions of the theory: apparently, white Mississippians are "humiliated" by learning about structural racism in a state where apartheid was enforced officially well into the late twentieth century.[7]

According to Professor Robert B. Horwitz, "The victim has become among the most important identity positions in American politics. Victimhood is now a pivotal means by which individuals and groups see themselves and constitute themselves as political actors. Indeed, victimhood seems to have become a status that must be established before political claims can be advanced."[8] Horwitz further argues that victimhood became a central aspect of American politics after the Civil Rights Movement in the 1960s.[9] According to Horwitz, critics—namely white conservatives—condemned the Civil Rights Movement as "a self-serving alliance between minorities and the new class of liberal elites in and out of government . . . as white men especially began to lose some of their systemic privileges in the wake of minority rights and women's revolution, they condemned the revolution as politics of victimhood."[10] However, in making this argument, conservatives thus contended that *they* were the *true* victims: the victims of victimhood.[11] They were the true victims of liberal policies that "provided unfair advantages to African Americans and other designated minorities—thus violating universalistic, color-blind norms of individual merit. The rejoinder to the policies of racial redress was the condemnation of victimhood while asserting true victimhood."[12]

A recent example of this phenomenon can be found in political commentator Dinesh D'Souza. As one writer observed, D'Souza "has made a career reviling those who deploy group oppressions to impose codes of acceptable speech and behavior on everyone else. Political correctness, for D'Souza, *is* the politics of victimhood."[13] Yet when D'Souza was convicted of violating campaign finance laws, he claimed to be a victim of political persecution, a victim of "Obama's anti-colonialist rage."[14] When Anita Hill appeared before the Senate Judiciary Committee during Justice Thomas's confirmation hearings, Thomas claimed that he was the true victim in the situation and that his victimizers included Hill, the media, liberal lobbying groups, and the Senate committee.[15]

Being a "true victim" has become a sort of currency within the modern U.S. political framework, not merely among those on the right.[16] Identifying oneself as a victim (or one's group as victims) is beneficial in many regards. For one, according to Horwitz, "victim status authorizes an aggrieved party to proclaim injury and demand recognition and reparation. . . . The wound of being acted upon by powerful, hostile forces has become a form of identification now performed by virtually all comers."[17] Other experts have argued that victims are "seen as morally and socially superior" and that with a sense of victimhood comes a sense of belonging.[18] Because victims are seen as morally superior, society is more willing to listen to them versus nonvictims. Moreover, perceiving oneself as a victim allows a person to blame external factors for things like personal failures or other such difficulties of life.[19] There is an element of blamelessness attached to the perception of victims that is no doubt desirable. According to Martha Minow, law professor and former dean of Harvard Law School, "The stories of victims are attractive because they arouse attractive emotions. . . . [V]ictimhood is attractive in the sense that it secures attention in an attention-taxed world."[20]

One might question whether the VRM has played a role in the right's attempt to weaponize victimhood status. The answer is almost certainly yes. Think back to the discussion of Frank Carrington's role in advancing victim rights. He along with many fellow travelers like then–vice president Spiro Agnew tapped into the anger of the Silent Majority. They, not criminal defendants (and, hint, Black people), were victims and needed to claim the high moral ground.[21]

Despite being increasingly linked to modern conservative ideologies, the victimhood mentality is not exclusive to the Republican Party. After former New York governor Andrew Cuomo resigned, he launched an ad campaign that portrayed him as a victim of politically motivated attacks.[22] Similarly, for years after former president Bill Clinton's impeachment saga, he attempted to portray himself as a victim as well.[23]

Professors Miles Armaly and Adam Enders's recent study identified two subsets of self-defined (or "perceived") victimhood that are rampant in American politics.[24] Their data tend to show that these two subsets of perceived victimhood—egocentric victimhood and systemic victimhood—"meaningfully impac[t] a number of political attitudes, orientations, and choices."[25] Egocentric victims tend to internalize a general feeling that they deserve more than what they get and that "they, personally, have a harder go at life than others." Systemic victimhood is more external. Systemic victims see "the system," that is, the government and societal structures, as victimizers that harm them but benefit others.[26]

Armaly and Enders's data show that these subsets of perceived victimhood tend to underlie support for certain political beliefs and that while some people may naturally be prone to feelings of victimization, "elites," namely political figures, can also stoke feelings of victimhood, changing "the extent to which one feels victimized or alter the salience of previously felt victimhood."[27] Put another way, Armaly and Enders's study tends to show that "political elites can rhetorically weaponize victimhood" on either end of the political spectrum and can make individuals perceive themselves as victims, regardless of their *actual* legal or sociopolitical victim status.[28] Interestingly, the participants of the study who scored higher as egocentric victims, regardless of whether they were liberal or conservative in practice, were more likely to support Trump than those who scored higher as systemic victims.[29]

Returning to Horwitz's assertion that the conservative "true victimhood" framework was largely a reaction to the Civil Rights Movement, Horwitz also observes that the VRM is another example of conservatives taking a "true victim" stance against liberal policies:

> The liberal effort to afford arrestees basic constitutional rights by the Warren Court sparked a reaction that they received more solicitousness than their victims—thus triggering the crime victims' movement. Here again, those who suffered from crime were seen as *true* victims. This move was more politically complicated, however, inasmuch as it was fed also by a feminist critique of how rape victims typically were treated. Notwithstanding the feminist angle, the main ideological thrust of the crime victims' rights movement was the righteous call for vengeance on behalf of the victims of crime.[30]

Professor Aya Gruber argues that the focuses of the VRM on the part of feminists and conservatives became "distinctly neoliberal and carceral" in the 1980s.[31] Crime-control discourse at this time seemingly weaponized victimhood, but the movement latched onto an extremely narrow vision of who the ideal victim was: "an innocent, brutalized, middle-class white woman or child, who (or whose family) could receive closure only through the swift and severe punishment of the monstrous offender."[32]

At least in the political arena, claiming victimhood seems to benefit someone who is seen as a victim. That may be the case despite the fact that the claim may be ludicrous. This chapter now turns to how "victim" may be defined in legislation, before examining whether seeing oneself as a victim is psychologically healthy.

A Look at Defining Victimhood

Before reading the previous section, one might have thought that defining a term like "victim" or "victimhood" was simple, perhaps captured by Justice Potter Stewart's famous line about hard-core pornography: "I know it when I see it."[33] Defining victim turns out to involve important policy questions. This section offers a sampling of those questions. Others have written far more extensively about these questions.[34]

A defendant commits an unprovoked act of violence against another person. No one doubts that the person against whom the crime was committed is a victim. But what if the victim is a drug dealer and the defendant robs the dealer because the person is a drug buyer who feels cheated by the defendant? Or the defendant is a battered woman who kills her abuser in his sleep? Or the defendant and the victim engage in mutual combat, but at trial, the defendant prevails on a claim of self-defense, making the victim the aggressor in the eyes of the law? Or what about family members who lose a relative when the defendant negligently kills their relative? Yet another question is whether an organization can be a victim, say, of fraud or an antitrust violation? Examples proliferate, but one gets a sense of some complex questions that arise in determining the meaning of the term "victim."[35]

Given that legislatures have created victims' rights statutes, the questions posed above are resolved through statutory construction and legislative intent. Typical statutes include a definition of the term. Congress, for example, defines a "crime victim" as the "person directly and proximately harmed as a result of the commission of a federal offense or an offense in the District of Columbia."[36] California defines victim to be "a person who suffers direct threatened physical, psychological, or financial harm as a result of the commission of a crime or delinquent act."[37] Massachusetts makes clear that only a "natural person" qualifies as a victim and defines the term as one who "suffers direct or threatened physical emotional, or financial harm as the result of the commission or attempted commission of a crime or delinquency offense, as demonstrated by the issuance of a complaint or indictment, the family members of such person if the person is a minor, incompetent or deceased."[38] Michigan law applies to "a sole proprietorship, partnership, corporation, association, governmental entity, or any other legal entity that suffers direct physical or financial harm as a result of a misdemeanor."[39]

The sources cited above include extensive discussions of legal issues created by the various statutory definitions. Of course, many of those issues turn on specific statutory language and are beyond the scope of this discussion. At times, the analysis is challenging. For example, the Arizona Supreme Court had to determine whether a wife of a man charged with murdering their two daughters was a victim within the meaning of the state's constitutional Victims' Bill of Rights. The complicating feature was that the wife may have been the person committing the murders.[40] Another example, this case arising under Virginia law, posed the question of whether a murder victim's coworkers and friends were victims within the meaning of the relevant legal provision.[41]

Typically, some seemingly injured parties fall outside the definition of victim. A suspect, even if wrongfully accused, is not a crime victim. Nor is a person wrongfully convicted and later exonerated. That is also true of a person charged with a crime who later interposes a successful claim of self-defense. In effect, the prosecutor in the latter case has made the decision about who is a victim by bringing the charges against the defendant.[42]

One ought to ask what is at stake in the cases described above. In some cases, like the Virginia case described above, the question is who may make a victim impact statement. The Arizona case turned on whether the wife was a victim entitled to refuse to be deposed by her husband. Other cases are about access to victim compensation funds.[43] The different contexts matter.

Chapter 6 provides an extensive critique of victim impact statements. Reading a definition of victims narrowly makes sense if one doubts the wisdom of such evidence. Basic fairness to a defendant militates in favor of a narrow reading of a provision like the Arizona provision in *Knapp*, despite the court's ruling there. Too broad a reading of such a provision might violate a defendant's Sixth Amendment constitutional right to a defense.[44] Most importantly, however, are cases where a person wants to qualify as a victim to gain access to compensation funds and other victims' rights services.[45]

Among the VRM's successes is the creation of compensation funds for victims. But here, by statute or court ruling, some individuals in need of funding are excluded based on narrow statutory language or construction. Imagine a woman, suffering from battered woman syndrome, who kills her husband. In the best-case scenario, she is exonerated if she successfully prevails on a claim of self-defense.[46] The typical statute excludes her from funding needed to address her psychological disability. Of course if she succeeds only in reducing the grade of her offense from murder to voluntary manslaughter, she is even less likely to receive psychological help in many prison systems.[47]

Yet another question about defining victim is whether the law recognizes one's status as a victim only if one cooperates with the police. In fact, that is a typical requirement.[48] Despite what may seem like a sensible requirement, it masks practical impacts of such a provision. For example, members of minority communities are less likely to cooperate with police for a host of credible reasons.[49] In *The Feminist War on Crime*, Professor Aya Gruber discusses examples where victims of spousal abuse refuse to cooperate at trial. Unlike wealthier women with adequate resources to escape their abusers, many of the women discussed by Gruber are financially dependent on their abusers and may rationally balance continued abuse with economic hardship.[50] Consciously or unconsciously, legislatures that require cooperation with the police have created another law with significant negative racial impacts. Of course, a narrow definition of victim excludes less affluent victims from health care and living expenses that others can access from victim compensation funds.

As seen in this section, defining victims in legislation presents complex policy questions. Perhaps Justice Stewart's "I know it when I see it" mantra does not work well in assessing who is a victim. Indeed, as argued in chapter 8, many individuals who victimize others have been victims at some point in their lives. Chapter 8 explores the implications of that reality.

While defining victim presents challenges, the next section picks up an even more challenging question: are victims well served by emphasizing their victimhood?

Victimhood and Psychological Well-Being

Experts have found that people who have experienced severe trauma or "true" victimization are not necessarily doomed to developing a victimhood mindset. Meanwhile, people who have not experienced any severe trauma can still develop a victimhood mentality. Certain people can be prone to feelings of victimization, such as those with anxious attachment styles. Experts have also shown that victimhood can be learned from external channels as well.[51] Psychologists have found that individuals with a "tendency for interpersonal victimhood," whether or not they have experienced severe trauma, exhibit four characteristics: (1) constant need for recognition of one's victimhood, (2) moral elitism, (3) lack of empathy for others, and (4) constant rumination about their past victimization.[52]

According to psychologist Scott Barry Kaufman, most of these characteristics are normal responses to severe trauma. For example, "Recognition of one's victimhood is a normal response to trauma and can help reestablish a person's confidence in their perception of the world as a fair and just place to live. Also, it is normal for victims to want the perpetrators to take responsibility for their wrongdoing and to express feelings of guilt." But the more severe degree to which people with a tendency for interpersonal victimhood exhibit these characteristics can be harmful.[53]

Stark moral elitism, according to Kaufman, can stunt personal growth and inhibit people from being able to see the world as more than one-dimensionally good versus evil.[54] Additionally, "a group that is completely preoccupied with its own suffering can develop what psychologists refer to as an 'egoism of victimhood,' whereby members are unable to see things from the perspective of the rival group, are unable or unwilling to empathize with the suffering of the rival group, and are unwilling to accept any responsibility for harm inflicted by their own group."[55]

Kaufman ponders what might happen if society could instill in individuals a "personal growth mindset" instead of a victimhood mindset.[56] According to Kaufman, "Seeing reality as clearly as possible is an essential step to making long-lasting change, and I believe one important step along that path is to shed the perpetual victimhood mindset for something more productive, constructive, hopeful and amenable to building positive relationships with others."[57]

As discussed below, these insights find support elsewhere as well. Holocaust survivor Viktor Frankl's book *Man's Search for Meaning* examines the way in which he thrived in life by refusing to see himself as victim.[58] Prominent psychologist Martin Seligman emphasized the value of positive thoughts in overcoming depression.[59] Carol Dweck's book *Mindset: Changing the Way You Think to Fulfill Your Promise* taps into the same insights. It relies on data that demonstrate, for example, that a positive mindset increases the likelihood of academic success.[60]

Some feminist scholars have made this point in the context of sexual violence. Gruber argues that this version of victimhood is reductive and harmful, especially as it relates to sex-related crimes, because it encourages women to be seen as objects acted upon by a wrongdoer.[61] Seeing victims as more than just passive objects who were acted upon by an evil wrongdoer "undermines the claim of victimhood, because victimhood depends on a reductive view of identity," according to Harvard professor Martha Minow.[62] The VRM, according to Gruber, gained success based on a particular view of victims:

> The victim image driving the war on crime was very specific. It actively excluded the marginalized men and women, often defendants themselves, who disproportionately suffered from crime but viewed the criminal system with a jaundiced eye. Victims instead were innocent women and children—preferably white—who were subjected to men's unspeakable brutality—preferably sexual. Victims were devastated, angry, and vengeful, and they defined themselves by that one bad moment in life. Victims felt oppressed by insufficiently zealous prosecutors, prying defense attorneys, due process protections, and lenient judges. Victims desired and benefited from greater participation in the criminal process and were satisfied with the sole reward of the perpetrator's incarceration.[63]

This characterization of crime victims as singularly defined by the injustice done to them is harmful for victims and can lead to the development of an unhealthy victimhood mentality.[64]

If the VRM wants to ensure that victims can have a healing experience, some believe that the traditional criminal law courtroom is not providing the kind of catharsis that victims need.[65] A Harvard Civil Rights–Civil Liberties Law Review article argues that the criminal system was not meant to be a space for restoration and that "the project of healing should not be undertaken at the defendant's expense."[66] The movement's close ties to criminal prosecutors have led to its shortcomings: stories exist of prosecutors ignoring crime victims' wishes not to press charges or engage in the criminal justice system for their healing.[67] Professors Lara Bazelon and Bruce Green highlight one particular instance of a prosecutor ignoring the wishes of a victim not to move forward with a criminal case. The victim was then traumatized by the criminal justice system and subsequently fell into a deep depression.[68]

Bazelon and Green argue that the VRM needs to shed its view of victims as monolithic—the view that all victims require their victimizers to be convicted and receive harsh punishments.[69] They contend that there is a lack of evidence supporting the proposition that harsh punishment of offenders helps to reduce a victim's suffering. Instead, studies show the opposite, "that any satisfaction victims may experience from such an outcome is temporary and not conducive to the healing process."[70] Perhaps a restorative justice framework would be more likely to ameliorate victims' suffering and allow them to heal, which would in turn make it less likely that they would fall prey to the negative attributes of interpersonal victimhood.[71] The reality is that restorative justice plays at best a minor role in the United States.[72]

There are many ironies in the debate about victimhood. One example is the position taken by many conservative scholars in criticizing pain and suffering damages in tort law.[73] Some scholars and tort defense lawyers have argued that pain journals, where a tort victim recounts the daily struggle to function, impair healing. In the criminal context, law-and-order conservatives seem to forget such concerns about victims. Instead, they realize that victimhood plays well to juries and sentencing judges.[74]

The chapter began with examples where many readers would agree claimed victimhood seems outrageous. Yes, Donald Trump lost the election, and his claim of victimhood is deranged. But beyond the hope to gain political advantage by claiming victimhood, this section has explored a more important question: do we help victims by emphasizing their status as victims, or do we demonstrate greater concern by helping them see themselves as positive actors who have survived victimhood? The thrust of this section argues for the latter conclusion. The next section uses a case that made international headlines to explore how these ideas play out in that scenario.

A Case Study in Victimhood

Does a victim of a crime benefit psychologically by focusing on her status as a victim? This section explores that question by examining a newsworthy case.

In 2015, Brock Turner, a Stanford University athlete, sexually assaulted Chanel Miller after they met at a fraternity party. Two international students at Stanford saw Turner lying on top of a woman who seemed to be unconscious.[75] Turner ran when the other students confronted him. They pursued him and tackled him, detaining him until campus police arrived.[76] A deputy sheriff believed that the woman was unconscious; she was unable to speak coherently for three hours after police found her. A medical examination revealed that the woman had suffered "significant trauma," including "penetrating trauma."[77]

While some details about the case were in conflict, the victim was clearly severely intoxicated. Turner's blood alcohol concentration exceeded .17 percent, over two times the legal limit for, say, driving.[78] Worse, the victim's blood alcohol concentration when finally measured several hours later was .12 percent, leading experts to conclude that at the time of the incident it was between .220 and .249 percent, three times the legal limit.[79]

The prosecutor initially charged Turner with two counts of rape as well as with assault with attempt to rape and two counts of sexual assault.[80] The prosecutor dropped the rape charges because of a lack of any evidence of penile penetration.[81] The controversy about the Turner case emerged after the jury convicted him of the three remaining charges and the judge sentenced him.[82]

Consistent with California law, a probation officer prepared a presentencing report, taking into consideration several factors prescribed by the California Penal Code.[83] In the modern era, courts have relied on risk-assessment measurements to help determine criminal sentences.[84] Turner's youth and lack of prior criminal record contributed to a score that predicted a low chance of recidivism.[85] The probation report included Turner's statements of remorse for the harm to the victim.[86] The probation officer also relied on the victim's initial statement in recommending that a short sentence be imposed.[87] Notably, the victim stated, "I want him to know it hurt me, but I don't want his life to be over. I want him to be punished, but as a human, I just want him to get better. I don't want him to feel like his life is over and I don't want him to rot away in jail; he doesn't need to be behind bars."[88] Judge Persky's sentence largely tracked the probation report's recommendations.[89]

The case became a cause célèbre for several reasons. Turner's sentence included six months in a county jail, not prison, which meant that he could be released after three months.[90] He was also sentenced to a term of probation.[91] He will remain a registered sexual offender for the rest of his life.[92]

The judge's sentence launched a firestorm. During the sentencing hearing, as allowed in most U.S. states and encouraged by victims' rights supporters, the victim made an additional victim impact statement at the sentencing hearing.[93] The victim's seven-thousand-word statement included a powerful attack on Turner.[94] Here are a few of the most dramatic statements: "You don't know me, but you've been inside me, and that's why we are here today."[95] She targeted criticism at the defense team and Turner's decision to testify in his own defense: she asserted that Turner's testimony revictimized her.[96]

The victim, now identified as Chanel Miller, seems to have had a change of heart between her statement to the probation officer and her victim impact statement at the sentencing hearing.[97] As Professor Gruber has summed it up, now she "sought retribution, not restraint. [Miller] attributed the change of heart to Turner's lack of remorse in his probation statement, but some believe she was influenced by the heady publicity surrounding the case."[98] One author, writing under a pseudonym, has speculated that Stanford Law professor Michele Dauber wrote Miller's victim impact statement.[99] The suggestion there and elsewhere is that Miller's status as an idealized victim changed her view of the case.

Turner and Judge Persky became pariahs and Miller a social media celebrity through the efforts of one of Miller's family friends.[100] Dauber orchestrated a social media campaign that resulted in an outpouring of criticism of Judge Persky. Through Dauber's connections, *BuzzFeed* published a story about the case, resulting in eleven million hits in four days.[101] At a time of increased concern about sexual assault, an articulate victim, backed by celebrities and a prominent academic, became emblematic of America's rape culture.[102] Starting with that kind of publicity and what appeared to be a good victim-monster defendant story, subsequent efforts to recall Judge Persky from the bench were a foregone conclusion.[103]

Efforts to defend the judge's sentence or to raise questions about Miller's role in exposing herself to harm led to claims of victim blaming. As suggested above, the VRM benefits from the public perception of idealized victims for many reasons, including adding to the political clout of the movement. But the Turner case allows a deeper discussion of the psychology of victimhood.[104]

Assume that a victim in a similar case sought psychological help. One controversial issue might be to explore why the victim engaged in severe binge drinking on more than one occasion. Apart from the context of sexual assault, surely most would agree that binge drinking is unhealthy and reflects underlying psychological issues. Members of the VRM who support MADD's efforts definitely agree on that point.

But there is far more to emphasizing one's status as a victim. Still debated among feminist scholars is whether society ought to abandon the characterization of someone who has been sexually assaulted as a victim or as a survivor. The argument against victimhood focuses on the need to give women agency and a positive vision about their lives and experiences. Many women, for example, subjected to violence in their personal relationships have gone on to lead successful lives. Focusing on victimhood, by contrast, emphasizes helplessness and passivity. Posed differently, victimhood invites focusing on weakness rather than strength.[105]

One can find examples outside the context of sexual assault where seeing oneself as a survivor, rather than as a victim, is inspiring. Viktor Frankl's 1946 book *Man's Search for Meaning* recounted his experience as a Holocaust survivor. His therapeutic method included focusing on positive imaging that could then give meaning to life. Such an attitude not only was essential to his survival in a Nazi concentration camp but almost certainly increases one's longevity.[106]

Psychological literature focuses on similar positive attitudes that lead to greater mental and physical health. For example, Martin Seligman, who had been studying depression, began to focus on well-being. He developed a new field of psychology, premised on the idea that well-being can be measured and taught, with remarkable success. He and those following his method had patients focus on the good and on positive blessings in their lives and on their strengths rather than their failures. A good bit of research supports the mental health benefits of such an approach.[107]

One can speculate whether Chanel Miller saw herself as a victim or survivor prior to and after Turner's trial. Compare her statement to the probation officer and her victim impact statement. While the former indicated the victim's anger at Turner, it included the following: "I want him to know it hurt me, but I don't want his life to be over. I want him to be punished, but as a human, I just want him to get better. I don't want him to feel like his life is over and I don't want him to rot away in jail; he doesn't need to be behind bars."[108] The tone of her seven-thousand-word victim impact statement was far more punitive. By the end of the trial, she wanted Turner to be punished. She criticized the probation officer for cherry-picking her statements during the officer's interview with her: "Now to address the sentencing. When I read the probation officer's report, I was in disbelief, consumed by anger which eventually quieted down to profound sadness. My statements have been slimmed down to distortion and taken out of context."[109] She accused Turner, in effect, of lawyering up and allowing his attorney to put her on trial.[110] Although a closer reading of several of Turner's statements suggests greater remorse on his part, Miller's statement at the sentencing hearing portrayed him as clueless about the harm he had caused.[111] She wanted greater punishment than the probation officer's recommendation, seemingly for the sake of punishment.

One can only speculate why Miller's attitude changed. Humane Justice, the pseudonym of the author of Collateral Damage, argued that Michele Dauber, not Miller, wrote her victim impact statement.[112] Humane Justice implies that through Dauber's efforts, Miller's case became a cause célèbre of the VRM and that influenced Miller's view of the case and of herself. Her victim impact statement is about victimhood, not survivorship. If Humane Justice's inference is true, one can ask whether her involvement with the VRM served Miller well.

Happily, at least based on some news reports, Miller is healing from the trauma that she experienced.[113] Published reports and her memoir suggest that she sees herself as a survivor, not as a victim.[114] Less clear is the form that her trauma therapy took in helping her develop a fuller life than many sexual assault victims achieve. Reframed, did her therapy emphasize victimhood or survivorship?

Closely related to whether a person is encouraged to see herself as a victim or survivor is whether her supporters urge her to forgive or to demand punishment for the person who harmed her. On that point, moral philosophers and criminal law scholars disagree among themselves about the importance of forgiveness. Worth noting, however, is that many scholars believe that the rejection of strict retributive principles is a positive development.[115] As Professor Martha Nussbaum argued in *Anger and Forgiveness*, and contrary to earlier positions that she had taken, the demand for anger reflected in the demand for retribution impairs social progress.[116] She cites examples of some of the world's most inspirational leaders, including Mahatma Gandhi, Martin Luther King Jr., and Nelson Mandela, who inspired change by overcoming their anger. As developed in chapter 6, which deals with victim impact statements, yielding to anger has contributed to mass incarceration, now seen as a failed policy. The trade-off benefit of demanding payback probably does not come about. For example, in homicide cases, the demand for payback obviously fails. Punishment does not bring the decedent back to life.

Beyond the scope of this book, but worth noting, is the sentiment captured by poet Alexander Pope: "to Err is Human, to Forgive is Divine."[117] Many Christians see forgiveness as part of Jesus's message.

One might argue that Miller was right to remain angry at Turner because he showed a lack of contrition. Her seven-thousand-word victim impact statement suggests as much.[118] As indicated above, however, those statements ignore much of what Turner said to the probation officer and others.

Miller's statement also suggested that Turner lacked contrition because he allowed his attorney to raise questions about her conduct.[119] Restorative justice advocates raise a parallel concern about the criminal justice system. It is not designed to help defendants accept responsibility and to seek their victims' forgiveness.[120] Turner's case demonstrates why. On the merits, whether Turner committed the crimes charged was a close question. Charged with attempted rape, he could interpose intoxication to negate his mens rea.[121] On the other charges, his belief of consent was relevant to whether he committed the crimes.[122] No doubt, the victim experienced harm, but whether the defendant committed a crime raises distinct issues. Had the case been resolved through a restorative justice process, a defendant like Turner could have demonstrated genuine contrition. But the case was not tried in such a setting.

Conclusion

Consider how best to help a crime victim to recover psychologically. The VRM has helped establish an elaborate structure to help victims. Some innovations are helpful, including providing funding to help some victims. But what about the core message that a person is a victim? That is more controversial.

As developed in this chapter, claiming the status as a victim has become a political gambit. It allows the "victim" to claim the right to special moral status. In the criminal justice context, that heightened moral status is important. Discussed in chapter 6 in more detail are questionable uses of victim impact statements. Often, prosecutors select family members of homicide victims because they favor the death penalty. Such cases demonstrate that actors in the system often care less about victims than about increasing punishment. Also, as that chapter explores, VRM advocates promise victims more than they can deliver. Victims are, they promise, going to experience "closure" by confronting their victimizers. Yet closure is both a questionable psychological experience and an unlikely result of a one-off confrontation with the person who harmed the victim.[123]

Most importantly, backed by psychological literature, this chapter suggests that feminists, for example, who urge sexual assault victims to see themselves as survivors, not as victims, have it right. The prolonged experience as a victim may prevent the person from developing a stronger sense of self. One need not agree with Alexander Pope that to forgive is divine in order to realize the benefits of forgiving and giving up the desire for revenge.

4

The Warren Court's Criminal Procedure Revolution and Its Inspiration for the Victims' Rights Movement

As developed in chapter 1, the Warren Court's criminal procedure revolution unintentionally fueled the Victims' Rights Movement's agenda. According to Frank Carrington, the father of the VRM,[1] the Court contributed to rising crime rates through its decisions that mollycoddled criminals and ignored crime victims. As summarized by Professor Paul Cassell, the most prominent academic supporter of the VRM, "Law and order conservatives decried the seemingly single-minded focus of the judicial system on the rights of criminal defendants and inattention to countervailing interests."[2]

The perception that the Warren Court ignored victims of crime led Carrington and the VRM to demand that victims be afforded rights comparable to those that the Court provided for defendants. As VRM supporters stated their concern, "We are seeking a balance between the rights of victims, who are primarily ignored, and the accused."[3] In effect, they claimed that victims were denied due process rights to which they were entitled. In Carrington's view, providing rights to criminal defendants was a zero-sum game, depriving victims and their families their rights to due process.[4]

This chapter focuses on the attack on the Warren Court and on the role that attack played in undoing many of the Court's progressive rulings. Whether the Warren Court unfairly tilted the criminal justice system toward defendants remains debatable.[5] Presidential candidate Richard Nixon won the 1968 election in part because he was able to attack the Court. Within Nixon's first two-plus years, he appointed four justices to the Supreme Court. Nixon and his advisors chose those judges with an eye toward unraveling the Warren Court's criminal procedure revolution.[6] Thus, even if one accepts the questionable view that the criminal justice system was ever tilted inappropriately toward criminals, post-Warren Courts have gutted so many of the pro-defendant rulings that one can no longer say with a straight face that the Court mollycoddles criminal defendants.

This chapter examines what happened to *Miranda v. Arizona* and *Mapp v. Ohio*, two of the Warren Court's most controversial decisions. Law-and-order conservatives demanded Chief Justice Earl Warren's impeachment because they saw *Miranda* as a dangerous decision.[7] By 2000, after the Court seemed to have teed up *Miranda* to be overruled, a 7–2 majority "reaffirmed" the decision as constitutionally based in an opinion written by the new chief justice, William Rehnquist, chosen by Nixon with an expectation that he would vote to overrule *Miranda*.[8] *Mapp* held that the exclusionary rule was the appropriate remedy for Fourth Amendment violations. The Court's critics claimed that the ruling would be a disaster. For many reasons, their claims proved exaggerated. As with *Miranda*, the post-Warren Courts have chipped away at *Mapp*.

After a discussion of *Miranda* and *Mapp*, this chapter explores one more important Warren Court decision. Although even Carrington and many law-and-order commentators acknowledged the wisdom of *Gideon v. Wainwright*, extending the right of Sixth Amendment counsel to indigent defendants charged with felonies in state courts,[9] this chapter explores how states have gutted *Gideon*'s promise. Many states provide at best overworked, underfunded legal services for indigent defendants.

The criminal justice system has evolved, in part, as a result of VRM's policies to give prosecutors enormous power to compel defendants to plead guilty and to give judges the power to impose extreme sentences. Today, anyone viewing the available court-appointed representation for many indigent defendants would be hard-pressed to claim that the system tips in favor of criminal defendants.

Despite the reality that our court system now provides criminal defendants with diminishing constitutional protections, victims' rights supporters continue to claim that the system favors criminal defendants over victims. They argue unabashedly for due process for victims, typically with little concern for the diminished rights of defendants. After all, they continue to see this as a zero-sum game.[10]

The first section analyzes the role that the Warren Court played in changing the direction of the Court. It reviews Carrington and others' attacks on the Court and the role that the Court played in Nixon's presidential victory in 1968. The second section describes how the post-Warren Courts gutted *Miranda*. The third section examines how the Court has narrowed *Mapp*'s exclusionary rule. The fourth section highlights *Gideon*'s failed promise to provide indigent defendants with competent counsel. The overall theme of this chapter is that any objective observer today is hard-pressed to claim that the system tips in favor of criminal defendants. Indeed, some commentators have raised concerns about how the system now often pressures innocent defendants to plead guilty to avoid severe prison terms that may result from a conviction.

The Warren Court and the Evolution of the VRM

While many commentators cite Carrington's 1975 book *The Victims* as the start of the VRM, one can trace its origins to 1966, when Carrington formed Americans for Effective Law Enforcement to protest the Warren Court's criminal procedure revolution.[11] That revolution began in 1961 when the Supreme Court held that the exclusionary rule, whereby evidence seized in violation of the Fourth Amendment had to be suppressed at trial, applied as a limitation on state power.[12] However, while the Court extended other protections in the Bill of Rights, Carrington along with many Americans focused on *Miranda v. Arizona* as a particularly egregious decision.[13]

Among its many decisions giving fuller effect to protections for criminal defendants found in the Bill of Rights, *Miranda* created a special firestorm. Critics contended that it would dry up confessions and that confessions were needed to secure criminal convictions.[14]

Carrington's organization and then his book *The Victims* argued that the Warren Court and other judges were soft on crime. His rhetoric resonated among conservative politicians in particular.[15] Carrington and other organizers wanted to create a counterbalance to the American Civil Liberties Union and other liberal organizations and instead support police and "law-abiding" citizens.[16] California governor Ronald Reagan took note.[17] Importantly, so did Richard Nixon, then engaged in his bid to become president.

The Warren Court played a decisive role in the 1968 presidential election. Even prior to the election, Chief Justice Warren's *Miranda* opinion led to calls to "IMPEACH EARL WARREN."[18] With crime rates rising, avowed segregationist George Wallace, also a candidate for president in 1968, made crime a major issue of his campaign, often using overtly racist rhetoric. Richard Nixon was somewhat more restrained in his rhetoric, but his use of the "dog whistle" racist message could not be missed. Law and order, Nixon's key message, targeted the Supreme Court and its pro-defendant (often seen as pro–Black American) rulings.[19]

Once elected, Nixon was able to make four Supreme Court appointments between 1969 and 1971. Nixon might not have had the chance to alter the Court's direction so quickly but for a particularly impactful political gaffe on Lyndon Johnson's part.[20]

Although both were California Republicans, Warren and Nixon despised each other. Fearing that Nixon would win the election, Warren announced his retirement with time for Johnson to appoint his successor. Johnson nominated his longtime friend Abe Fortas, then a sitting associate justice, to replace Warren as chief justice. He also nominated fellow Texan Homer Thornberry, a judge on the U.S. Fifth Circuit Court of Appeals, to fill the spot that Fortas would vacate if he became chief justice. Fortas's nomination opened up inquiries into his questionable business dealings. His nomination floundered when senators successfully filibustered the nomination. More revelations about his relationship with a Wall Street financier led to Fortas's resignation.[21]

Warren and Fortas's resignations gave Nixon two appointments to the Court. First, he appointed Warren Burger to replace Earl Warren as chief justice. He chose Burger because of his hostility toward many of the liberal Warren Court rulings.[22] Second, although Nixon's first two nominees ran into political trouble,[23] he eventually appointed Harry Blackmun, who, although he would later be considered by some commentators as a constitutional liberal (at least by comparison to an increasingly right-wing Court), often took positions to the right of Fortas.[24]

Justices Black and Harlan's retirements in 1971 gave Nixon the chance to reshape the Court. Nixon's appointments, Lewis Powell and William Rehnquist, like Burger and Blackmun, were to the right of the justices whom they replaced. Nixon and his advisors' strategy was clear: the expectation was that the Court would either overrule or limit Warren Court precedent.[25]

Speculation that the Court would make a sharp turn to the right and immediately overturn Warren Court precedent was overly optimistic or pessimistic, depending on one's perspective. Unlike some of the more extreme justices appointed to the Court later, the new appointees adhered to traditional notions of stare decisis. Instead of swift overruling of prior case law, the Court refused to extend some holdings or began chipping away at others.[26] The next section turns to ways in which the post-Warren Courts eroded *Miranda*.

Miranda's Vanishing Act

As indicated above, even when the Warren Court decided cases like *Miranda*, its critics overstated anticipated harm, like the inability of the police to secure confessions, and undervalued why the Court provided extended defendants additional rights, like those provided in *Miranda*. But that is largely a historical debate. More importantly, the VRM continues to claim that the system is unfairly balanced in favor of defendants. As developed in this chapter, in light of what has happened after the end of the Warren Court, a fair commentator cannot make such a claim.

Unintentionally, Chief Justice Warren aided Carrington and other law-and-order conservatives' attack on *Miranda*. Warren made two statements in his majority opinion that gave its detractors a foothold in their attack. According to the *Miranda* Court, Congress or state legislatures could come up with alternative remedies to deal with coercive police practices that the Court condemned in *Miranda*. Critics also pointed to Warren's acknowledgment that, in some of the companion cases to *Miranda*, the confessions would not have been inadmissible under the Court's voluntariness case law.[27]

The chief justice's two statements opened two channels of attack: one argument was that if a legislature could replace *Miranda* with alternative procedures, *Miranda* warnings were not grounded in the Constitution. Even before the 1968 presidential election, Congress had enacted the 1968 Omnibus Crime Control Act, aiming to overrule *Miranda* in §3501. That provision reinstated the voluntariness standard as the controlling test for determining admissibility of a confession.[28]

Warren's second concession that some of the confessions in *Miranda*'s companion cases would not have been suppressed under the Court's voluntariness added to the claim of constitutional illegitimacy: the Court's rulings applied to the states as well as to the federal government. The

Court could dictate that states had to follow its voluntariness case law only if the state violated the Constitution. Absent a constitutional violation, the Court acted without authority.[29]

Almost from the outset, the Burger Court began eroding *Miranda*. While the Department of Justice did not attempt to rely on §3501, the provision in the 1968 Omnibus Crime Control Act that purported to overrule *Miranda*,[30] the Court routinely chipped away at almost every aspect of *Miranda*. In the 1970s, the Court characterized *Miranda*'s protections as merely "prophylactic." If only prophylactic, the argument went, the protections were not mandated by the Constitution and could not legitimately be imposed on the states. And because merely prophylactic, the protections were not coterminous with the voluntariness protections: those protections, now recognized as found in the Fifth Amendment, were the core protections. *Miranda* was not part of that core protection.[31]

More than once, the Court seemed to have teed up *Miranda* to be overruled. For example, in *Brewer v. Williams*, a case involving a brutal sexual assault and murder of a young girl, the Court seemed on the verge of abandoning *Miranda*. Iowa secured Williams's conviction in part based on his statement to a police detective that led authorities to the victim's body. Williams prevailed on his motion for writ of habeas corpus in the federal district court on three grounds: the police conduct violated the Sixth Amendment right to counsel, *Miranda*, and due process voluntariness.[32] The Court of Appeals agreed on the first two grounds. In a 5–4 decision, written by Justice Stewart, a *Miranda* dissenter, the Court found that the state violated Williams's Sixth Amendment right to counsel. As a result, the majority did not reach the question of *Miranda*'s constitutional status. Given that Williams won in the lower courts, one can draw the obvious inference: justices voting to grant review did so because the case, with its horrific facts, would make overruling *Miranda* possible. Instead, the Court resuscitated the relevance of the Sixth Amendment in the custodial setting.[33]

Efforts to overrule *Miranda* did not end with *Williams*. Almost alone, Professor Paul Cassell kept pressure on the Department of Justice to invoke §3501 as a vehicle for overruling *Miranda*.[34] By the time the Court granted review in *Dickerson v. United States*, where the lower courts considered §3501's applicability, a lot had changed since 1966.

The Burger and Rehnquist (and, since then, Roberts) Courts almost nonstop narrowed *Miranda*.[35] Other than instances in which a suspect invoked the right to *Miranda* counsel,[36] the Court did not extend or, more frequently, severely limited *Miranda*.[37]

As a measure of how effectively the post-Warren Courts eroded *Miranda*, consider the Court's 7–2 decision in *Dickerson v. United States*. Cassell's efforts to get the Court to overrule *Miranda* and to uphold applicability of §3501 seemed to have come to fruition when the Court granted review, in effect, to decide that question. The clear majority, over Justice Scalia's full-throated dissent, found that *Miranda* was grounded in the Constitution.[38]

Dickerson was noteworthy for several reasons. Anyone familiar with *Miranda*'s role in tipping the 1968 presidential election to Richard Nixon must realize the irony that Chief Justice Rehnquist wrote the decision. Nixon appointed him with an eye toward overruling *Miranda*.[39] While Rehnquist's "endorsement" of *Miranda*'s constitutional foundation was tepid at best, *Miranda*, as rewritten over thirty plus years, still lives. It has survived largely because the Court had so thoroughly eroded *Miranda* that it bore almost no relationship to *Miranda* as authored by Chief Justice Warren.[40]

Even now, Cassell continues to argue that *Miranda* comes with an unwarranted cost, leading to suppression of some significant number of confessions.[41] Despite that continuing debate, *Dickerson* reflected the reality even in 2000: law enforcement has learned to live with *Miranda*. Its rules are sufficiently clear, and police can give warnings without fear of invocation of *Miranda* rights in most cases. *Miranda*'s erosion is so complete that many constitutional liberals have little faith in its ability to protect suspects most in need of rights that the *Miranda* Court sought to protect. For example, *Miranda* provides little help for inexperienced and frightened suspects, potentially pressured into making false confessions. Whatever the reality in 1966, today no one can seriously contend that *Miranda*-lite helps to mollycoddle suspects.[42]

Mapp's Continuing Erosion

Other Warren Court case law has suffered similar erosion during the past fifty-plus years. *Mapp v. Ohio* provides another example of an opinion that Carrington and other VRM advocates cited as proof that the system favored defendants over victims.[43] As with *Miranda*, claims that *Mapp* would do violence to the criminal justice system were greatly exaggerated. Also as with *Miranda*, the post-Warren Courts have eroded *Mapp*, leaving it as a far less robust remedy than its critics claimed.

As is the case with many constitutional provisions, the Fourth Amendment speaks in broad terms. It includes no express remedy for violations of its provisions.[44] As early as 1914, in *Weeks v. United States*, the Supreme Court held that when federal authorities violate the Fourth Amendment, courts should exclude the evidence. It found that the mere return of illegally seized property was an insufficient remedy.[45]

Consistent with the Court's long-standing position that the protections in the Bill of Rights were limitations on federal, not state, power, the Court rejected the petitioner's argument in *Wolf v. Colorado* that the exclusionary rule applied to state officials when they violated the Fourth Amendment.[46] According to Justice Frankfurter, *Wolf*'s author, states needed to have some effective remedy for Fourth Amendment violations; but the exclusion of evidence was not part of the Fourth Amendment's core protection. A mere twelve years later, the Court revisited that question in *Mapp v. Ohio*.[47]

Mapp's facts offered the Court a vehicle to question *Wolf*'s holding. There, police were acting on a tip that a bombing suspect lived in Mapp's home. When they arrived at her home, Mapp resisted their efforts to enter her home on advice of counsel. Although the historical record differs from the facts reported in the Court's decision, police falsely claimed to have a search warrant. After Mapp grabbed the paper that an officer waved at her, officers wrestled it from her. When her attorney arrived at the scene, officers refused to allow him entrance and ignored his protests that their conduct was illegal. Officers found not a bomber but pornographic material in Mapp's possession. The state pursued charges that Mapp was in possession of pornographic material.[48]

By the late 1950s, when Ohio officials pursued charges against Mapp, litigants were challenging pornography laws on First Amendment grounds. Mapp's core claim was that her prosecution violated the First Amendment.[49] Raised in passing was the argument that the Court adopted: the state had to adhere to the exclusionary rule when police violated the Fourth Amendment. Justice Clark's slim majority in 1961 ushered in the Warren Court's criminal procedure revolution. At root was whether a protection found in the Bill of Rights was fundamental to the American scheme of justice to require that states adhere to those rights as part of Fourteenth Amendment due process.[50]

Unlike *Miranda*, *Mapp* did not suggest arguments that would undercut its legitimacy. The Court stated that although the Fourth Amendment was silent on the appropriate remedy, the Constitution required the exclusionary rule as the remedy for its violation. While the Court recognized that the police need incentives to comply with the Fourth Amendment and would be deterred from violating its provisions by the threat of evidence suppression, the Court also grounded its holding on the need for judges to comply with the Constitution. Thus, the argument went, if judges allowed use of illegally seized evidence to be used in criminal proceedings, they became parties to illegality. Judicial integrity required judges to deny the use of such evidence.[51]

Like *Miranda* would do five years later, *Mapp* produced a serious attack from law-and-order conservatives. *Mapp* was open to some legitimate criticism: for example, the Court seemed to decide an issue not fully litigated by the parties.[52] The Court also overruled recent precedent, violating the traditional principle of stare decisis.[53] Exclusionary rule opponents saw *Mapp* as undercutting effective policing practices. Among its most vocal critics was then-judge Burger. His law review article *Who Will Watch the Watchman?* contributed to Nixon's interest in appointing him as chief justice.[54] Once on the Court, Burger's distaste for the exclusionary rule was in evidence almost immediately. In his words, the rule is a "Draconian, discredited device in its present absolutist form."[55]

The Court set the stage for *Mapp*'s erosion even before the beginning of the Burger Court. In *Linkletter v. Walker*, the Court refused to apply *Mapp* retroactively. The Court treated the primary purpose of the exclusionary rule to be deterrence of police misconduct, largely ignoring the judicial integrity argument.[56] That focus would become the Court's mantra in subsequent exclusionary rule case law.

Since *Mapp*, the Court has repeatedly limited application of the exclusionary rule. Justices and commentators opposing the exclusionary rule cited several arguments to overrule or narrow its application. At core, the post-Warren Courts focused on the deterrence-as-the-rationale argument to find that the rule does not apply. For example, in *United States v. Calandra*, the Court held that a grand jury witness could not refuse to answer questions even if the questions were based on evidence discovered in violation of the Fourth Amendment. The majority concluded that any deterrent value was outweighed by the cost of the rule's application.[57]

The Court's cost-benefit analysis, focusing only on deterrence as the possible justification for suppression, has continued. That analysis has led to the Court rejecting the use of the exclusionary rule in, for example, civil tax assessment proceedings[58] and federal habeas corpus cases, as long as a defendant had a full and fair opportunity to litigate the Fourth Amendment claim in state court.[59]

By ignoring the judicial integrity rationale and focusing only on deterrence, members of the Court focused on an argument that would ultimately narrow the exclusionary rule: only an officer who is aware that their conduct is illegal can be deterred. Therefore, the argument went, the Court should adopt a good-faith exception to the exclusionary rule. When the Court squarely addressed whether the exclusionary rule applies only when officers are aware that their conduct is unlawful, the Court adopted a different formulation of its test. In *United States v. Leon*, the Court permitted the use of evidence at trial that was seized pursuant to a technically defective search warrant. Despite the technical illegality of the police conduct, *Leon* held that the inquiry into the officer's good faith required an inquiry into whether "a reasonably well-trained officer would have known that the search was illegal despite the magistrate's authorization" of the warrant.[60]

The Court continued its narrowing of the rule, culminating with *Herring v. United States*. There, while Herring was at the Coffee County Sheriff's Department, an officer asked the county clerk to see if the department had any outstanding warrants for Herring's arrest. When the clerk did not find a warrant, the officer had the clerk check with the Dale County Sheriff's Department. That department's clerk indicated that an outstanding warrant was in effect. That information was stale.

Chief Justice Roberts's opinion in *Herring* included provocative dicta. He suggested that the extreme police misconduct in *Weeks* and *Mapp* explained the Court's adoption of the exclusionary rule in those cases. Because the exclusionary rule was premised on such extreme misconduct, said the chief justice, "To trigger the exclusionary rule, police conduct must be sufficiently deliberate that exclusion can meaningfully deter it, and sufficiently culpable that such deterrence is worth the price paid by the justice system."[61] Thus, according to *Herring*, the exclusionary rule is premised on a showing of "deliberate, reckless, or grossly negligent conduct, or in some circumstances recurring or systemic negligence."[62] Given that the officer in *Herring* acted reasonably, that language was dicta. To date, the Court has not formally adopted *Herring*'s dicta.[63]

The Court has ignored the effectiveness of the exclusionary rule. As one author has demonstrated, the application of the exclusionary rule led to increased professionalism within police forces.[64] Further, justices who have voted to narrow the exclusionary rule and law-and-order advocates in the VRM ignore a different kind of victim: victims of illegal police conduct.[65]

Cases like *Leon* and *Herring* demonstrate the ways in which the post-Warren Courts have whittled down the application of the exclusionary rule. Fears raised by law-and-order conservatives that the exclusionary rule would have a devastating effect on the criminal justice system were overblown from the outset. Critics like Burger claimed that the rule would allow the release of countless criminals.[66] When data showed that few defendants had evidence suppressed as a result of the exclusionary rule, the attack on the application of the rule changed in tone, but not in intensity.[67]

Miranda and *Mapp* are not the only Warren Court opinions that Carrington and other VRM critics of the Warren Court claimed tilted the system toward criminals, requiring a rebalancing of the system to protect victims. Many of those holdings have been reshaped by post-Warren Courts as well.[68] Thus, claims about the ways in which the criminal justice system mollycoddles criminals are wildly overstated today and almost certainly were overstated at the time.[69] But, as developed below, even without the erosion of pro-defendant rights, a panoply of rights provides little benefit if defendants lack competent counsel to advance those rights. Today, indigent defendants often lack adequate access to effective assistance of counsel.

Gideon's Failed Promise

Between 1961 and 1969, the Warren Court held that most of the protections afforded criminal defendants in the Bill of Rights applied to the states as well as to the federal government. Although many law-and-order supporters followed Carrington's lead in questioning the Court's legitimacy, the American criminal justice system, at least for a time, offered a rights-based model worthy of imitation. As argued by Professors Geoffrey Stone and David Strauss in *Democracy and Equality*, the Warren Court pursued truly democratic values.[70] The Court's criminal procedure revolution often demonstrated that commitment.

Not all of the Warren Court's decisions raised questions of legitimacy. One opinion that gained widespread support was its decision in *Gideon v. Wainwright*, holding that the Sixth Amendment required a state to provide competent counsel to an indigent defendant charged with a felony.[71] Observers of the criminal justice system have begun to acknowledge that *Gideon's* promise has failed.

In *Powell v. Alabama*, decided in 1932, the Court found that the state violated due process when it failed to provide competent counsel to indigent defendants faced with capital murder charges.[72] The Court did not hold that Alabama violated the Sixth Amendment right to counsel; under the then-prevailing view of the Bill of Rights, the Sixth Amendment was not a limitation on state power.[73]

The Court's analysis in cases like *Powell*, based on fundamental fairness, produced ad hoc results, depending on a myriad of factors in specific cases. For example, in *Betts v. Brady*, decided in 1942, the Court held that only upon a showing of a variety of factors did a state have to appoint counsel for an indigent.[74] Hence, someone who was illiterate or of limited intelligence or was facing a particularly complex charge might be entitled to counsel.[75] In dissent, Justice Black urged incorporation of the Sixth Amendment, requiring adherence to its command of a right to counsel in all felony cases. As he stated in *Betts*, the idea is that an innocent person should not be forced to risk conviction because of his poverty.[76]

Justice Black prevailed in *Gideon*. Gideon, a drifter with an extensive record of minor criminal offenses, requested counsel when he was charged with committing a burglary. The trial court denied his request based on state law that required appointment of counsel only in capital cases. Gideon represented himself, leading to his conviction. He eventually petitioned the Court for review. The Supreme Court appointed prominent D.C. lawyer and later Supreme Court justice Abe Fortas to argue the case for Gideon.[77] A unanimous Court found for Gideon.[78] On retrial, with competent counsel, Gideon was acquitted.[79]

The Court's unanimity suggests that the result was widely viewed as correct. Even many law-and-order conservatives view the right to counsel as fundamental, including Carrington, who observed that *Gideon* was rightly decided.[80] Summarizing the United States' commitment to providing competent counsel for all defendants, former attorney general Eric Holder stated that "our criminal justice system, and our faith in it, depends on effective representation on both sides."[81] Professional groups like the American Bar Association echo that view.[82]

That is the good news. On the ground, the system has not worked as well as the Court hoped it would in 1963. States vary on how they provide indigent defendants with counsel. Some states and the District of Columbia have created highly regarded public defender offices.[83] Other states use one of two other systems: a contract system, whereby the county contracts with a private firm to provide indigent counsel, or a system of ad hoc court appointment of attorneys willing to handle indigent cases.[84] In theory, these systems comply with *Gideon*'s command. In practice, many states and local governments fail miserably in their obligation to provide indigent defendants with competent counsel. Two significant problems erode the effectiveness of public defenders and other court-appointed counsel systems. The first problem is that as a result of years of increased sentences and mandatory minimum sentences, prosecutors can pressure even innocent defendants to plead guilty to avoid long prison terms.[85] The second problem is economic: many states and local governments underfund their systems that provide counsel for indigents.[86] Often, even the best attorney's caseload is so heavy that she cannot provide meaningful assistance to many, if not most, of her clients.

The VRM, among other interest groups, has contributed to decades of increased use of prisons as the remedy of choice in criminal cases. While a broad coalition of politicians and interest groups have contributed to the process, the VRM has encouraged legislatures to enhance sentences and to create minimum sentences for many crimes. Since the end of the Warren Court, the criminal justice system has become addicted to guilty pleas. Well over 90 percent of all defendants plead guilty. Prosecutors confront defendants and their overworked attorneys with plea agreements that even innocent defendants may not be able to resist. One major report summarized the problem in the federal system: "There is ample evidence that federal criminal defendants are being coerced to plead guilty because the penalty for exercising their constitutional rights is simply too high a risk."[87] Similar concerns exist about state systems as well.[88] To be clear, the risk is not simply that *guilty* defendants plead guilty but that innocent defendants do so as well.[89]

Anecdotes demonstrate why an innocent person might plead guilty and why such a plea may become part of a downward spiral in that person's life. As the Department of Justice demonstrated in its 2015 investigation of the Ferguson, Missouri, Police Department , following the police killing of Michael Brown, the impact is especially severe in minority communities. Imagine an innocent defendant who is unable to make bail.[90] Delays in bringing the defendant to trial leave that person at risk of losing his job. Even though innocent of the charges, he may accept a plea offer because he has the chance of going home immediately.[91]

In the previous scenario, even if the plea is only to a misdemeanor, the conviction by guilty plea may begin a downward spiral in that person's life. He may have lost his job because of time away from work. His criminal record may make him less employable when he looks for another job. Part of the plea agreement may include paying a fine. The economic reality may mean that the now-unemployed person might have to borrow money to pay the fine. Failing to pay may lead to exorbitant interest and costs accruing, furthering the downward spiral.[92] As the Department of Justice report demonstrated, some local governments use such fines to fund their court systems. Poorer and minority community members are far more likely to be trapped in such a downward spiral.[93]

The second, closely related problem with the criminal justice system's commitment to provide a defendant with adequate counsel is the failure to fund the system adequately. Sufficient funding has become a chronic problem in many jurisdictions. The problem has been so severe that some litigants have sued governmental entities based on the claim that inadequate funding means that services provided by overworked attorneys violate indigent defendants' Sixth Amendment right to competent counsel.[94]

Plaintiffs base such claims on facts like the sheer size of attorneys' caseloads, their inability to meet with clients except briefly before discussing the proffered plea offers, and their inability to do adequate investigations to find exculpatory evidence.[95] Other allegations include lack of training for attorneys representing indigent defendants, lack of independence, and frequent cases in which counsel is forced to represent multiple defendants whose interests are in conflict. In some instances, plaintiffs have filed on behalf of juvenile offenders and argued that the Sixth Amendment requires, at a minimum, that court-appointed counsel be familiar with the juvenile justice system.[96] Some cases raise the reality of unequal funding from community to community, leading also to claims of violations of equal protection: for various reasons, indigent African American defendants end up with inadequate counsel.[97] Other suits raise concerns that courts do not appoint counsel until defendants have already been in jail for a year or more awaiting trial.[98]

The picture is grim enough in the run-of-the-mill criminal case. But imagine similar problems when defendants face the death penalty. Surely, one might expect that courts would appoint highly experienced and competent counsel in capital murder cases. Again, some jurisdictions have well-funded death penalty public defender offices or attorneys with extensive death penalty litigation experience. That kind of specialized training is essential. Substantial evidence indicates that juries are unlikely to impose the death penalty when competent counsel represents the accused.[99]

Professor Brandon Garrett's *End of Its Rope: How Killing the Death Penalty Can Revive Criminal Justice* provides detailed examples of how competent attorneys, along with trained investigators and experts, prevent clients from receiving the death penalty.[100] Perhaps the most impressive example is the case of James Holmes, the Aurora, Colorado, murderer who killed twelve moviegoers in 2012. His careful planning of the crime to maximize casualties made the liability question, that is, premeditation, a foregone conclusion. Despite that, the well-trained defense team succeeded in sparing Holmes's life. His case is hardly unique in capital cases where the death penalty team consists of competent personnel and is adequately funded.[101]

Unlike Holmes's case, many offenders who end up on death row lack anything comparable to competent counsel. Again, Garrett's book collects anecdotes that anyone familiar with death penalty literature knows are far too common. For example, Garrett described lawyers who slept through much of the trial or who were drunk or on drugs during the trial. In North Carolina, one in six death row prisoners was represented by counsel later disbarred or disciplined for misconduct.[102] Death row inmates now are likely to be housed in states that grossly underfund the court-appointed counsel system. Amazingly, courts have affirmed death penalties in some cases even when the court accepted the allegations that counsel was drunk, on drugs, or asleep during key parts of the case.[103] One appellate court, for example, suggested that co-counsel let his colleague sleep as a strategic move.[104]

Of course, indigent defendants are at risk not only for unequal treatment. For a host of reasons, our current system is ingrained with racial inequality: race matters when juries decide who will end up on death row.[105]

So think back to Carrington and other victims' rights advocates' central thesis. Initially, they argued, the Warren Court skewed the criminal justice system in favor of criminal defendants. The system had to be rebalanced to protect victims. Whether the Warren Court's rulings ever tilted the system unfairly in favor of defendants is doubtful. The Court's decisions have been so cabined by post-Warren case law that making those claims today is unsustainable.

Even in areas like the need for states to provide competent counsel for criminal defendants facing jail or prison time that are widely acknowledged as correctly decided, the current picture of our criminal justice system hardly looks like a cakewalk for indigent defendants.

Despite widely recognized realities of our criminal justice system in the modern era, many victims' rights advocates continue to argue that the system is unbalanced in favor of criminal defendants. That perspective is hard to reconcile with the realities of our criminal justice system. As discussed in chapter 2, the VRM can rightly take credit for some important changes to the law. But demanding more rights for victims on the theory that the system has tipped so far in favor of defendants is implausible.

5

Eliminating and Extending Statutes of Limitations

For years, officials in organizations like the Catholic Church and the Boys Scouts of America worked hard to hide sexual misconduct by their members. Only after years of investigation and litigation did the extent of misconduct come to light.[1] Similarly, men like Harvey Weinstein, Jeffrey Epstein, and Bill Cosby engaged in gross sexual misconduct that largely went undetected for years.[2]

By the time the crimes of sexual predators came to light, many victims felt unheard. Despite broad support for prosecuting such egregious conduct, many prosecutions were time-barred because of relatively short statutes of limitations for sex offenses.[3]

Many victims' rights groups support eliminating or extending statutes of limitations. While such proposals are limited typically to sex offenses, not to other crimes like robbery, the Victims' Rights Movement generally supports such efforts. Traditional VRM members like district attorneys and their professional associations are strong supporters of such measures.[4] That is, those measures are not part only of a feminist agenda.[5]

Such measures find broad support among members of the public and policy makers.[6] Victims' rights groups make several arguments to support such changes. As also discussed in chapter 6, they argue that victims need closure by participating in the prosecution of their sexual predators. They claim that traumatized victims do not become aware of their trauma for many years and need the extension of time to achieve justice.[7] They deny that the lapse of time impairs memory. Despite intuitive sense to the contrary, some advocates claim that memory remains intact, reducing the risk of criminalizing innocent defendants.[8]

The case in favor of eliminating or extending statutes of limitations seems so compelling that one might ask why anyone would object. Any claim of unfairness to men like Weinstein and Cosby seems questionable at best. At least if allegations are true, both were serial sexual abusers.

As happened in their prosecutions, they were able to hire high-powered criminal defense lawyers to present their defenses.[9]

But policy makers and courts should be concerned about eliminating or extending statutes of limitations. Long ago, legislatures in the United States created statutes of limitations, often for policy reasons still at play. Focusing on dramatic cases of uber-wealthy defendants like Weinstein and Cosby skews one's view of the fairness of measures to abandon limitation periods. Often, the VRM has driven policy based on headline cases. Those cases are often atypical, resulting in laws that create prejudice for more typical defendants, unable to afford superstar counsel, often dependent on overworked public defenders.

The first section describes the statutes of limitations in the United States. The second section discusses the headline cases propelling the move to eliminate or expand statutes of limitations and the arguments proponents make to explain such changes. The third section examines those arguments with a critical eye. The discussion focuses on what at least some legal commentators and members of the public think are unacceptable risks to convicting innocent defendants.

Statutes of Limitations: An Overview

Statutes of limitations, as implied by the term, are creatures of statutes. They did not exist as part of common law. Despite the adoption of English common law, the first U.S. Congress enacted legislation creating specific statutes of limitations.[10]

Given that the United States consists of fifty state criminal systems and the federal system, statutes of limitations vary from jurisdiction to jurisdiction. Yet some generalizations are possible.

In the federal system, by legislation, capital offenses may be brought without time limitations. Congress created a catchall provision creating a five-year statute of limitations for other federal crimes and specific statutes of limitations, dealing with particular crimes. For example, the theft of artwork has a twenty-year statute of limitations, arson a ten-year one.[11] The pattern varies, depending on unique policy considerations for other crimes or circumstances that may make detection difficult.

Federal law now contains two major provisions extending the statute of limitations in child sex abuse cases. One provision eliminates the statute of limitations for certain child sexual abuse cases. Another provision allows charges to be brought within the longer of ten years or the life of the victim.[12]

States vary considerably with regard to their statutes of limitations. Most include no statute of limitations for murder. Various policies support such a rule for murder (or in some states, first degree murder). Most importantly, statutes of limitations advance the general goal of prompt reporting. In many murder cases, the only person who might report the crime is dead. Additional policies include the complexity of some murder cases, requiring more investigation than involved in other cases. Sometimes cited is the argument that in instances where an innocent person is convicted and exonerated, the murderer remains at large and should be subject to punishment for the crime.[13]

States vary on the length of the statutes of limitations for other felonies. Alaska, for example, has two tiers of crimes: for some the statute of limitations is five years, for others ten years. Arizona's general statute of limitations is seven years. California sets the limitations at six or three years, depending on the crime. Connecticut has a patchwork: for the most serious felonies, there is no statute of limitations. For most other felonies, the statute of limitations is five years. For sexual assault, abuse, or exploitation, the statute of limitations is thirty years. In cases of the abuse of minors, the statute of limitations runs for five years after the victim gives notification to the police. One can find a comprehensive list of state statutes of limitations at the website cited in the endnotes.[14]

Most jurisdictions recognize equitable exceptions to the more rigid time limits implied by statutes of limitations. Statutes of limitations may be tolled if a defendant has fled or otherwise frustrated reasonable efforts of police to locate him.[15] Typical is a federal statute that provides that "[n]o statute of limitations shall extend to any person fleeing from justice."[16] State statutes vary. For example, some require a showing that the offender was fleeing or hiding. Other statutes toll the limitation period for any amount of time that the offender is absent from that state. Yet another variation tolls the statutes of limitations when the suspect is out of state, but the relevant provision may set out deadlines for prosecution.[17]

Importantly, these kinds of laws reflect a balance of competing policies. As summarized in the Working Papers of the National Commission on Reform of Federal Criminal Laws, "The primary reasons for restrictions of time revolve around universally accepted notions that prompt investigation and prosecution insures that conviction or acquittal is a reliable result, and not the product of faded memory or unavailable evidence; that ancient wrongs ought not to be resurrected except in some cases of concealment of the offense or identity of the offender; and that community security and economy in allocation of enforcement resources require that most effort be concentrated on recent wrongs."[18] As indicated above, on the other side of the ledger are equitable considerations. The law should not encourage an offender to frustrate the legitimate efforts to pursue the offender's arrest and prosecution. At the same time, all jurisdictions today maintain statutes of limitations for most crimes, except murder, with limited exceptions. But, as developed below, states and the federal government have rethought that balance in child sexual abuse and sexual assault cases.

Pressure to Eliminate or Extend Statutes of Limitations in Sex Offense Cases

One does not need to look far to find headlines about demands to extend statutes of limitations in sex offense cases. Even before the #MeToo Movement,[19] revelations about years of cover-ups regarding child sexual abuse by Catholic priests and other men in positions of power have incensed members of the public.[20]

In the United States, claims of sexual abuse by Catholic priests surfaced in the mid-1980s.[21] Books and articles about the abuse began to appear in the 1990s, culminating with an important series published by the *Boston Globe*.[22] The cases continue to surface with several themes: Church officials routinely reappointed priests to other dioceses; they seldom reported abuse to public officials; and Church officials seemed more concerned about the Church's reputation than the harm to young victims of abuse.[23]

Lawsuits mounted against the Church. Many of those suits settled, costing the Church billions of dollars. Often, Church officials were not forthcoming during discovery but attempted to shield the Church and its priests from public scrutiny. Another tactic was to attempt to acknowledge the abuse scandal but engage in damage control. For example, even as recently as 2008, years after the cases began to mount, Church officials contended that "only" about 1 percent of its priests worldwide were involved in abuse.[24]

In 2018, a Pennsylvania grand jury reported its findings about abuse within the church in that state. In its 884-page report, the grand jury found over a thousand claims of abuse by about three hundred priests in six of the eight dioceses in Pennsylvania. The report speculated that there were likely thousands more cases that went unreported.[25]

Despite obvious criminal violations, the state pursued only two criminal cases. That was because the statute of limitations had run on most of the crimes. Among several recommendations, the Pennsylvania grand jury urged that the statute of limitations for criminal violations be eliminated.[26]

Stories continue to emerge that enrage the public. For example, in 2019 the Associated Press published a report revealing that about seventeen hundred priests, monks, and other Church members accused of sexual misconduct were "living under the radar," unsupervised by Church or police authorities. Many of those individuals were working with young people in positions of trust or authority.[27]

The COVID-19 pandemic pushed many stories off the front page. But another headline story during 2020 concerned the Boy Scout sex abuse scandal. That scandal dates back many years but recently has picked up momentum. Civil suits resulted in significant jury verdicts, eventually leading the organization in February 2020 to file in federal court to seek Chapter 11 bankruptcy protection. By November 2020, over sixty thousand men had come forward to make claims against the organization, while many more victims chose not to join the proceedings.[28]

As with the Catholic Church, the Boy Scout officials tried to deny claims of abuse for many years. Also like the situation with regard to criminal prosecutions of priests, few criminal charges have been brought against sex abusers within the Boy Scouts.[29]

COVID-19 pushed yet other sex scandals off the front page. The powerful movie mogul Harvey Weinstein first came under public scrutiny for sex offenses in 2015. He was convicted of two counts of sexual misconduct in February 2020 and sentenced to twenty-three years in prison in March 2020.[30] Many claims of other acts of sexual misconduct have surfaced against Weinstein. While he faces trial in Los Angeles in late 2022, many of the other charges are time-barred.[31]

Charges against once-beloved actor Bill Cosby also focused national attention on difficulties faced by women who have been assaulted by prominent men. Despite more than fifty women coming forward with charges against Cosby, prosecutors were barely able to proceed against him because the statute of limitations almost ran on the charges eventually brought against him.[32]

Before his suicide in jail, Jeffrey Epstein was yet another prominent man facing many charges of sexual abuse. As with Weinstein, Boy Scout leaders, and Catholic priests, Epstein would have been able to avoid prosecution on many of the charges because the statute of limitations would have run.[33]

Cases like these make powerful headlines. Beyond the headlines, a number of interest groups, notably victims' rights organizations, have been able to advance their policy positions in part because of the headlines. That agenda includes lengthening or abandoning statutes of limitations in sex and child sex offense cases.[34]

Backed by victims' rights organizations, policy makers have advanced several arguments to justify lengthening or abandoning statutes of limitations in sex and child sex offense cases. Here are their most important arguments.

Victims' rights organizations point to other legislative changes as part of their contribution to the law. Most states now allow victim impact statements and evidence as part of the sentencing process in criminal cases. Such evidence can be powerful, as manifest in some widely reported cases. Importantly, many victims' rights supporters argue that participating in criminal proceedings where victims can confront their abusers produces "closure" for the victims.[35]

Beyond closure for victims, victims' rights advocates argue that eliminating or extending statutes of limitations protects against rapists creating more victims. For example, according to a spokesperson for the Rape, Abuse, and Incest National Network (RAINN), "The act of rape doesn't change over time—just because a certain amount of time has passed doesn't mean that someone is less culpable." Some offenders are serial offenders, creating a continuing public safety issue. As the RAINN spokesperson stated, "We don't want to reward a rapist for being good at not getting caught."[36]

Typically, statutes of limitations find support in the argument that the lapse of time makes defending charges difficult for defendants. Memory fades and evidence may be lost. Victims' advocates argue that abuse victims suffer from repressed memories that prevent them from making timely reports and that when the memories surface, they are accurate. A website for a group of attorneys representing victims of child molestation states, "Our legal team of child molestation attorneys cannot even begin to count how many victims with whom we have spoken with that convey, in their 40's and 50's, little pieces of memories come at them bit by bit. . . . Eventually, like a jigsaw puzzle, they put together these pieces until they come to the realization that, 'Oh my God, I was sexually abused by my coach!'"[37] Apparently, the average age for childhood and adolescent abuse victims to reveal their abuse is fifty-two years old.[38] Some psychologists explain that young people delay reporting abuse because they do not trust adults; only when children age do they feel independent enough to disclose the facts of their abuse.[39]

Advocates for victims of sexual and child sexual assault believe that "statutes of limitations are a bitter impediment to justice." Contrary to conventional teaching, some advocates contend that "our brains are actually wired to hold on to the details of stressful and traumatic experiences."[40]

Some legislatures single out for special treatment cases where DNA evidence exists. While a state might keep in place statutes of limitations for other offenses, it might create an exception if DNA evidence is available.[41]

These efforts often go hand in hand with legislation to extend the statute of limitations in civil cases. As indicated above, in some instances, as with the Boy Scouts, extending the statute of limitations has led to a flood of case filings, pushing the organization into bankruptcy. Some victims' rights advocates argue that reality supports extending or abandoning the statute of limitations in criminal cases.

Cases like those highlighted above produce broad public support. What is objectionable about efforts to support victims of such egregious crimes? I turn to that question below. First, however, one needs to understand the role that the VRM has played in the development of criminal justice policy in the United States.

Counterarguments to VRM's Claims about Statutes of Limitations

As developed in chapter 1, the VRM has benefited from policy makers' rejection of expertise and willingness to vote in favor of policies that were more popular than sound. This section explores how that general observation applies to these specific policy choices. Here, policy makers make popular policy choices rather than backing less popular, but more principled, policies ingrained in our criminal justice system. Here, "by principled" I mean policies consistent with the goals of a mature criminal justice system. Notably, here, the trend toward abandoning statutes of limitations in sexual assault cases increases the chances of convicting innocent defendants.

Closure

Years ago, jurisdictions in the United States bifurcated tort law and criminal law. The systems have different goals. Essentially, the tort system seeks to compensate innocent victims for harm caused by defendants, while the criminal justice system seeks to punish blameworthy defendants. Despite that, many advocates for eliminating or extending statutes of limitations argue that allowing participation in the prosecution of their abusers or putative abusers provides relief to victims.[42] That argument has a simple rebuttal and a more complex counterargument.

The simple rebuttal is that extending the statute of limitations in civil cases can provide victims much more meaningful relief than having the state pursue criminal charges against the alleged abusers. Indeed, states have extended statutes of limitations in civil cases, which have resulted in compensation funds for victims.[43] That makes sense because trauma victims need access to good medical and psychological care. Victims may lack access to such care. That would seemingly respond to concerns about allowing victims to participate in criminal proceedings long after their injuries. Criminal proceedings are not well designed to remedy personal harm; civil damages should address that kind of harm.[44]

The more complex argument advanced by victims' rights advocates is that participation in the criminal proceedings gives victims closure. As discussed more fully in chapter 6, many listeners now believe that "closure" is a well-recognized psychological term. But, as Professor Susan Bandes has shown, it is not. Instead, "[c]losure is a term with no accepted psychological meaning. It is, in fact, an unacknowledged umbrella term for a host of loosely related and often empirically dubious concepts."[45] Further, victims who expect to experience "closure," if by that one means healing of the victims' trauma, are likely to be disappointed with the results of their participation in court proceedings.[46]

Many crime victims suffer from posttraumatic stress disorder (PTSD). No serious psychological professional would contend that confronting one's abuser in an unregulated courtroom setting is the recognized treatment for PTSD.[47] At best, such a freewheeling confrontation might be helpful if made part of a more carefully controlled treatment modality. But that is not how courtroom drama plays out.

Similarly, the idea that all sexual assault victims are traumatized is inaccurate. For those who have adjusted to life without confronting their abusers or who have received sufficient care to go on with their lives, participation in criminal proceedings years later would seem at best to be unnecessary and perhaps even retraumatizing.[48]

Serial Rapists and Culpability

Nonetheless, victims' rights advocates might respond, as suggested above, by arguing that eliminating or extending statutes of limitations for sex offenses may prevent other victims in the future. Or as cited above, they might argue that some offenders are serial offenders, creating a continuing public safety issue.

Similar to other arguments widely advanced by victims' rights advocates and widely accepted by members of the media and general public, the view of the unrepentant and untreatable sexual pervert is largely untrue. Headline cases fuel the view of sexual predators beyond the capacity for reform. Often, legislatures respond to such headline cases by enacting restrictive sex offender laws typically based on the aberrational case.[49]

As I have observed elsewhere,

A young child vanishes from her home. After frantic efforts to locate the child, her body is found, with evidence of sexual assault. Police eventually arrest a convicted sex offender, who lives in her neighborhood. In another episode, police find an abducted child's severed head. In yet another headline case, the police learn that the perpetrator, another convicted sex offender, buried his victim alive.

Who cannot react with outrage to such stories? Despite the infrequency of such abductions and murders, they command the public's attention, often staying in the headlines for weeks. Cases like these, although statistical aberrations, have driven America's policies in dealing with sexual offenders for over a decade.[50]

Similarly, as Professor Katharine Baker has observed,

A 1989 Bureau of Justice Statistics recidivism study found that only 7.7% of released rapists were rearrested for rape. In contrast, 33.5% of released larcenists were rearrested for larceny; 31.9% of released burglars were rearrested for burglary; and 24.8% of drug offenders were rearrested for drug offenses. Only homicide had a lower recidivism rate than rape. It is true that released rapists are more likely than other released prisoners to be rearrested for rape, but that rapists are more likely than others to rape again does not distinguish rapists from other criminals. Larcenists are twenty-five percent more likely to be rearrested for larceny than rapists are to be rearrested for rape. Arguing from the statistics, a crime-based prior act exception is better suited to larcenists and drug offenders than to rapists.[51]

Data like these undercut the claim that one needs to extend statutes of limitations because most rapists are serial offenders.

The RAINN spokesperson raised a second issue: just because time has passed does not mean that the rapist is not culpable. That is true but raises complex questions about the purposes of punishment within our criminal justice system. Beyond the scope of this chapter is an extensive discussion of justifications for punishment. Even a few words about the different justifying goals of punishment suggest why extending the statutes of limitations may be unwarranted. Criminologists have demonstrated that many offenders "age" out of their criminal years; in effect, they self-rehabilitate.[52] As such, the criminal law no longer needs to intervene to rehabilitate such offenders. Similarly, the idea that the prospect of facing criminal prosecution many years in the future would deter a prospective offender is not persuasive. Studies demonstrate that certainty of punishment is more important than severity of punishment.[53] In addition, experts know that young offenders are impulsive, not thinking about the long-term consequences of their actions.[54] Retributive arguments point in different directions: perhaps, one must punish an offender long after the crime because he deserved punishment. Alternatively, if a rehabilitated offender has become a "different" person, does the new person still deserve punishment for conduct done long ago? More critically, the retribution argument assumes the guilt of the person accused of rape. As discussed below, the lapse of time increases the risk of convicting innocent defendants.

Faulty Memory, Convicting Innocent Defendants

Shouldn't legislatures and courts be concerned that expanding or eliminating statutes of limitations will lead to the conviction of more innocent defendants? Memory fades over time, doesn't it? Access to exculpatory evidence may be lost with the passage of time. Victims' rights supporters claim otherwise.

Victims' rights advocates who urge expanding statutes of limitations for sex offenses argue that memory of essential details does not fade over time. For example, in an article summarizing the arguments for abandoning statutes of limitations in sex offense cases, the author cited Jim Hopper, a Harvard professor of psychology, as supporting the claim that our brains hold onto details occurring during stressful events.[55]

Hopper argues that traumatic memories involve three processes. First is encoding, whereby the brain retains central details, but not peripheral details. The second stage is storage. Again, the brain retains central details more completely than peripheral details, which may be gone within a day of an incident. Finally, a person's retrieval of details of traumatic events depends on whether the fact was central or peripheral. Thus, one can recall with some clarity central details, but not peripheral details.[56]

Victims' rights supporters' claims are contrary to established theory about memory.[57] Even Hopper's discussion of memory raises questions about expanding statutes of limitations. In any given case, the victim will have focused on different central details. Whether those details will be essential to key issues in a case is speculative, as discussed in connection with modern acquaintance rape cases below.

Further, Hopper's argument about memory is hardly accepted doctrine among psychologists and other researchers. For years, the leading scholar in the field has been Professor Elizabeth Loftus. Her early research focused on the weaknesses of eyewitness identification. Relevant to this discussion, Loftus found that information received by witnesses after the event influenced their accounts.[58]

Even more directly relevant to this discussion are her later works involving false memories, even in cases where an event did not take place at all. Her work has dealt with false memories in trauma cases, and her widely accepted results contradict Hopper's claims. Loftus served as a defense witness in a case involving a defendant accused of raping and murdering his daughter's childhood friend. Loftus suggested that the "memory" recovered during the daughter's therapy was a false one, a product of suggestion and possible because of the malleability of memory.[59] Elsewhere, she has described cases of memories "recovered" from young children that seem contradicted by the lack of any physical corroboration in instances where, had the events taken place, massive physical injuries would have occurred.[60]

Unable ethically to engage in research in which she would attempt to implant false memories of sexual abuse, Loftus conducted other research that established that one can implant false memories. She and her assistant used a "lost-in-the-mall" technique whereby they suggested to subjects that they had gotten lost in a mall as young children. Significant percentages of participants were convinced that the events had taken place, when in reality the memories were implanted by researchers.[61]

Here, considering two modern sexual assault cases helps understand the relevance of Hopper's arguments. Even on the assumption that he is correct, one should be cautious about extending the statute of limitations because memory of details unimportant to the victim may have significant legal relevance. More importantly, because his view is not widely accepted, more traditional studies suggest the real risk to defendants accused long after events took place.

Until the 1980s, most prosecutions involved a male offender, typically unknown to the victim, who used violence to compel the victim's submission.[62] Many feminists and other victims' rights advocates pushed to change the legal landscape. Today, some of the hardest cases involve date rape or other cases between acquaintances. Often on college campuses, students end up having sex, often fueled by alcohol consumption.[63] While frequently characterized as cases involving "he said, she said," such cases are more appropriately understood as cases where a male may have engaged in intercourse without consent but where he lacked a culpable mens rea.[64]

Many leading criminal law casebooks include *Commonwealth v. Berkowitz*, a case that arose in Pennsylvania.[65] There, two college students had sexual intercourse. The defendant was initially convicted of violating the state's rape statute, which included an element of "forcible compulsion."[66] Some uncontested facts included these: the woman involved had been drinking early in the day and went to the defendant's dormitory room. She was looking for the defendant's roommate. She ended up staying in the room. The defendant asked her to join him on his bed. She declined.[67]

During the interlude, the woman told the defendant no when he began kissing and fondling her. The court of appeals that reversed the defendant's conviction reported interaction between them as follows:

> Ten or fifteen more seconds passed before the two rose to their feet. Appellant disregarded the victim's continual complaints that she "had to go," and instead walked two feet away to the door and locked it so that no one from the outside could enter.
>
> Then, in the victim's words, "[appellant] put me down on the bed. It was kind of like—he didn't throw me on the bed. It's hard to explain. It was kind of like a push but no. . . ." She did not bounce off the bed. "It wasn't slow like a romantic kind of thing, but it wasn't a fast shove either. It was kind of in the middle."[68]

The act of intercourse followed once the defendant placed the woman on his bed.

The court found that the preceding conduct did not amount to a sufficient act of force to bring the defendant's conduct within the statutory term of "forcible compulsion." That is, the only force used by the defendant was that incidental to an act of intercourse.[69]

The case provides a good example of additional issues, including the importance of mens rea in sexual assault cases. The record included evidence about prior interactions between the defendant and the woman with whom he had intercourse. After a lecture at their university on sexual behavior, she inquired about the size of his penis. She stopped by his room on more than one occasion. During one of those visits, "she had laid down on his bed. When asked whether she had asked [the defendant] again at that time what his penis size was, the victim testified that she did not remember."[70]

Similar prosecutions exist in many U.S. states.[71] Such cases present difficult questions: a woman (typically, although male victims exist as well) engages in intercourse without her consent. But based on surrounding circumstances, a man may believe that he has acted with consent, a fact relevant to whether the prosecution can prove mens rea as required by state law.[72]

What about cases like these if a state has abandoned or extended its statute of limitations for rape offenses? Victims' rights supporters contend that women often do not come forward for years. As argued by proponents of expanding statutes of limitations, victims may not trust the system and may not come to grips with their trauma for many years.[73]

Expanding the statute of limitations in such cases increases the risk of convicting innocent defendants. Imagine a case like that described above being tried many years after the events. A defendant might need to find friends of his accuser who might remember details relevant to the woman's conduct. For example, she inquired about the defendant's penis during a speakerphone call with the defendant and his roommate, evidence relevant to his mens rea.[74] Years later, would his roommate remember the phone call, even if the roommate would still be available to testify? What about other witnesses, like friends of the woman to whom she might have made statements relating to the events prior to or after the act of intercourse?

Also, memory is malleable. In the case described, already clouded by intoxication, the woman *might* have a good recollection of the events. But years later, her recollection may be altered in ways described by cognitive psychologists like Loftus.[75] As it seems to have happened in the Brock Turner case, victims' rights advocates may influence the woman's perception of events.[76] Turner, of course, is the Stanford swimmer, often referred to inaccurately as the "Stanford rapist." Unlike claims discussed above by some victims' rights supporters, trauma does not produce clear memories. Instead, memories are subject to manipulation and seem to become crystal clear despite the reality that the events did not take place as recalled.[77]

Cases like those pose a classic balancing act between competing, often compelling, goals. Protecting victims of sexual assault is obviously an important goal. But the United States historically made a commitment to establishing the rights of criminal defendants designed to protect the innocent from being convicted.[78] Extending statutes of limitations does not seem justified in light of that risk.

Those concerns exist in cases involving adults. They are as compelling when the victims were children when events took place. Again, Loftus has worked with cases involving alleged victims of child sexual abuse. The most notable and one of the longest trials in U.S. history involved defendants who ran a preschool.[79] The family members were accused of committing a host of sexual acts with the children as part of Satanic rituals. The long and expensive trial resulted in zero convictions. The prosecution eventually dropped all charges against the family members.[80] The young witnesses confirmed a variety of perverse acts, but experts like Loftus challenged the suggestive techniques used to interview the children. The general consensus is that the interviews, using such techniques, resulted in false memories and testimony.[81]

Although not a child sexual assault case, *Cooper v. Brown* offers another example of post-event distortion of memory.[82] In 1983, California charged Kevin Cooper with four brutal murders. Only an eight-year-old child survived, despite massive injuries. Cooper remains on death row despite substantial evidence of his innocence.[83]

One person remains convinced of Cooper's guilt, the then-child, now-adult who survived the bloody event.[84] Not long after the events, the witness indicated that three or four white men committed the murders. Today, he is adamant that Cooper was the killer.[85]

What happened in the interim between the child's initial statement and his current views? He participated in a trial in which the prosecution amassed enough evidence to put Cooper on death row. That included DNA evidence that may have been fabricated by police.[86]

Even timely interviews with crime victims can result in false memories and other distortions about critical events. Good law enforcement practices can reduce such risks. Beyond the scope of this chapter is a larger concern within the criminal justice community: even apart from questions about extending statutes of limitations are concerns about interviewing techniques by the police generally. Critics of common police interviewing techniques argue that relying on the typical question-answer format of police interviews distorts facts toward the interviewers' version of the events.[87] Critics urge that best police practices include interviews that asks witnesses and victims for narratives of events, rather than for responses to officer-framed questions.[88]

My concern with extending statutes of limitations is that long gaps between events and prosecution leave putative victims open to unmeasurable influences that can distort memory.[89]

Concluding Thoughts

VRM advocates' arguments are appealing to members of the public. As suggested above, who can defend sexual abusers, especially child abusers? The answer to that question is that legal scholars and those interested in protecting innocent defendants and developing sound public policy must do so.[90]

Relying on newspaper headlines does not make for good public policy.[91] Anyone who knows the name Brock Turner will tell you, most likely, that he was the Stanford rapist who received an inappropriately lenient sentence because he was a spoiled college athlete.[92] Much of that is a false narrative.[93]

Victims' rights advocates' proposals to expand statutes of limitations in sexual crimes can lead to the conviction of some innocent defendants.[94] Unlike popular misperceptions about sex offenders, most sex offenders are not repeat offenders, and those who are most likely can be convicted on current charges without extending the statutes of limitations.[95]

The widely accepted notion that victims' participation in the criminal justice process gives them closure is questionable at best.[96] Adhering to such "truths" has led to prison sentences longer than necessary for social protection.[97] Mass incarceration has diverted billions of dollars from other, more socially useful programs.[98] We might start with developing a better health care system that might genuinely assist crime victims.[99]

Defendants accused of sex offenses evoke little sympathy.[100] Crime victims do.[101] Allowing criminal justice policy to be based on popular sentiment comes with costs to the basic values of our criminal justice system.[102] Notably, the United States has touted adherence to principles like the presumption of innocence and guilt beyond a reasonable doubt as ways to protect defendants from erroneous conviction.[103] Expansion of statutes of limitations increases the risk of convicting the innocent and cannot be justified by countervailing policies.[104]

6

Victim Impact Statements and an Assessment of the Value of a Human Life

One as-of-yet-unfulfilled agenda item of the Victims' Rights Movement is the passage of the Victims' Rights Amendment, which would amend the U.S. Constitution, ensuring certain victims' rights permanently. Among the amendment's provisions is one that would guarantee a victim's right to present written or oral testimony prior to the sentencing of a defendant.[1] Despite the fact that Congress has not passed legislation adopting the amendment, many states have amended their constitutions to include a set of victims' rights. Congress and most states also have enacted legislation creating a right for victims to give personal statements prior to the imposition of a sentence on a defendant.[2] Several of those provisions have found wide support among members of the public and many judges.[3] This chapter focuses on the debate concerning victim impact statements specifically and, to a lesser degree, victim impact evidence.

The first section recounts the original steps leading to laws allowing victim impact evidence. It details the Supreme Court's initial holdings, largely rendering such statements inadmissible because, according to the Court, they violated the Eighth Amendment's prohibition against cruel and unusual punishment. It turns then to the Court's almost immediate repudiation of those holdings, a decision that has virtually removed any constitutional restraints on the use of victim impact evidence.

The second section begins with examples of victim impact statements and then turns to VRM supporters' arguments in favor of such evidence. Supporters make several arguments, both normative and practical, about the importance of victim impact evidence. They argue that such evidence gives sentencing judges a full picture of the harm caused by a defendant's conduct. They contest claims that the use of victim impact evidence leads to longer prison sentences. They also contend that victim participation provides victims with "closure," that is, psychological healing.

The third section delves into the other side of the debate and concludes that the opponents to victim impact statements make the stronger case, both normatively and empirically. VRM proponents do not have an effective rebuttal to the argument that victim impact evidence inappropriately treats some victims' lives as more valuable than others. Supporters of victim impact statements conflate criminal law, which is primarily focused on offender culpability, and tort law, which is primarily about risk allocation and compensation for injured parties. Given the realities of income inequality and racial bias, victim impact statements, in theory, can lead to racial and other forms of discrimination in sentencing. While VRM members and their opponents cite conflicting empirical evidence, this chapter argues on balance that, again, opponents have the better arguments that victim impact statements result in longer prison sentences—sentences that are unnecessary to protect the public. This section also examines the debate about closure and concludes that VRM supporters falsely promise a benefit that is not likely to result from participation in most criminal cases.

The fourth section returns to a different aspect of the debate about victim impact statements: opponents have claimed that it increases the length of prison sentences, improperly so. They further contend that they also do so in ways that are racially discriminatory. Victims' rights advocates dispute those claims. This section deals with that discussion.

Finally, the fifth section turns to a question much debated in the literature about the VRM: the role of democracy in establishing appropriate punishments for crimes. This section argues that adherence to popular opinion in assessing criminal punishments results in sentences that are unnecessarily punitive.

The Early Days

The 1982 President's Task Force on Victims of Crime was pivotal in advancing the VRM's agenda. Prior to the report, few states required judges to consider victim impact information prior to sentencing.[4] Shortly before completion of the Task Force's work, Congress passed the Victim and Witness Protection Act of 1982. That law required inclusion of such evidence in presentencing reports.[5] The law also ensured that victims could participate in the process. As summarized in a treatise on crime victims and their rights, "the Task Force noted that the crime victim's life, as well as the defendant's life, is profoundly affected by the sentence imposed. It felt that the court must hear from both sides to make an informed sentencing decision."[6]

The Task Force made clear that the victim's views were relevant to the sentence to be imposed. As the report stated, judges should "give appropriate weight to[] input at sentencing from victims of violent crime."[7] Inclusion of such information was important, in effect, to level the playing field between defendants, who, according to critics like Frank Carrington, were heavily favored in the criminal justice system, especially as a result of liberal Warren Court criminal procedural decisions. As the report stated, "Victims, no less than defendants, are entitled to their day in court."[8]

After Congress enacted the Victim and Witness Protection Act of 1982, states followed suit. Not all states allow oral victim statements. Some limit the kinds of crimes related to which a victim may provide an impact statement.[9] An occasional state allows victim impact statements but does not allow sentencing judges to consider them in assessing the appropriate punishment. Several states have amended state constitutions to guarantee various victims' rights, including the right to present evidence at sentencing hearings.[10]

As described below, initially the Supreme Court found that the use of such statements in death penalty cases violated defendants' Eighth Amendment right to be protected against excessive punishment. The Court's decision to overrule its earlier precedent has given policy makers a green light to expand victims' participation at sentencing.[11] Legislation in 2015 adds a victim's right to confer with the prosecutor and to be heard at the sentencing hearing, although both rights are limited to what is reasonable.[12]

One can find a detailed discussion of variations among state laws in *Crime Victim Rights and Remedies*. For purposes of this discussion, victim participation at the sentencing phase is now settled law in most states and in federal courts.[13]

In the late 1980s, the Supreme Court addressed the constitutionality of such evidence in death penalty cases. In *Booth v. Maryland*, Booth and a co-felon broke into the victims' home to commit a robbery. Because he knew that the victims could identify him, Booth killed the elderly couple. The prosecutor sought the death penalty in Booth's murder trial.[14]

After Booth's conviction, the state parole department compiled a presentence report. That report contained a victim impact statement, including the impact of the murder on the victims' family. The lower courts upheld the use of the victim impact statement as relevant to the full extent of the harm that the defendant caused.[15]

A divided Supreme Court reversed the lower court decisions. It found that, as a general matter, the victims' personal characteristics and impact on the family of the victims were irrelevant to determine whether the death penalty was warranted.[16] By the 1980s, after *Furman v. Georgia* put in question the constitutionality of the death penalty,[17] the Court had upheld capital punishment but imposed restrictions aimed at ensuring that only the worst-of-the-worst murderers were subject to death.[18] Consistent with that view, the Court held that evidence relating to the victims' personal characteristics and to the impact on the family was irrelevant in a capital sentencing hearing. The function of the capital sentencing hearing was to "express the conscience of the community on the ultimate question of life and death,"[19] and the key to such a determination was the defendant's blameworthiness. Specifically, a jury must make an "individualized determination whether the defendant should be executed, based on the 'character of the individual and the circumstances of the crime.'"[20] Focusing on the character of the victim or the impact on the family might lead to the imposition of the death penalty based on a facts unknown to the accused at the time of the crime. According to the Court, factors not relating to culpability are irrelevant in assessing whether an individual may be subjected to the death penalty.[21]

The Court suggested that victim impact evidence might be relevant under a narrow set of circumstances. For example, an offender might kill his victim with the intent to punish the victim's family. The Court also questioned whether different human worth of the victim was a permissible basis to mete out the death penalty. It rejected the obvious implication of relying on the victim's character—that some members of society are entitled to greater protection than others.[22]

Two years later, the Court extended its holding in *Booth* in *South Carolina v. Gathers*.[23] As in *Booth*, the murder in *Gathers* was gruesome. During the prosecutor's closing argument in the death penalty phase of the case, the prosecutor referred to the victim's life to humanize the victim.[24]

The South Carolina Supreme Court found that "the prosecutor's remarks conveyed the suggestion that appellant deserved a death sentence because the victim was a religious man and a registered voter,"[25] and found that the argument violated the Court's holding in *Booth*. The Supreme Court granted certiorari in order to reconsider its holding in *Booth*. Instead, the Court extended *Booth* beyond admission of a victim impact statement to include the prosecutor's closing argument. Again, absent a showing that Gathers was aware of his victim's personal characteristics, the evidence and reliance on the evidence during capital sentencing violated the Eighth Amendment.[26]

The Court would never resolve a question left open in *Booth* and *Gathers*: did their holdings apply only in capital cases? By 1991, the composition of the Court had changed, with Justice Brennan, a leading death penalty opponent, no longer on the bench.[27] The Court granted review in yet another victim impact evidence case, again involving powerful facts for the state.

Payne v. Tennessee involved a defendant who committed a particularly brutal murder. He reacted violently when his neighbor refused his sexual advances. Payne not only stabbed the woman repeatedly but also killed her young daughter and nearly killed her young son. The description of Payne's acts makes one wonder why the prosecutor would have needed additional victim impact evidence—a statement by the mother of the murdered woman and grandmother of the two young children. She testified about the little boy's suffering and loss of his mother.[28]

Although the Court could have avoided the issue of whether to overrule *Booth* and *Gathers*, for example, by finding the error harmless,[29] the facts were so compelling that the Court addressed the core issue. Despite the fact that its precedents were only two and four years old, the Court rejected the application of stare decisis. Writing for a six-justice majority, Chief Justice Rehnquist echoed many arguments advanced by VRM proponents.

At the core of the dispute about victim impact statements and evidence is the role of harm in criminal sentencing. Chief Justice Rehnquist focused on the premise, central to *Booth* and *Gathers*, that victim impact evidence does not "reflect on the defendant's 'blameworthiness,'" and the related premise that "only evidence relating to 'blameworthiness' is relevant to the capital sentencing decision."[30] The chief justice adopted an argument from Justice Scalia's dissent in *Booth* and *Gathers* that, in fact, "the assessment of harm caused by the defendant as a result of the crime charged has understandably been an important concern of the criminal law, both in determining the elements of the offense and in determining the appropriate punishment."[31] He borrowed Justice Scalia's example in his *Booth* dissent, of two equally culpable bank robbers, each of whom fires a gun at a guard. If the gun fires and the guard dies, the defendant is guilty of murder and may be subject to the death penalty. If the gun misfires, the defendant is obviously not guilty of the substantive offense of murder and is not subject to the death penalty.[32] Even absent the death penalty, jurisdictions typically punish attempts less severely than they do completed crimes. In the Court's view, victims' lives are unique as well as defendants' lives, making such evidence about the value of their lives relevant.[33]

With an indirect nod to the VRM, the chief justice expressed concern about a perceived unfairness to the state.[34] Under the Court's earlier holdings preventing the state from barring mitigating evidence, capital defendants typically introduce evidence aimed at creating jury sympathy for the defendant. The Court cited a somewhat ambiguous statement by the Tennessee Supreme Court that in light of the "parade of witnesses who may praise the background, character and good deeds of Defendant . . . , *without limitation as to relevancy*,"[35] fairness required that the state be allowed to introduce evidence relating to the character of the decedents.

One cannot overstate the importance of *Payne* in advancing the VRM's agenda. *Payne* has ushered in an era in which prosecutors use such information frequently. Indeed, the admissibility of victim impact evidence has created a cottage industry. Companies produce highly polished videos about the lives of victims and their families. The use of such evidence is most notable in death penalty cases; but victims often make statements in noncapital cases as well.[36]

After *Payne*, the prosecution does not need to demonstrate that a defendant has any knowledge about harm to living relatives or friends. Moreover, the prosecution can use evidence entirely unknown to an offender as long as that evidence demonstrates harm caused by the crime.

Payne has spawned a variety of issues currently unresolved by the Supreme Court. The chief justice's opinion suggested that evidence during a capital sentencing might violate due process because the evidence was so unfairly prejudicial.[37] Application of such a standard leaves broad discretion to lower courts. One treatise on victims' rights and remedies has observed that state courts generally uphold trial court rulings on admissibility.[38] Federal trial courts allow not just family members but also coworkers, friends, and neighbors to testify. They do draw a line between permissible testimony about the victims' personality and impact on their lives on one hand and recommendations about the appropriate sentence on the other hand.[39]

Given that *Booth* and *Gathers* left open their holdings to noncapital cases, it is not surprising that lower courts now routinely allow such evidence in noncapital cases. Other important questions have arisen: Must a victim testify under oath? Must the witness be subject to cross-examination? Does admission of a written victim impact statement violate the Confrontation Clause? These and other similar questions have generated a substantial body of lower court case law, yet to be resolved by the Supreme Court. But most often, courts side with prosecutors.[40]

At least in jurisdictions where courts have generally favored the prosecution's use of such evidence with few constraints, one can see how powerful such evidence might be. Some reported cases, for example, have allowed extensive photo montages of the decedent's life or professionally produced videos detailing the victim's life and impact on family members.[41] Especially defendants who rely on court-appointed counsel may have difficulty countering such powerful evidence. But such concerns anticipate the debate surrounding victim impact evidence.

Support for Victim Impact Evidence

The success of the VRM in getting the federal government and all fifty states to allow victim impact evidence invites a question: in effect, given such broad support, how can one contest the use of such evidence?[42]

Former federal district court judge and now professor Paul Cassell is the most prominent legal scholar who supports the VRM. In one of his articles, Cassell laid out four justifications for victim impact statements: "First, they provide information to the sentencing judge or jury about the true harm of the crime-information that the sentencer can use to craft an appropriate penalty. Second, they may have therapeutic aspects, helping crime victims recover from crimes committed against them. Third, they help to educate the defendant about the full consequences of his crime, perhaps leading to greater acceptance of responsibility and rehabilitation. And finally, they create a perception of fairness at sentencing, by ensuring that all relevant parties—the State, the defendant, and the victim—are heard."[43] This section examines these arguments in more depth.

The True Harm

Cassell has coauthored a casebook on victims' role in criminal procedure, along with other prominent academics who are active VRM advocates.[44] In the book's chapter on the role of victims during sentencing and parole hearings, the authors introduce readers to a victim's impact statement made by former U.S. Circuit Court judge Michael Luttig, a statement made at the trial of two defendants charged with murdering Luttig's father. The two adult defendants attempted to rob Luttig's father along with the gunman, Napoleon Beazley. The killing occurred during a failed carjacking.[45] The statement is extraordinarily powerful. That is not surprising, given that Luttig is an educated, highly successful lawyer. While Luttig's statement is particularly powerful, one can readily find other heartbreaking statements made by bereaved parents, spouses, and children of murder victims.

In one of his many VRM articles, Cassell cites other examples of similarly moving victim impact statements.[46] In an article supporting the proposed victims' rights constitutional amendment, he states, "Read an actual victim impact statement from a homicide case all the way through and see if you truly learn nothing new about the enormity of the loss caused by a homicide. Sadly, the reader will have no shortage of such victim impact statements to choose from. Actual impact statements from court proceedings are accessible in various places."[47] Anyone who reads the material that Cassell cites cannot avoid feeling the pain that victims and their families experience.[48] (Relevant to a discussion below, most of the cited cases involve white victims and family members.)[49] Indeed, VRM advocates make the emotional harm a central tenet of their support for victim impact evidence.

Cassell's argument tracks Chief Justice Rehnquist's analysis in *Payne*. The chief justice asserted that "the assessment of harm caused by the defendant as a result of the crime charged has understandably been an important concern of the criminal law, both in determining the elements of the offense and in determining the appropriate punishment."[50] As described above, a classic conundrum from the law of attempt liability compares two identically culpable offenders who shoot at their intended victims. If one gunman misfires, he faces a less severe penalty than does the successful killer, despite equally culpable mental states.[51]

Cassell and other advocates of the use of victim impact evidence share the chief justice's view about the role of such evidence. In *Payne*, the Court claimed that *Booth* misunderstood the way in which such evidence functioned. The *Booth* Court rejected such evidence because it invited juries to compare the value of one victim with that of another. Thus, a jury might impose the death penalty because the victim was well loved or wealthy or white but might not do so if the victim was unpleasant or poor or a member of a minority group. Not so, said the chief justice: "[V]ictim impact evidence is not offered to encourage comparative judgments of this kind—for instance, that the killer of a hardworking, devoted parent deserves the death penalty, but that the murderer of a reprobate does not. It is designed to show instead *each* victim's 'uniqueness as an individual human being,' whatever the jury might think the loss to the community resulting from his death might be."[52] As the chief justice believed and as Cassell continues to believe, at least in death penalty cases, the state needs such evidence to level the playing field with the defendant. As indicated above, current death penalty case law allows a defendant in a capital case to introduce almost without limits mitigating facts to show that he is not among the worst of the worst. But the state has a countervailing interest to mitigate such evidence "'by reminding the sentencer that just as the murderer should be considered as an individual, so too the victim is an individual whose death represents a unique loss to society and in particular to his family.'"[53]

Closure

Perhaps the most important argument in favor of victim impact statements is the claim that victims will experience "closure" by participating at the sentencing phase of a trial. VRM advocates contend that various policies are appropriate to secure closure, presumably a type of psychological benefit that victims experience by participating. For example, as discussed in chapter 5, they also argue that states should eliminate or extend statutes of limitations in sex offense cases to help victims achieve closure.[54]

Cassell and others in the movement argue that victims may receive psychological benefits from participating in the sentencing process. Judge Rosemarie Aquilina's comment to one of Larry Nassar's victims reflects how closure is supposed to work: "Leave your pain here and go out and do your magnificent things."[55] At least some studies suggest that participation in the sentencing process helps victims. Summarizing that literature, Cassell has stated, "One thorough assessment of the literature on victim participation explained, 'The cumulative knowledge acquired from research in various jurisdictions, in countries with different legal systems, suggests that victims often benefit from participation and input. With proper safeguards, the overall experience of providing input can be positive and empowering.' Thus, the consensus appears to be that victim impact statements allow the victim 'to regain a sense of dignity and respect rather than feeling powerless and ashamed.'"[56] Recognizing that not all victims want to participate in the criminal justice process for many reasons, Cassell suggests that participation should be voluntary.[57]

While victims' rights advocates frequently cite "closure" as a justification for victims' participation at the sentencing stages, Cassell recognizes the reality that the promise may be overblown. As he stated in one of his articles on victim impact statements: "The point should not be overstated. Occasionally the claim is made that victim impact statements will automatically bring 'closure' to victims from a crime. It is not clear that 'closure' ever really occurs after a violent crime—especially when extreme violence is at issue. But victim impact statements need not deliver total closure to nonetheless be a desirable part of the criminal justice process. [A victim may] . . . desperately like the chance to make a victim impact statement. Unless there is some compelling countervailing concern, the system ought to accommodate her request."[58] Not entirely clear from reading victims' rights advocates' arguments for participation is whether they would endorse a provision allowing such statements but only after a judge has determined the appropriate sentence.[59] The distinction becomes important when one considers whether victim participation increases criminal sentences generally and creates racial inequity specifically. As developed below, victims' rights advocates dispute claims that victim participation increases criminal sentences.

Rehabilitating Offenders

Victims' rights advocates advance another argument to support victim impact statements: they may help to rehabilitate an offender. As Professor Marcus Dubber, a critic of victim impact statements, has recognized, "[I]f a victim impact statement helps a defendant understand and gain empathy towards the victim, it may serve as the first step towards his effective rehabilitation. A victim impact statement can thus be justified because it may be beneficial for the offender."[60] As developed below, this argument may have broad support if the victim and defendant are participating in a restorative justice confrontation. But the argument seems not to apply in death penalty cases and in most traditional criminal trials that lack the special procedures used in restorative justice proceedings. In that sense, the argument is not at the core of claims by victims' rights supporters.

Basic Fairness

Finally, again as Cassell has argued, victim participation is about basic fairness: given the structure of contemporary criminal justice systems, fairness requires victim impact statements. The President's Task Force on Victims of Crime Final Report explained the point forcefully in concluding that "[w]hen the court hears, as it may, from the defendant, his lawyer, his family and friends, his minister, and others, simple fairness dictates that the person who has borne the brunt of the defendant's crime be allowed to speak."[61]

Recognizing that a defendant has some rights that victims do not have, victims' rights advocates urge that allowing victim participation advances the appearance of fairness. Participation is appropriate to advance the victim's and the public's acceptance of the ultimate sentence that a judge may impose.

These various justifications do not all require that victims speak before a judge determines the appropriate sentence or that victims speak in person. Nonetheless, typically victims' rights advocates advance the right of victims to speak in person and in advance of a judge's determination of the appropriate sentence.[62]

The Counterarguments

This section addresses each of the arguments laid out above. The theme of this section (and chapter) is that the VRM has it wrong.

Purposes of Punishment

In *Booth*, Justice Powell focused only on the use of victim impact evidence in death penalty cases. As Cassell has observed, drawing the line between death penalty cases and other crimes makes no sense.[63] Analytically, Cassell is right: if victim impact evidence is irrelevant in death penalty cases, it is because such evidence does not reflect on the defendant's culpability. That core principle should apply to all crimes, absent some compelling counterarguments.[64]

That invites the question of why the *Booth* majority found that the evidence was inconsistent with the purposes of punishment. According to the Court, without more, victim impact evidence does not relate to an offender's blameworthiness.[65] Not surprisingly, Cassell and other victims' rights supporters disagree. Cassell relies on the well-documented fact that legislatures do grade criminal conduct based on harm. Thus, penalties are typically higher for crimes of violence than for property crimes. Punishments are longer for completed acts than for attempted crimes. Thus, concludes Cassell, "If [victim impact statements] do shed light on harm, they relate to the purposes of punishment."[66] A lot is going on in Cassell's statement, requiring one to unpack a number of arguments.

As developed below, while harm still matters in criminal law, early in Anglo-American justice systems, harm played a greater role than it does today. Sorting out the role of harm in the criminal justice system requires historical background.

In common law in England, an injured person could choose between different remedies, roughly corresponding to tort and criminal remedies as understood today. The early common law distinguished crimes and torts but not as done in the modern era. In early common law, most prosecutions were brought by private parties and the remedy sought was for monetary damages. Some but far fewer cases were brought in the name of the government.[67] Several factors led to the erosion of the system of private prosecutions.

Theoretically, Enlightenment philosophers argued that crimes are public wrongs against the state and against public order. Injured parties could seek remedies for their personal harm in tort actions. Apart from a theoretical explanation for the shift, it is likely attributable to "public pressure in response to growing urban crime, as victims 'frequently did not prosecute because it was expensive, time consuming, and brought few benefits other than the satisfaction of revenge or justice.'"[68] Urbanization was accompanied by the development of professional police departments, which were increasingly charged with maintaining public order, not remedying private disputes. A closely related development was the adoption of public prosecutors. Again, like professional police departments, public prosecutors sought to remedy harm to the public generally, not necessarily harm to individuals.

Not only did public prosecutions become the norm, but also goals of the criminal justice and tort systems increasingly bifurcated. A few examples demonstrate those differences: a criminal prosecution may proceed without a victim's consent, while a person must choose to be a tort plaintiff. Tort law compensates (typically) innocent victims for their losses and allocates risk between the parties. For example, courts often determine which party is in a better position to insure against a risk of harm.[69] Increasingly, the criminal law has focused on punishing culpable defendants. Blameworthiness, not harm, has emerged as the modern measure of the criminal law. The result of a successful criminal prosecution is often imprisonment of the defendant, justified because of the defendant's moral blame. Not only is culpability a threshold question of whether the criminal law should impose liability on a person, but it also determines the proportionality of that punishment.[70]

Here, I want to expand the previous discussion by reference to an article that I published in the NYU *Annual Survey of American Law* and to explain why the *Booth* Court got it right:[71] In *The Victim Impact Statements: Skewing Criminal Justice Away from First Principles*, I described a discussion with my criminal law class from several years ago.[72] Well into the semester, we were discussing Pennsylvania criminal code §3124.1, which provides that "a person commits a felony of the second degree when that person engages in sexual intercourse with a complainant without the complainant's consent."[73] The discussion was far-ranging, including a discussion of the relevant sentence for a felony of the second degree under Pennsylvania law (up to ten years in prison).[74] It then focused on the absence of a mens rea term in the statute and whether it should be read as a strict liability offense.[75] A student raised her hand and asked, "What would be wrong with making the offense strict liability?"

Many students and members of the public have trouble understanding why harm alone does not justify punishment. The harm to a victim remains the same whether the defendant acted without a culpable frame of mind. What is the counterargument for requiring a guilty mind, even when harm occurs?

Every modern criminal law casebook includes a few introductory chapters.[76] They lay out the first principles of the criminal law. Among those essential aspects of criminal law are principles that focus on an offender's culpability,[77] on proportional punishment,[78] and on the reasons for standards like guilt beyond a reasonable doubt.[79] Some casebooks include a chapter on lenity,[80] which focuses on rules that favor defendants and their liberty when the meaning of a statute is unclear.[81] Casebooks raise questions about alternatives to criminal law, like tort law or other civil sanctions, to avoid imposing the weight of criminal law on some individuals.[82]

These are not transient notions, as the Supreme Court has observed.[83] For example, while analyzing whether a statute includes a mens rea element, courts recognize that an offender's culpability is essential to the criminal law.[84] Punishment is not measured by harm to the victim, but instead the major focus is on the offender's culpability.[85] Indeed, that notion has constitutional status: in assessing whether an offender's sentence is grossly disproportionate, the Court looks to the gravity of an offense, measured in terms of *social* harm and the offender's level of culpability.[86] Indeed, some commentators have questioned whether the law should even criminalize negligent offenders; after all, someone unable to achieve the standard of a reasonable person may be subject to punishment for their stupidity rather than for their individual fault.[87] As a result, the criminal law not only disfavors strict liability but also shuns ordinary negligence, typically requiring more than the kind of risk that can lead to tort liability.[88] The discussion above of the bifurcation of tort and criminal law helps put this discussion in context. The criminal law is not about risk allocation and compensation for victims. It is about individual culpability and punishment for culpable conduct.[89]

The criminal law is concerned with liberty.[90] Hence, in recognizing that the Constitution includes the requirement of a presumption of innocence and of guilt beyond a reasonable doubt, the Court recognizes the preference for liberty.[91] Thus, our criminal justice system has long recognized, if not literally, as a metaphor, that we would rather acquit ten guilty offenders than convict one innocent offender.[92]

Liberty matters. Not only is the preference for liberty part of constitutional protections, it also explains the principle of lenity.[93] Unless a legislature abandons the principle of lenity, the principle requires courts to interpret ambiguous statutes in favor of the defendant.[94] If the choice is between favoring the powerful state or the individual, the court should side with liberty; if necessary, the state can rewrite its laws.[95] In the interim, close calls go to accused individuals.[96]

Social harm still counts in criminal law. The *Payne* Court noted that the law makes the victim's harm relevant, without reference to offender culpability, in any number of cases: "For example, if the defendant physically injured the victim, the victim could describe the nature and extent of the injuries-facts that are clearly relevant to sentencing under virtually any conceivable sentencing scheme. The federal sentencing guidelines, for example, assign various recommended penalties depending on whether the victim suffered 'bodily injury,' 'serious bodily injury,' or 'permanent or life-threatening bodily injury.'"[97] These are uncontroversial examples. They describe elements of graded offenses. Thus, most criminal codes distinguish simple aggravated crimes, like battery or rape. Notably, typically those are crimes where an offender cannot plausibly claim that he did not know that he was causing the more extensive injury.[98] Or, for example, if a defendant fights a person with a thin skull, a classic example where a tort defendant takes her victim as she is, the criminal law would not typically treat the offender as guilty of the crime with elevated, unforeseen damages.[99]

The prior point is consistent with the modern criminal law. The movement toward modern criminal law saw the shift in focus from social harm to the offender's culpability.[100] *Regina v. Cunningham* captures this change in the criminal law.[101] There, the defendant stole a gas meter to extract the coins.[102] In doing so, he broke the gas line, leading to the asphyxiation of a resident of the other home in a duplex. He was charged with maliciously administering a noxious thing to another person, thereby endangering that person.[103] The trial court instructed the jury that it should find the defendant guilty as long as he did a wicked thing.[104] Of course, he did so by committing the theft. The appellate court construed the statutory term "maliciously" as the equivalent to recklessness.[105] It then parsed the statute to determine whether the mens rea term attached to the social harm.[106] In a compact way, the court signaled the change in modern criminal law: the social harm remains whether or not the offender was aware of the risk that he created. But an offender who was aware of the risk is more culpable than one who failed to recognize the risk.[107]

The Supreme Court has increasingly recognized the same principle through its interpretation of modern criminal statutes. For example, in *Staples v. United States*, the Court inferred that Congress must have intended a malum prohibitum statute to include a mens rea term in light of the possible long prison term.[108] The majority ignored precedent that upheld a term of imprisonment even absent a mens rea term for such public welfare statutes.[109] Increasingly, the Court has read statutes silent on mens rea as requiring some mens rea to be read into its language.[110] Similarly, in its death penalty case law, even in cases where the defendant has killed another person, the Court has required some significant level of culpable mens rea.[111]

The Model Penal Code offers more examples of the modern trend. For instance, strict liability offenses are disfavored,[112] and prison time is not suitable in such cases.[113] Absent a stated mens rea, under the code's default provision, the court must read into the statute a minimum of recklessness.[114] While retaining negligence as a possible mens rea term, the code's drafters rejected that level of culpability as generally acceptable.[115] Indeed, the drafters debated whether a negligent actor, one who lacks subjective awareness, is ever a suitable subject for punishment.[116]

Strong arguments suggest that a state cannot constitutionally imprison an offender, at least for a significant period of time, based on strict liability.[117] As suggested above, the Court has skirted the issue on occasion by reading statutes to include mens rea, which requires the prosecution to prove some level of culpability.

While the criminal law does not ignore harm, culpability has emerged as the primary basis for punishment. Anomalies exist in the criminal law. Its treatment of attempted versus completed crimes is such an example. But those are just that, anomalies.

Felony murder may be the best counterexample to the principle that an offender must have some culpable mental state as to the harm for which he is held responsible. Thus, an offender who agrees to participate in a robbery with no reason to know that his associate is armed is liable for murder, not merely robbery, if a death occurs during the commission of the robbery.[118] Similarly, a defendant who commits a burglary with no reason to know that anyone is home is liable for murder when a resident dies unexpectedly during the course of the burglary.[119]

Reliance on felony murder as a counterexample misses the point: courts and commentators see felony murder as outdated because it violates the core principles of culpability and proportionality.[120] For years, California courts limited felony murder, openly acknowledging that they did so because an offender's culpability might not be proportional to the crime of murder.[121] Almost all the scholarly literature concurs.[122] The drafters of the Model Penal Code concurred with that view. According to the MPC Commentary, felony murder is indefensible as a matter of principle.[123] More recently, following this trend, the California legislature has narrowed the application of felony murder to require a mens rea commensurate with the punishment for homicide.[124]

The *Booth* majority reflects modern criminal law principles. To pursue the point more thoroughly, consider a hypothetical, hardly unrealistic in our criminal justice system: in a killing spree, a defendant kills multiple victims. One is a wealthy white person; another is an unemployed African American; a third is an elderly person living on a pension. The killer knows nothing about the victims or their families and did not kill because of the race of his victims. Without embarrassment or accusation that one is a racist, could one seriously argue that the punishment should be greater for killing a wealthy white person than for killing an unemployed African American or an elderly pensioner? Or consider a spin-off of that example: imagine in one instance the victims' family insisted on the death penalty because of the killer's race or because of their hatred of the defendant. Should such desires be recognized by the law?

Although increasingly controversial, tort law considers such factors as employment history and future harm in assessing damages. Some critics of tort law governing assessment of damages argue that, given the long history of racial discrimination, Black lives are valued less than white lives. But even in tort law, as reflected in discussions about Minneapolis's agreement to pay George Floyd's family $27 million, many observers now criticize how the tort law has treated Black lives as less worthy than white lives.[125] That debate is beyond the scope of this chapter.[126]

The hypothetical above underscores the strength of Justice Powell's argument in *Booth*. Absent some intent or knowledge on the killer's part, the victim's traits seem irrelevant to the offender's culpability. No one—at least not the *Booth* majority, most criminal law scholars, and many courts—would seriously contend that the criminal law should treat innocent victims' lives as of unequal value. Indeed, courts and policy makers often eschew such arguments. Even as the American Law Institute extended the defense of necessity to homicide cases, the comments made clear that all innocent lives were to be treated equally.[127]

Given what seems indisputable, one needs to ask how the *Payne* Court and victims' rights advocates deal with that argument. According to Chief Justice Rehnquist, the use of victim impact evidence does not invite a comparison of the value of different victims' lives: "It is designed to show instead *each* victim's 'uniqueness as an individual human being,' whatever the jury might think the loss to the community resulting from his death might be."[128] Thus, the *Payne* Court and victims' rights advocates like Cassell argue that somehow, the jury or sentencing judge is not comparing the value of victims' lives but just assessing the magnitude of the loss of a particular victim.[129]

That distinction is hard to understand. Go back to the hypothetical from above. A killer who knows nothing about his victims will receive a longer sentence based on factors beyond the killer's knowledge. For example, he may have no idea whether the victim has a family or, if so, whether the victim's family will experience a grave loss. The *Payne-Cassell* approach allows extensive information, often beyond the defendant's awareness, reflecting on victims' characteristics that, of course, lead the jury or judge to assess the value of the victims' lives. That process leads to valuing some victims' lives more than others, even if the jury and sentencing judge do not explicitly compare those values.

What then, victims' rights advocates might ask, of Chief Justice Rehnquist and Justice Scalia's example concerning different treatment for offenders who are guilty only of an attempted crime and those who complete the crime? Borrowing from Justice Scalia's earlier dissent, the chief justice offered the following example to show that harm matters, without regard to an offender's culpability: "[T]wo equally blameworthy criminal defendants may be guilty of different offenses solely because their acts cause differing amounts of harm. 'If a bank robber aims his gun at a guard, pulls the trigger, and kills his target, he may be put to death. If the gun unexpectedly misfires, he may not. His moral guilt in both cases is identical, but his responsibility in the former is greater.'"[130] The example provides a classic conundrum, often debated by criminal law scholars. Some scholars have tried to explain why the law traditionally punishes attempted crimes far less seriously than it punishes completed crimes.[131]

Apart from whether one can make a principled, rather than pragmatic, argument to support the distinction is beyond the scope of this chapter. Notice two points, however. First, Justice Scalia's example is an exception in the criminal law that has roots in early criminal law. Attempt liability worked its way into the criminal law when, absent physical injuries, policy makers saw no harm. The days of such formalism are long gone.[132]

The second observation about the Scalia-Rehnquist example is that modern criminal law scholars argue that the punishment should be the same because modern criminal law turns on offender culpability, not random results. In developing the Model Penal Code, for example, the drafters focused on that issue. Dominated by scholars who were "subjectivists," many of the members of the drafters urged equal punishment for offenders.[133] Those scholars saw no difference between the two hypothetical offenders. As is often the result of a collaborative drafting process, the drafters compromised: for the most serious felonies, punishments for attempted crimes would be lower than those for completed offenses. But innovatively, the punishments for attempted crimes for lesser felonies would be the same as those for the completed offenses.[134]

One parting thought about this aspect of the debate: Cassell and other victims' rights advocates point to *Payne* as support for their endorsement for victim impact statements. The question in *Payne* is different from the policy question at issue: *Payne* dealt with the meaning of the Constitution. One might agree that, as a matter of constitutional law, the Eighth Amendment should be read narrowly to allow states to use victim impact evidence, but also agree as a matter of policy, such evidence is not appropriate.

Some VRM supporters argue that the criminal justice system should go back to the era when private individuals had a greater role in the criminal justice system.[135] That would be unfortunate. In addition to arguments above, public prosecutors who are committed to doing justice, not just advocating for someone pursuing personal harm, seem like a virtue of the U.S. criminal justice system.[136]

What about other arguments supporting victim impact statements and evidence? Perhaps, one might argue that, even if such evidence raises theoretical problems, other more practical justifications make such evidence worthwhile. The next subsection turns to claims that victims need closure and that their participation in criminal cases provides them that relief.

Closure

Victims' rights advocates invoke the need for victims and their families to experience closure to justify many of their policies. As Professor Susan Bandes, a prominent critic of the VRM, has stated, "Closure is offered—often successfully—as an argument to impose death sentences, trim procedural protections, permit victim impact statements, deny appeals and clemency petitions, speed up executions, televise executions, and grant the bereaved access to the execution chamber."[137] Despite that, much about the idea of closure is controversial.

Do victims benefit by making statements as part of criminal sentencing? One might have theoretical objections to the use of victim impact evidence but conclude on consequentialist grounds that courts should allow victims to make their voices heard. For example, perhaps, on balance, victims benefit more by making such statements than offenders are harmed. Thus, one might argue that the costs to offenders are outweighed by the benefits to victims, who may not have been at fault in being injured. That argument seems implicit in some of the language used by victims' advocates.[138]

Before addressing whether victims and their families experience closure, one ought to ask what it means to experience closure. Here, despite common usage and the public's general acceptance that the term has fixed meaning, its meaning is far from clear. As Frank Zimring demonstrated in *The Contradictions of American Capital Punishment*, the term is a new addition to the criminal justice arena. VRM advocates began using the term in the late 1980s.[139] By 2001, members of the public believed that closure for victims' families helped justify the death penalty.

As Professor Bandes has argued, "Closure is a puzzle. Its parameters are fuzzy, its dynamics are murky, and its origins seem to have more to do with law and politics than with psychology." For example, it may be "a set of legal aspirations for the conduct of criminal proceedings."[140] Often, the term seems to be equated with "catharsis," a purging of emotion that has some long-term curative effect. Short of that, one wonders how victims' rights advocates can urge so many procedural reforms, with risks to convicting or executing innocent defendants, if those reforms will not produce lasting, meaningful benefits to victims or their families. As quoted above, Judge Rosemarie Aquilina's comment to one of Larry Nassar's victims reflects this curative notion: "Leave your pain here and go out and do your magnificent things." Similarly, victims' rights advocates seem to be promising victims a cathartic experience when they encourage victims to participate in criminal proceedings.

What about the empirical data, then, that support the idea that victims experience closure when they make statements in open court? Here, the evidence is open to debate.

Victims' rights supporters rely on anecdotal evidence to support such claims. For example, after hearing one victim's statement, a judge reassured her that she was not to blame for the incident, thereby acknowledging her suffering.[141] The victim said, "Because of what the judge said, it was so easy just to walk out of that court and start my life."[142] One report noted that when judges make statements to the defendant in front of the victim, like "I can't believe how much damage you have caused here," it can help victims as well.[143]

Elsewhere, one victim of the Boston Marathon attack wrote to the defendant that making her statement aided her even though he failed to make eye contact with her when she spoke.[144] As she stated, "Today I looked at you right in the face and realized I wasn't afraid anymore. And today I realized that sitting across from you was somehow the crazy kind of step forward that I needed all along."[145] This suggests that victims' impact statements may benefit victims by allowing them to confront defendants for the pain and suffering that the defendants have caused.[146]

The evidence cited above is anecdotal. More substantial empirical studies provide less support for the VRM position. Professor Cassell has characterized the empirical support for benefits to victims as follows: "There may be therapeutic aspects to a victim giving a victim impact statement. . . . These healing effects are not unusual. One thorough assessment of the literature on victim participation explained, 'The cumulative knowledge acquired from research in various jurisdictions, in countries with different legal systems, suggests that victims often benefit from participation and input. With proper safeguards, the overall experience of providing input can be positive and empowering.' Thus, the consensus appears to be that victim impact statements allow the victim 'to regain a sense of dignity and respect rather than feeling powerless and ashamed.'"[147] His characterization is more measured than many victims' rights advocates' claims about closure. Cassell is right to be measured. The data do not support a general cathartic effect of victim participation.[148] Hence, Cassell suggests that participation "may be therapeutic" and that victims *seem* to regain a sense of dignity. He does not assert that the benefits are long-lasting. Many surveys of victims and their families suggest, for example, that they express satisfaction with their participation at the time of trial. Or, as one study of homicide victims' family members concluded, the family members equated "closure" with the end of the process, not with long-term healing.[149] Again, that is a far cry from lasting benefits. A question about feelings after trial is entirely different from longitudinal studies to measure long-term benefits.

On the flip side, some empirical studies suggest that closure is an illusion. Marilyn Armour, director of the Institute for Restorative Justice and Restorative Dialogue, has spent twenty years researching crime victims and writes that "[t]hey'll tell you over and over and over again that there's no such thing as closure."[150]

Further, psychological studies have found that executions do little to heal the victims' families.[151] A Marquette University study compared the effects of executions on victims' families in Minnesota and Texas. Minnesota has no death penalty; Texas leads the nation in executions. The study found that families of victims in Minnesota had higher levels of physical, psychological, and behavioral health and more satisfaction with the criminal justice system than victims' families in Texas.[152]

Some victims' families have formed a group, Murder Victims' Families for Reconciliation, whose mission statement is to mobilize "victim families and help them tell their stories in ways that disrupt and dismantle the death penalty and create pathways for wholeness, reconciliation, and restoration."[153] This suggests that executions do not in fact provide the alleged closure that victims' rights advocates claim as a justification for victim impact statements.[154]

Apart from empirical data, one should be skeptical about long-term healing through participation at trial. Consider why victims and their families are not likely to experience catharsis by participating in the criminal justice system: criminal violence causes trauma.[155] The victims most in need of help are suffering from posttraumatic stress disorder (PTSD).[156] Even a cursory review of the literature concerning treatment modalities for PTSD indicates that effective treatment takes time with a skilled therapist.[157] Mental health professionals have developed a variety of treatment modalities.[158] All require extensive treatment with a health care professional. For example, cognitive processing therapy lasts twelve weeks, with each session taking between sixty and ninety minutes.[159] Other treatments take longer.[160]

While allowing a victim to speak to her victimizer in open court might be part of a therapeutic regime, that is not what happens in the criminal justice system.[161] Instead, a victim speaks her mind but then is likely to be back on her own without additional therapeutic help.[162] Some judges—for example, Judge Aquilina, Larry Nassar's sentencing judge—show extraordinary sympathy during victims' statements, but that is hardly the rule. Even then, a day in court with a sympathetic judge does not look like the therapeutic modalities described in the PTSD literature.[163]

One can compare the process in a traditional criminal case and the ways in which restorative justice programs work. Restorative justice programs involve the willing participation of victims and offenders. They also involve an extended discussion between the victim and offender and possible conduct by the offender to help the victim heal. Such measures include restitution and open acknowledgment of the harm that the offender caused.[164] While victim participation in the traditional criminal law increases restitution, the other benefits of restorative justice are lacking there. By comparison, a defense attorney would be hard-pressed to allow a client to make such an open acknowledgment of guilt in a criminal trial.[165] A victim's statement in open court is not necessarily accompanied by any therapy in any meaningful sense.[166]

Two final points are worth considering before moving on to the next justification for victim impact statements. As developed below, victims' rights advocates and opponents debate whether such evidence improperly increases criminal sentences.[167] But if such evidence does improperly increase punishment, one might argue in favor of victim impact statements *after* a judge announces the appropriate sentence. As indicated, that is not the VRM's position, however.

The other thought about closure is that prosecutors and victims' rights advocates typically (but not exclusively)[168] support victims who want to participate if they want the jury to impose the death penalty or to impose a long prison term. In some well-publicized cases, family members have opposed the death penalty. Matthew Shepard's parents opposed the prosecutor's decision to seek the death penalty; they were ignored.[169] Similarly, parents of eight-year-old Martin Richard, killed by the Boston bombers, opposed the death penalty. Again, prosecutors ignored their request.[170] No doubt, not all prosecutors value victim participation only to increase punishment or leverage in securing guilty pleas. But that certainly seems to be one reason that prosecutors support such evidence. Even if the Boston prosecutor argued that other victims' families needed the death penalty to achieve closure, the Laramie, Wyoming, prosecutor could not make such a claim: both parents of Shepard, the only murder victim, needed closure by avoiding the protracted death penalty proceedings.

The previous paragraph taps into a larger theme, discussed in chapter 1: one of the recommendations of the 1982 President's Task Force on

Victims of Crime was that states provide greater services for victims. But that promise has not been fulfilled in many states.[171] Victims may need physical and psychological help. Many states lack adequate health care provisions for victims. Instead, the primary "rights" of victims are participation at sentencing and in parole hearings. Viewed objectively, victim participation seems to be more about punishing defendants than about helping victims.[172]

Rehabilitating Offenders

The argument in favor of victim impact evidence as a way to advance rehabilitating an offender seems odd in many contexts. Given the context in which many victims' family members make victim impact statements, namely capital cases, one cannot take too seriously the argument that supporters want offenders rehabilitated. They want them dead.[173]

In other cases, often in restorative justice settings, one might hope that such a confrontation between victim and offender can have some rehabilitative effect. As noted above, some restorative justice programs involve much more than is involved in the typical courtroom setting. Restorative justice may involve professionals who can facilitate the confrontation between victim and victimizer. Most cases do not resemble the restorative justice model. As Danielle Sered has observed, the traditional criminal justice setting is ill suited for offenders to accept responsibility for the harm that they have caused.[174] Hearing supporters of the VRM urge rehabilitation as a benefit of victim impact statements is not without irony: again, early VRM members succeeded in overturning rehabilitation as a goal of imprisonment and in making the U.S. criminal justice system extremely punitive.[175] Given the VRM's role in abandoning rehabilitation and often continuing to oppose it today, this argument seems at best a makeweight, if not hypocritical.

Finally, as with closure, one could achieve whatever possible rehabilitative effect might come from victim impact statements without risking increased criminal sentences. Such statements might take place after the judge has decided on a sentence. Thus, urging rehabilitation as a benefit of victim impact statements and evidence seems like a makeweight.

Basic Fairness

Cassell also argues, based on the President's Task Force Report, that "[w]hen the court hears, as it may, from the defendant, his lawyer, his family and friends, his minister, and others, simple fairness dictates that the person who has borne the brunt of the defendant's crime be allowed to speak."[176] The argument appeals to "basic fairness" for victims.

Chapter 4 focused on Frank Carrington's role in creating the VRM. Carrington as well as many law-and-order conservatives attacked the Warren Court for mollycoddling criminals. In that context, Carrington argued that the playing field had to be leveled.[177]

As argued in chapter 4, the rapid change in Court personnel began decades of retrenchment. Even Carrington acknowledged that some of the Warren Court's holdings, like *Gideon v. Wainwright* (requiring the state to appoint counsel for indigent defendants), were warranted.[178] But even *Gideon* has not fulfilled its aspirational goals. Today, many public defender offices or other state-funded defender programs are stretched far too thin to provide meaningful representation. The shift in power to prosecutors through legislation creating long prison sentences and the Court's permissive stance on plea bargaining leave many defendants with few options other than accepting plea deals dictated by prosecutors. Some have voiced concern that a significant number of innocent defendants plead guilty, lest they face much longer sentences for asserting their right to a trial.[179]

Beyond the grim reality of our criminal justice system, Cassell's argument about basic fairness invites much greater scrutiny. General appeals to fairness require asking more basic questions: how should one define fairness? In this context, that question takes one back to the earlier discussion about the purposes of our criminal justice and tort systems. If the purpose of the system is to compensate victims, then victim participation, including victim impact statements, is needed to achieve fairness. But that is not the core function of the criminal justice system. Fairness, in that context, requires an assessment of blameworthiness as a core question. If, as I have argued, victim impact evidence distracts the decision maker from offender culpability, the VRM position is not fair because it may lead to punishment that is disproportionate to the offender's blameworthiness.

Increasing Sentencing and Racial Injustice?

Longer Sentences and More Death Penalties

Much of the debate about victims' participation in the criminal justice system may be much ado about nothing if their participation provides them marginal benefits and comes with little cost. Thus, one might ask whether it matters if a victim's participation in the process makes no difference if the defendant's sentence remains fixed. Here, some victims' rights advocates contend that victim participation does not lengthen prison sentences.

Again, Professor Cassell disputes claims of opponents that victim participation via victim impact statements and evidence increases punishment. After reviewing data, which Cassell claims indicate that such evidence does not increase the likelihood of imposition of the death penalty, he addressed noncapital sentences and concluded as follows: "Moving to the larger body of research on the effect of victim impact statements on non-capital sentences, the empirical evidence also finds little effect on sentence severity. . . . A careful scholar recently reviewed all of the available evidence in this country and elsewhere, and concluded that 'sentence severity has not increased following the passage of [victim impact] legislation.'"[180] Indeed, Cassell and other victims' rights advocates disclaim that the goal of victim participation was to increase criminal sentences. Instead, their goal was therapeutic. Quoting Professor Edna Enez, Cassell argues that increasing criminal sentences was never the goal of victim impact legislation. Instead, "[h]istorically, and at the present, the primary function of the [victim impact statement] legislation has been expressive or therapeutic—to provide crime victims with a 'voice,' regardless of any impact it may have on sentencing."[181] On the latter point, one might want to revisit the discussion about closure and question the assertion that victim impact statements are, in fact, therapeutic. Here, the focus is on the Enez-Cassell argument that such laws were not intended to increase criminal sentences.

Also, in the same breath, Cassell then argues that even if such evidence increases punishment, so be it. That is appropriate, he says.[182] He cycles back to the claim discussed above: such evidence eliminates distortion in the sentencing process because the judge has a complete view of the harm caused by the defendant. On this latter point, I would simply refer back to the discussion above: focusing on harm without any showing that the defendant acted with mens rea as to the harm is irrelevant to the core question in modern criminal law: offender culpability. But here, one needs to focus on the arguments about why victims' rights advocates have pushed for laws allowing victim participation in sentencing and what the effect is.

Before turning to the empirical data on whether victim participation increases criminal sentences, the assertion that the drafters of victim impact legislation did not intend for judges to impose more death penalties or longer terms of imprisonment is a difficult conclusion to accept. True, one can be a victims' rights advocate without believing that longer sentences or the death penalty should be imposed.[183] But the Enez-Cassell argument ignores history.

Noted earlier, Frank Carrington was the most important figure at the outset of the Victims' Rights Movement. His seminal work *The Victims* argued for the expanded use of the death penalty. Several organizations, which formed in the late 1970s and early 1980s, advanced Carrington's work. They pushed for harsher sentences along with greater participation by victims in the criminal justice system.[184] Some of their proposals included abandoning parole, thereby forcing defendants to serve their full sentence. They also urged limiting death penalty appeals, thereby increasing executions.[185] As described by Raphael Ginsberg, organizations like the National Organization for Victim Assistance conflated victim services with tough-on-crime policies. Conviction and punishment became the rights of victims.[186]

Ginsberg cites yet another example where legislation advanced to protect victims aimed to increase criminal sentences, not merely to advance therapeutic participation. Roberta Roper's work began after the rape and murder of her daughter. She worked to get Maryland to pass legislation narrowing mitigating circumstances in first-degree murder cases and adopting life without benefit of parole as an alternative to life with parole, to expand the death penalty to include coconspirators, to make victim impact statements mandatory, and to limit parole.[187]

Other VRM organizations advance proposals to increase criminal sentences. Think about Mothers Against Drunk Driving, whose clearest policy goal was to get states to increase punishments for drunk drivers.[188] Chapter 7 offers a fuller exploration of the Three Strikes movement in California. Beyond question, the goal of Three Strikes advocates was to increase the length of criminal sentences.[189]

What then about Cassell's statement that "the empirical evidence also finds little effect on sentence severity"? Cassell's statement reflects his position as an advocate and ignores competing data. As stated by the authors of *Crime Victim Rights and Remedies*, "Based on studies primarily conducted during the 1980s, research in this area, however, have been quite mixed."[190]

Outside the context of the death penalty, relatively few victims present victim impact statements.[191] But their participation may have an effect on sentences not fully measured in sentencing data: when victims testify during the guilt phase of trials, their participation is likely to increase the chance of convictions.[192] Jurors, like most of us, have empathy for victims. A victim's emotional testimony creates an empathic bond between jurors and the victim, increasing the desire to find the defendant guilty.[193] As explored in the discussion about race and victim impact evidence, data also show greater empathy for victims of the same race as the jurors, adding to racial inequity in convictions and sentencing.[194]

Some of the data about the impact of victim participation are anecdotal, based on questioning judges and prosecutors about what they believe the effect of hearing such evidence is. That is, do judges and prosecutors consider victims' preference for longer or shorter sentence? Not surprisingly, most judges find victim input an "effective means of obtaining useful information."[195] Most judges found information about financial, physical, and psychological information useful, but found unnecessary victims' recommendations with regard to particular sentences. Polls focusing on whether judges and prosecutors believe that victim evidence influences sentencing also produce mixed results.[196]

Three factors may explain why victim participation may not have a profound effect on the length of many prison sentences. Most cases are resolved through plea bargaining.[197] Judges may be hesitant to unravel a plea deal by increasing the sentence in light of victim impact evidence. Often, as well, the impact on the victim is built into the criminal charge: aggravated rape and aggravated assault require evidence of greater harm than do rape or assault generally. That is, the determination of guilt may include a measure of the impact on the victim. Finally, judges' discretion may be limited in states with mandatory sentences or rigid sentencing guideline criteria.[198]

The empirical studies cited above focus on sentences generally, including the overwhelming number of cases resolved through the guilty-plea process. Of course, the most important area where victim impact evidence matters is in capital cases.[199] As indicated above, many of the most visible victims' rights advocates favored imposition of more death penalties.

Researchers have used mock juries to assess whether victim impact statements produce more punitive responses. Professors Deise and Paternoster have concluded that mock jurors were more likely to impose the death penalty when jurors heard victim impact testimony than if they were not provided that evidence. They also tended to believe, unquestionably inappropriately, that the prosecutor's case was stronger if they heard the evidence than if they did not have that evidence.[200] Aware of the limitations of mock jury research, the same coauthors reached similar conclusions by using subjects from a list of potential jurors who were death-penalty-qualified.[201]

Apart from uncertain empirical data, one ought to consider the likely effect of victim participation as long as a judge has discretion about the length of the sentence. One can reexamine some of the victim impact statements cited by Cassell in his coauthored casebook or in his scholarly writings.[202] How could a judge or jury (in death penalty cases) not be moved to increase the sentence or to impose the death penalty? Prosecutors exclude statements from victims who do not seek sufficiently punitive sanctions. They urge juries to help victims and their families receive closure, now a widely assumed role that the death penalty or other severe punishment can provide.[203] Any listener capable of empathy must be moved by such evidence, and data suggest that is the case.[204]

Earlier in this chapter, I referred to Michael Luttig's statement at Napoleon Beazley's codefendants' murder trial. He also spoke at Beazley's trial.[205] Factors weighed against imposition of the death penalty in Beazley's case. At the time of the murder, Beazley was only seventeen years old. Not long thereafter, the Supreme Court found that the imposition of the death penalty on an offender under eighteen years old at the time of their crime was cruel and unusual punishment.[206] Even at the time of Beazley's trial, jurisdictions following the classic balancing of aggravating and mitigating factors considered youth as a mitigating factor.[207] Further, the crime was a botched carjacking, not a planned murder. Beazley committed his crime with two adult offenders who testified against him. They received terms of life in prison. While Beazley was the shooter, evidence that a youthful offender committed his crime alongside older offenders often works as a form of mitigation.[208] Other evidence in Beazley's favor seemed to weigh against imposition of the death penalty, including his lack of a violent criminal record.[209] As discussed below, Beazley was an African American, whose race may have been a factor leading to imposition of the death penalty. Considering factors that often mitigate against imposition of the death penalty, one can fairly assume that Luttig's powerful victim impact statement influenced the jury.

Before turning to questions of race and victim impact evidence, consider one more thought about the role of victim impact evidence. Studies indicate that prosecutors find victim impact evidence relevant.[210] At least in notable instances, prosecutors ignore victims and their family members who, for example, oppose the death penalty.[211] That suggests that experienced prosecutors believe that they can increase criminal sentences, especially in death penalty cases, by relying on such evidence when it favors longer sentences.

Thus far, as argued above, empirical evidence may leave one uncertain about the extent to which victim impact statements increase criminal sentences. But many VRM supporters seem to believe that they do: like Carrington, many VRM supporters are law-and-order proponents who helped usher in decades of expanding prisons filled with offenders given extremely long sentences. VRM advocates cannot run away from that history easily. Whatever doubt one might have about the empirical data, one ought to keep one fact in mind: would prosecutors be such strong supporters of victim impact evidence if they did not believe that it did not increase criminal sentences?

Racial Injustice in Sentencing

Today, substantial research demonstrates that our criminal justice system discriminates based on race and ethnicity.[212] People of color receive longer sentences than their white counterparts.

One can find studies coming to the opposite conclusion. But today, the debate has largely been put to rest. For example, in 2004, pursuant to a Department of Justice grant, Ojmarrh Mitchell and Doris L. MacKenzie published a meta-analysis of studies addressing the role of race and ethnicity in criminal sentencing. The authors examined existing studies by using "a quantitative (i.e., meta-analytic) synthesis of empirical research assessing the influence of race/ethnicity on non-capital sentencing decisions in U.S. criminal courts."[213] Not surprising to many of us, they concluded that African Americans and Latinos were generally sentenced more harshly than white offenders.

While the Mitchell-MacKenzie report focused on terms of imprisonment, others have found disparities in the death penalty as well. The Baldus study (actually two studies conducted by David Baldus and George Woodworth), the most famous research concluding that race matters in determining who ends up on death row, was at the center of the debate in the Supreme Court. The researchers examined almost twenty-five hundred homicide cases from Georgia during the 1970s and used multiple variables to determine whether race influenced the imposition of the death penalty. The procedures that the authors used are widely accepted in the academic literature.[214]

At least among defense attorneys and many academics, the Baldus study's conclusions were expected: race matters in the imposition of the death penalty. A bit surprising, the strongest correlation between imposition of the death penalty and race was between the race of the victim and the sentence imposed by the jury.[215] Juries imposed the death penalty in 27 percent of cases in which the victim was white, but only 7 percent when the victim was Black.[216] The correlation between defendant's race and imposition of the death penalty existed but was not as strong.[217] Those conclusions did not persuade the Supreme Court that the death penalty was unconstitutional.

In *McCleskey v. Kemp*, a divided Court upheld the death penalty. Even assuming the data were accurate, the Court held that the defendant needed to show intentional discrimination to establish an equal protection violation. The Court also found that the defendant failed to show that the imposition of the death penalty in Georgia was sufficiently arbitrary and capricious to violate the Eighth Amendment prohibition against cruel and unusual punishment.[218] The Court's holding was not necessarily inconsistent with the Baldus study's conclusions: the racial bias that existed did not arise to the extremely high level needed to show a constitutional violation.

Unlike the Supreme Court, the U.S. district court rejected the findings of the Baldus study. District court judge Forrester made several findings undercutting the validity of the Baldus study. For example, the authors used a forty-two-page questionnaire trying to identify variables that might have resulted in the imposition or failure to impose the death penalty. The judge found that the authors' questionnaire "could not capture every nuance of every case."[219] He also found that variables used in the study suffered from "multicollinearity," a situation when there is a high correlation between two variables.[220] Multicollinearity can increase confidence in correlations greater than merited. Specifically, Judge Forrester concluded that variables like aggravating circumstances in cases involving white victims and mitigating circumstances in cases involving Black victims demonstrated multicollinearity. The judge found other flaws in the analysis, allowing him to reject claims of racial bias in the imposition of the death penalty.[221]

In *Whom the State Kills*, authors Scott Phillips and Justin Marceau updated the Baldus study. Phillips and Marceau looked not at cases in which the death penalty was imposed but at those in which it was carried out.[222]

As the authors observed, "Baldus's research showed that the race of the victim was highly predictive of which defendants would be sentenced to death."[223] The authors found "[a] racially disparate execution-selection effect: the problematic sentencing disparity discovered by Baldus is exacerbated at the execution stage. Even among those already sentenced to death, persons who were convicted of killing a white victim were more than twice as likely to be executed." They found that almost no one was executed if the victim was Black. Their findings remained intact even after controlling for "confounding variables," like whether the murders of white victims were the most aggravated killings.[224]

As suggested by Phillips and Marceau, the overwhelming majority of scholars agree with the Baldus study conclusions. That includes academics familiar with statistical methodology. For example, Dr. Richard Berk described the Baldus study as "far and away the most complete and thorough analysis of sentencing ever carried out."[225] Professor Samuel Gross challenged the district court (and the Eleventh Circuit panel that affirmed the district court's analysis) as "simply false."[226] He argued that the thrust of the courts' rejection of the Baldus study was to suggest no statistical assessment could prove racial discrimination in sentencing.[227]

The occasional commentator who rejects the Baldus study does so largely by repeating Judge Forrester's criticism. That is the thrust of Kent Scheidegger's argument in *Rebutting the Myths about Race and the Death Penalty*. Scheidegger is the longtime director of the Criminal Justice Legal Foundation, a pro–death penalty, law-and-order organization established early in the days of the VRM.[228] His Ohio State Criminal Law Journal article largely tracts the district court's opinion. Similarly, Professor Cassell relies on Judge Forrester's opinion to reject claims of racial bias in the application of the death penalty.[229]

The Baldus study is consistent with findings concerning criminal sentencing generally. As discussed above, those data are ample and shameful: in a society where race matters and African Americans and other less affluent minorities have struggled generally, we should not be surprised about the data. We should acknowledge them and work to repair the system. One also ought to be aware that victim impact statements are not solely responsible for racial disparity in sentencing. But one can make a strong case that they contribute to those disparities.

Even if empirical studies leave room for debate on whether victim impact statements increase racial disparity in sentencing, one can examine their likely effect. Pinpointing causes for discriminatory sentencing presents difficult challenges. Many factors may contribute to discrimination, including economic inequality, which leaves poorer racial minority members represented by overworked public defenders. But one still ought to consider how victim impact statements may contribute to racial bias.

Nonwhites are far more likely to be victims of violent crime than are whites. Similarly, victims of violence are more likely to be poor than well-to-do.[230] Nonetheless, white victims are twice as likely as Black victims to make victim impact statements.[231] Many factors may explain such results, including the cost required to participate in a criminal trial, like taking time off from work. Education correlates with wealth and race in America; in many instances, education leads to greater confidence.[232] Victims like former Judge Luttig make ideal witnesses for the prosecution. Some states allow victims to have lawyers help them present their evidence;[233] but again, that skews participation away from poorer victims.

Although Chief Justice Rehnquist cautioned that victim impact statements were not supposed to lead to a comparison of the value of victims' lives, data suggest that juries consider the value of the victims' lives in ways that are legally wrong. As well documented in debates about the death penalty, prosecutors often exclude minority jurors.[234] Jurors find more compelling witnesses with whom they identify.[235] Not surprisingly, some jurors admit finding Black victims' testimony less compelling than testimony from white victims given the racial composition of juries.

Think back to Napoleon Beazley's trial. As discussed above, viewed objectively, Beazley did not seem to be among the worst of the worst, those for whom the death penalty is supposedly an appropriate punishment. He was only seventeen, almost universally considered a mitigating circumstance. Although he got caught up in drug dealing, he had no criminal record for any violent crime. His crime demonstrated incompetence, rather than the careful planning associated with an act of a cold-blooded killer. He committed the crime with two adult associates, often assumed to be more culpable actors. Beazley's victims were wealthy and white; Beazley was Black.[236]

The empirical evidence about racial disparity does not seem open to debate. But even if it is, the data are strongly suggestive that *Payne* got it wrong: victim impact statements result in inappropriate comparisons about the value of victims' lives. Jurors must care more about homicide victims whose family members testify articulately about their pain than they do about similar victims whose family members fail to testify or do so unartfully. For example, educational inequities in the United States and the racially disparate rates of participation at sentencing should create doubt about the Court's *Payne* analysis.

The Role of Democracy in Determining Criminal Penalties

In writing an article opposing critics of the Victims' Rights Amendment to the Constitution, Cassell suggested that VRM opponents saw members of the movement as "barbarians at the gates."[237] In doing so, Cassell tapped into some of the roots of the VRM. Carrington and members of the 1982 President's Task Force on Victims of Crime rejected expertise. Professionals in the criminal justice system were, in their view, out of touch with populist sentiment.[238]

As developed in chapter 7, cases that become media headlines often drive criminal justice policy. For most of the past fifty years, few legislators ran on platforms that emphasized that they were soft (or even smart) on crime. California's extremely expensive experiment with its "Three Strikes and You're Out" statute offers a case study in bad public policy. The Three Strikes initiative resulting in the statute passed with about 72 percent of the popular vote.[239]

Another example of the power of the Victims' Rights Movement is the reaction in California after Brock Turner's criminal sentence.[240] Turner, of course, is the Stanford "rapist" whose case garnered international headlines. Even at a time when the state had started to advance liberal sentencing reforms, California changed its law to mandate a minimum prison sentence for an offender convicted of sexual assault of an unconscious woman in reaction to the sentence imposed on Turner.[241] Turner's case also led to the sentencing judge's recall, despite the fact that the well-regarded judge, Aaron Persky, followed the probation report's recommendation when he imposed Turner's sentence.[242] The vote favoring Persky's recall was almost 60 percent.[243]

There is something wrong with having voters determine sentencing policy. Long ago, Jeremy Bentham argued that a criminal justice system should center on a government's properly developed penal code, not on public morals or outrage.[244] Scholars have demonstrated that Bentham was right and that public involvement in criminal sentences results in prison terms longer than needed for protecting public safety.[245]

The authors of *Punishment and Democracy* demonstrated the excesses of California's Three Strikes Law.[246] The authors found that, at best, it had only a minor deterrent effect for future criminal activity.[247] Further, offenders convicted of their third offense tended to be older and, in many instances, guilty of midlevel offenses.[248] The offenders whom Three Strikes proponents claimed would be subject to the law (murderers, rapists, and child molesters)[249] were already subject to very long terms of imprisonment or even the death penalty.[250] The offenders tended to be older because they had already served prison sentences for their qualifying strikes.[251] Hence, the most common offenders given very long sentences under the law were midlevel offenders who were no longer in their prime criminal years age-wise—namely, for most men, between nineteen and twenty-nine years old.[252] A twenty-five-years-to-life sentence imposed on a thirty-five-year-old midlevel offender results in many years of expensive incarceration that cannot be justified based on any resulting social protection.[253]

Similarly, many commentators who opposed Judge Persky's recall did so, in part, out of concern about judicial independence, especially relating to length of prison sentences.[254] Imagine, for a moment, another judge sentencing a defendant in a case like Brock Turner's after witnessing the successful recall effort. Consciously or unconsciously, the judge would have to consider the risk to his or her career if the sentence seemed to the public to be inadequate.[255] While recall supporters downplayed the impact on judicial independence, empirical data support the concern about judges imposing unnecessarily long sentences.[256]

In December 2015, the Brennan Center for Justice at New York University Law School published a study on state court judicial sentencing practices.[257] The report measured the effect of an upcoming reelection on a judge's sentencing practices and discussed the increased cost of judicial elections.[258] Much of the funding for election campaigns is from outside groups that typically fund negative ads.[259] Largely, those ads attack opposition candidates as soft on crime or tout candidates as tough on crime.[260] Relevant to this discussion, judges up for retention gave longer sentences as those judges got closer to reelection.[261] Keep in mind that in many states, victims' rights groups provide much of the money for judicial election ads.[262] In California, the prison guards' union, working closely with victims' rights groups, often provides funding to back tough-on-crime judges.[263] Not surprisingly, therefore, the political process ends up adding unnecessary years of confinement in many cases.[264]

While in recent years the public has seemed exhausted with mass incarceration,[265] the democratic process will almost inevitably result in sentences that are longer than necessary to protect public safety.[266]

Often lost in the reaction to Judge Persky's sentencing decision was his reliance on a detailed probation report.[267] That report, in turn, focused on the California legislature's criteria for determining the length of a criminal sentence.[268] Those criteria include a risk assessment instrument, which provides a reasonably accurate prediction of whether an offender will recidivate.[269] In light of his age and lack of prior criminal record, Turner's score indicated a low likelihood of reoffending.[270] The sentence imposed was not only lawful but also based on that substantial probation report.[271]

Like many, I read the headlines about the light jail sentence and assumed that the sentence demonstrated the worst kind of bias, a light sentence imposed on a well-to-do athlete.[272] After reading the probation report, I was less certain about the sentence. In addition, I was not in the courtroom and did not see the defendant when he testified. As a result, like most people who have heard about the case, I have no idea whether he was credible. Apparently, the judge found the defendant's testimony about some of the events to be credible, including the defendant's belief that the victim was consenting.[273] Over time, I became increasingly agnostic about whether Turner's sentence was too lenient.

My experience with the Turner case is illustrative: even someone who has written about excessive punishment and urged greater attention to limiting prison sentences and focusing on rehabilitation was initially moved by news headlines.[274] Most voters are not criminal law scholars and have little time or opportunity to read probation reports or to reflect on first principles of the criminal law. Many people learned about the case from headlines, often ones that misrepresented the facts of the case.[275]

Even worse were reports on social media that distorted the facts of the case. So many false accusations were made on largely unregulated social media sites that a law professor set up a web page to rebut misstatements or outright lies made about the case.[276]

The democratic process does not work in rightsizing criminal punishment. Anyone with empathy feels for victims. We may see ourselves or our loved ones as victims. Guilty defendants have done something wrong.[277] Getting past those realities to a position where one can assess appropriate punishment dispassionately is difficult. Explaining first principles of criminal law to members of the public takes one into a theoretical realm, which is harder to understand than the immediate pain of victims.

Concluding Thoughts

Allowing victims to confront the person who caused them harm and to tell that person of the suffering the victims have undergone seems like an unequivocal good thing. Anyone with a minimal amount of empathy would seemingly have to support such a process. But is that so clear?

Depending on the VRM's success in getting a federal constitutional victims' rights amendment past, such statements may be written in stone. For now, every state and the federal government allow some form of victim participation at the criminal sentencing stage.

Such evidence may be relevant. A man decides to kill his ex-spouse's child to make her suffer for leaving him. His desire to cause his ex-spouse pain relates to his level of culpability under current death penalty legal standards. A woman hits another person in the face with a bottle. The victim experiences severe injuries to the face. The victim's testimony about those injuries is legally relevant to whether the perpetrator committed simple or aggravated battery, where the dividing line focuses on the extent of the harm done to the victim.

Starting with *Payne v. Tennessee*, however, the Supreme Court opened the floodgates, allowing victim impact evidence that may have nothing to do with an offender's degree of culpability. Such evidence invites juries to impose harsher punishment when an offender kills a wealthy person whose family members appear in court and share their grief, even in cases where the offender had no reason to know anything about the victim or the victim's family. As such, punishing an offender for consequences that he could not have known violates two fundamental criminal law principles: the criminal law focuses primarily on an offender's mens rea as a measure of that offender's blameworthiness; it also focuses on the offender's mens rea to assess a proportional punishment. While victim impact statements are not supposed to invite a comparison of the value of different victims' lives, that is certainly the impact of such evidence as the system is administered.

Despite equivocation by some VRM supporters, victim participation by design is supposed to increase criminal sentences. In retrospect, the VRM shares responsibility for excessive use of prison as the first option upon conviction over most of the past fifty-plus years. Many policy makers across a broad political spectrum are now seeking to undo some of the harm caused by mass incarceration. As argued in this chapter, empirical studies point in competing directions about whether such evidence results in longer prison sentences and imposition of more death penalties. This chapter has argued why victim impact statements do increase punishment and increase the likely imposition of the death penalty.

The United States is having a moment of awareness about racial injustice. VRM advocates attempt to deny that victim impact evidence results in racial disparity in criminal sentencing. Attempting to do so requires ignoring a large body of empirical work, about both criminal sentencing generally and the death penalty in particular. In a society where one can see racism in so many areas, one must be in denial to believe that victim impact evidence does not exacerbate racial inequity in sentencing.

Any efforts to shift responsibility to the democratic process should fail. As a criminal law scholar who lectures and debates these issues, I know that explaining essential principles of the criminal law to many members of the public presents a challenge: victims who are suffering deserve our empathy. But leaving sentencing policy to the public is likely to lead, as it has for most of the past-fifty years, to excessive punishment. That comes at a massive cost to offenders, to their families, and to our society. In many instances, incarceration does little to help victims and reallocates resources away from health care toward prisons and the people who maintain them. From where I sit, that has been a tragic bargain.

7

California's Three Strikes and You're Out Legislation

A Case Study in the VRM's Excesses

The previous chapter discussed the debate about whether victim impact evidence increases criminal penalties. While some victims' rights supporters claim that such evidence does not increase punishment, this chapter examines an example where members of the Victims' Rights Movement unequivocally sought to increase prison terms. California's Three Strikes Law, a draconian statute that passed with the help of victims' rights organizations, helped bloat California's prisons and did so with little regard to any coherent theory of punishment. The resulting expansion of California's prisons was no accident.[1]

Not only is Three Strikes evidence of the VRM's role in increasing incarceration, but it also provides a case study of many themes explored elsewhere in this book. The law traces its origins to parents whose children were crime victims. As occurred elsewhere, passage of the law benefitted from idealized victims and misleading media campaigns. The law's drafters demonstrated distrust and, at times, open contempt for criminal justice experts.[2] Support came from diverse groups, joined together by varied interests regarding the issue. The law led to bad results.[3] Despite extravagant claims by supporters that the law caused sharp declines in crime rates, empirical data contradict such assertions. Instead, like many other VRM initiatives, the law has been excessively punitive, imposing sentences far greater than needed for the protection of society and often grossly disproportionate to an offender's culpability.[4] Apart from economic costs, the law has devastated many individuals, including offenders and their families.

Since passage of laws like Three Strikes, there has been an emerging recognition that the nation's reliance on prisons as a first resort has resulted in mass incarceration. Reformers from across a broad political spectrum have reversed, in part, that state of affairs, with efforts at changing drug laws, exploring other options to prisons, and expanding rehabilitative measures.[5] But countertrends exist. For example, at a time when many Americans see the need for reform, headline cases still result in knee-jerk legislative reactions, resulting in longer prison sentences. The widely (mis)reported Stanford "rapist" case is a case study in how media and social media can resort to draconian sentencing laws.[6]

The first section begins with a discussion of a senseless murder and a grieving father's efforts to reform criminal sentencing laws. It traces Mike Reynolds's slow progress from drafting the draconian Three Strikes Law to its eventual adoption by the state legislature and then a parallel initiative, approved with overwhelming support of state voters. Widely recognized is the fact that Reynolds's bill would have died on the vine but for the kidnapping and murder of another Californian, twelve-year-old Polly Klaas, the kind of photogenic victim whose tragic death drew national attention. Beyond that, Reynolds's efforts might also have failed but for the substantial backing of victims' rights organizations and other powerful interest groups like the National Rifle Association[7] and the California Correctional Peace Officers Association (CCPOA).[8] Finally, that section also explores Reynolds and his supporters' contempt for experts, reminiscent of Frank Carrington's rejection of experts and appeal to the "common man." Experts, including the occasional policy-wonk politician, who attempted to slow down passage of Reynolds's bill and initiative learned quickly to step aside or get bowled over.[9]

The second section focuses on the Three Strikes Law's impact on California. As observed by the authors of the most important empirical critique of Three Strikes, most habitual offender statutes promise more punishment than they deliver—or to borrow their analogy, most such laws have a louder bark than their bite. By comparison, California's Three Strikes Law, which included a less publicized two-strikes provision, had a greater bite than bark. In effect, the law was the greatest penological experiment in our history.[10]

The law's supporters claim that the experiment has been a major success. They contend that it resulted in the sharp downturn in crime rates in California.[11] The second section of this chapter visits those claims and reports the evidence to the contrary—that California's sharp decline in crime was, at best, only marginally the result of Three Strikes. Elsewhere, states experienced similar sharply declining crime rates without the budget-busting cost of building and maintaining prisons. Beyond the cost of the law was its lack of a coherent theory of punishment. Not only did the law impose disproportionate sentences but such cases began to make headlines.[12] Although the process took years, the law's excesses have started to produce pushback from several quarters.[13]

The third section examines ways in which Americans have become exhausted with overreliance on incarceration. Slow to join the national trend to sentencing reform, California got a boost from a three-judge panel of federal judges, which found that California's prison overcrowding violated prisoners' constitutional rights.[14] Both the voters through the initiative process and the legislature have chipped away at California's Byzantine and punitive sentencing scheme. Finally, with support from Governor Newsom, the increasingly liberal California legislature created a commission to study the state's penal code. Its recommendations include repealing the death penalty and the Three Strikes Law.[15] While it remains unclear whether California will adopt the commission's recommendations, they reflect the dramatic reversal of California's punitive stance.

The fourth section raises questions about the future. This chapter does not end with what criminal justice reformers would see as good news. Instead, the section discusses how easily they can unravel even if California achieves progressive reforms. As an example, it considers passage of a statute dramatically increasing penalties for distributing fentanyl and for a death resulting from that crime. The legislature did so at the same moment that it reduced drug enhancements for some crimes and gave judges broader discretion to "strike" some sentence enhancements when an offender used a weapon.[16] The chapter ends with a question: can progressive reforms survive a rise in crime rates that generate more headline cases?

Grieving Fathers and the Road to Three Strikes in California

In June 1992, Kimber Reynolds was leaving a Fresno, California, restaurant when a career criminal attempted to steal her purse. When she resisted, her assailant shot her in the head from close range. Briefly maintained on life support, she died about a day after the attack.[17]

Mike Reynolds, Kimber's grieving father, began his campaign to deal with her death immediately. Within hours of her death, he appeared on a Fresno-area right-wing talk show. Discussion of the case led to a police informant's tip that Joe Davis was her murderer. Davis was a repeat offender and meth addict, released from prison only two months before he killed Reynolds's daughter.[18] Within days of the crime, Davis died in a gun battle with police, a fact that brought satisfaction to Reynolds.[19]

About a month later, Reynolds hosted a group of Fresno area men known for their tough-on-crime stances. Among the group were two judges, Buck Lewis, a local municipal court judge, and James Ardaiz, a state appellate court justice, and local right-wing talk-show host Ray Appleton.[20] Part of the discussion was about what would sell to the public. Although they adopted the Three Strikes and You're Out language from a recently enacted Washington State law, as developed below, the law was much broader than Washington's statute.

Three judges, including Ardaiz, wrote a draft of the law thereafter. Initially, Ardaiz sought anonymity because, according to Reynolds, he and the other judges "might need to rule on a 'three strikes' case and they didn't want to [be] placed in a position of partiality."[21]

Armed with his proposed bill, Reynolds attempted to find support in the California legislature to get it passed. In 1993, Bill Jones, then a Republican assemblyman from the Fresno area, agreed to sponsor the bill.[22] In turn, Jones contacted the state's attorney general, Dan Lungren, and asked him to support the bill. With an eye toward the 1998 governor's race, Lungren, already a tough-on-crime advocate, readily agreed. He helped tweak Reynolds's bill to avoid some arguably unconstitutional language.[23]

Later in 1993, Reynolds began his efforts to get the bill passed in the California legislature. Despite traveling to Sacramento with several busloads of supporters and making a passionate plea before the Assembly Public Safety Committee, Reynolds's impassioned plea went unheard, at least for the moment.[24] Members of the legislature saw some of the less obvious expansive aspects of the bill. Despite claims that it was aimed at violent repeat offenders, the bill made residential burglary a qualifying prior strike and made any felony a third strike, including many crimes that could not be deemed violent under anyone's definition.[25] The law also included a Trojan horse, a second-strike provision, not widely publicized, which doubled many prison sentences.[26] Perhaps sensing the public's mood, the committee proposed letting a more modest bill, closer to Washington State's law, go to the Assembly floor. Reynolds rejected that offer, leading to the committee's decision not to send the bill to the Assembly as a whole.[27]

The committee's rejection of Reynolds's bill as written would have significant consequences for the state. He and his backers realized that resorting to the initiative process might lead to a state constitutional amendment, requiring a supermajority in the legislature to amend the law.[28]

The fate of Reynolds's bill was about to change. In July 1993, Richard Allen Davis, another repeat offender, had been released from state prison on parole. Davis had a long criminal record, driven in part by mental illness, no doubt the product of a long history of abuse and drug addiction. On October 1, he broke into a Petaluma, California, home with an intent to steal valuables. Instead, when he found three young girls in a bedroom, he kidnapped one of them. That was Polly Klaas.[29]

Her kidnapping changed the direction of Reynolds's campaign to enact Three Strikes. The Klaas family acted quickly in getting out information about the kidnapping with hopes that the police would find her alive. That included circulating her photo and a home movie of the preteen that captured the hearts of members of the public.[30] While her fate remained uncertain, news coverage intensified, ramping up public support for Polly's family. Winona Ryder, who grew up in Petaluma, offered a $200,000 reward for her return.[31] Despite the rarity of such crimes, they are often galvanizing, triggering the fears of parents and family members. Indeed, this case, occurring in an affluent community where one would expect freedom from crime, had the necessary elements to keep it on the front pages all over the country. The crime took place in "the heart of a prosperous small town. . . . The victim was an idealized version of everybody's daughter or sister, an innocent young girl at a slumber party."[32]

Before news of Polly's death, Reynolds's efforts to get the required signatures to place his initiative on the ballot had generated little interest. With only about twenty thousand signatures, Reynolds would almost certainly not have prevailed in his efforts. Shortly after Polly's death was discovered, Reynolds got Polly's dad's signature on his ballot petition.

Within days, Reynolds had over fifty thousand signatures, on the way to becoming the fastest qualifying initiative in California's history.[33] Of course, Davis's status as a repeat offender boosted public support for the law.

Before Polly's kidnapping, Reynolds needed funding for his efforts. The National Rifle Association was one of the first organizations to finance the Three Strikes proposal.[34] It did so after having just financed the successful passage of Washington's own Three Strikes law in 1992, to the tune of $90,000.[35] As described by one author, the NRA struggled in the early 1990s to maintain its image in western states like California and Washington, where citizens were (1) much more interested in sensible gun laws than those in other states and (2) beginning to realize that the NRA "was a huge impediment to that."[36] The NRA's involvement with the Three Strikes campaign in Washington and subsequently Reynolds's campaign in California were attempts to rehabilitate its reputation among voters.[37] The NRA's support of the Three Strikes initiative was "[a] strategy to win friends and influence people over the controversial issue of gun control. Through advocating harsher penalties for the victims of crime, the NRA used an effective strategy of diverting attention away from the public's easy access to guns, which are the weapons of choice for most criminals."[38] In a 1994 *Los Angeles Times* article, the vice president of the NRA boasted of their $40,000 direct contribution to Reynolds's campaign efforts, along with their indirect financial contributions in the form of "hundreds of thousands of dollars' worth of NRA magazine publicity promoting [the campaign] and countless California NRA members and activists all doing their part."[39]

Lost on many, seemingly Reynolds himself, was a certain irony about his acceptance of NRA money. His daughter was a victim of gun violence. Of course, the mantra of the NRA and law-and-order advocates is a familiar one: guns don't kill people, people do.[40]

At least in California, an even more powerful group with ties to the VRM is the California Correctional Peace Officers Association (CCPOA). Indeed, CCPOA is a major funder of many VRM groups in California.[41] It was the second organization to become heavily involved with the Three Strikes campaign in California, and its second most critical source of funds, with a direct contribution of over $100,000.[42] CCPOA's then-president Don Novey was reportedly hesitant to support the campaign in its early stages and asked Reynolds to "wait a year or so" to push for its legislation.[43] Eventually, however, Novey decided to support the campaign and described it as "the only right thing to do; it would get 'career criminals' off the street, people who were the dregs of society, [who] prey on their fellow citizens."[44] Novey also stated, "Mike Reynolds sought the assistance of CCPOA and we jumped on board—we were determined to help him rid our neighborhoods of violent felons. Three Strikes and You're Out became *our* initiative."[45] The association also donated $1 million to then-governor Pete Wilson after he began supporting the Three Strikes Law.[46]

Those critical of the CCPOA's involvement in the Three Strikes campaign contend that the organization likely had little interest in deterring criminal activity.[47] Rather, their interest was business oriented: the Three Strikes Law would ultimately mean more people incarcerated for longer periods of time, requiring more corrections officers who could then join the CCPOA, which would mean an increased flow of union dues to the organization and thus more political clout for the organization.[48] Lieutenant Kevin Peters, a member of the CCPOA, characterized it as such: "We've gone from 12 institutions to 28 in 12 years, and with 'Three Strikes' and the overcrowding we're going to experience with that, we're going to need to build at least three prisons a year for the next five years. Each one of those institutions will take approximately 1,000 employees."[49] The lieutenant's predictions seem to be accurate: according to the California Policy Center, by 1998 the state had already tripled its number of prisons since the early 1980s.[50]

The CCPOA's support for Three Strikes did not end after its enactment. In fact, the CCPOA actively lobbied against seven bills that would have reformed the Three Strikes Law between 1995 and 2003.[51] In 2004, the CCPOA also spent $1 million to defeat Proposition 66, which "would have limited the crimes that triggered a life sentence under the Three Strikes law."[52]

One might praise Reynolds for his "grassroots" campaign to change sentencing policy in California. But such grassroots efforts are likely to increase punishment unnecessarily, at considerable cost to the public.[53] Part of what led to the law's excess was the contempt of expertise demonstrated by Reynolds and his supporters. With echoes of Frank Carrington's appeal to the "common man" and rejection of expertise,

Reynolds spoke contemptuously of politicians who got in his way. Los Angeles–based right-wing radio talk show hosts John Kobylt and Ken Chiampou helped Reynolds gin up support for the initiative. Notably, they targeted the liberal members of the Public Safety Committee that had prevented the bill from coming to the full Assembly.[54]

Shows like the *John and Ken Show* made Reynolds a celebrity and gave him a power unlike any other actor in the legislative process. Prior to passage of AB 971, Reynolds's version of Three Strikes, a number of legislators proposed narrower versions of the law, including one initially backed by the powerful California District Attorneys Association. Reynolds was unrelenting, making clear in an election year that he would accept no compromise.[55]

Various legislators and organizations raised concerns about the cost and broad sweep of the bill. Alternative bills were proposed even by law-and-order legislative members. As I summarized elsewhere, "Reynolds refused to allow any amendments to the bill. Further, Reynolds' sway with the legislature was almost unprecedented. Reynolds was adept in using the press to intimidate those who raised questions about the legislation. Reynolds' judgment that a politician was soft on crime promised to be devastating."[56] Even critical reports from the body's own Legislative Analyst's Office did not slow down the process.[57]

Reynolds's efforts got a boost from Governor Pete Wilson. Wilson, involved in a difficult reelection campaign, made law and order and his support for Reynolds's bill cornerstones of his campaign.[58]

Even after passage of AB 971 without amendments, Reynolds remained so distrustful that he reneged on a commitment not to pursue his initiative if the legislature passed his bill. Reynolds and his supporters held members of the legislature in contempt. An example is his comment about members of the legislature. Still angry at the Public Safety Committee's rejection of his bill, after passage of the law, his comment summarized his view of California's legislative members: "The second time we went up there . . . those suckers saluted."[59]

His contempt for expertise, echoing Carrington's similar appeal to what Richard Nixon called the Silent Majority, was reflected not only in his comments. As one author summarized that contempt, "[N]o professional analytical input was permitted or given by criminologists and other social scientists, no hearings to receive their expert opinions were held. It was a complete triumph of fear, emotion, and political cowardice over reason."[60] Or as Professor Frank Zimring and his coauthors more tersely stated, the law passed "untouched by human hands."[61]

Less clear is whether anything could have stopped the passage of Three Strikes. For example, legislative Democrats and Republicans voted overwhelmingly for the law.[62] Even the fact that Marc and Joe Klaas reversed their early support for the law and eventually worked to oppose it had no effect.[63] Many Californians would soon realize that they had gotten more than they thought when they voted for the initiative.

The Impact of Three Strikes

As indicated above, the legislature and California voters approved Three Strikes "untouched by human hands,"[64] or perhaps more precisely, without input from criminal justice experts. That was, in part, Reynolds and his supporters' goal. It was also part of a trend in the United States.[65]

One might reasonably ask what is wrong with leaving sentencing policy to the public and to their elected officials, without the buffer of criminal justice experts. As Zimring and his coauthors explained: "The modern politics of criminal justice involves rhetoric that imagines criminal sentencing as a zero-sum game between victims and offenders. If one prefers victims, one believes that punishment should be increased. Those who oppose increasing punishments must, in this view, prefer offenders' interest to victims' interests. To live in this kind of world is to deny that expert opinion is of any real importance in making policy."[66] The authors' point invites some unpacking. Central to my thesis is that the VRM has contributed to increased and excessive punishment. The VRM's proponents have often been law-and-order conservatives following Frank Carrington's lead in the 1960s.[67] The VRM has succeeded in capturing public support with headline cases that seem to call for punitive sanctions. Zimring and his coauthors also place Three Strikes within that national trend. Three Strikes was not a one-off.[68]

Beyond suggesting that Three Strikes was part of a national trend, the quote from *Punishment and Democracy* invites a discussion of how the law led to excessive punishment. In one sense, California's law led to excessive sentences by bucking the national trend. This section develops those points more fully.

California adopted its Three Strikes Law at the same time as did many other jurisdictions. However, as often has been the case with get-tough-on-crime legislation, legislators talk tough but, through various constraints, end up producing less than promised impacts on the criminal justice system. For example, when Congress adopted its Three Strikes Law, the law had "loud bark, small bite."[69] That was not the case with California's law.

Reynolds and his supporters were "deliberately confrontational,"[70] as described earlier. They intended to change the system and tolerated no dissent. The result was to produce a Three Strikes Law like no other in the nation. While they were confrontational, they also participated in a campaign that was unlike the "loud bark, small bite" approach followed by members of Congress.[71] I have described elsewhere in detail misleading aspects of the Three Strikes campaign. At a minimum, supporters must have known that initiative campaign literature was misleading when it claimed that the law was aimed at "murderers, rapists and child molesters."[72] Punishments on the books for those crimes prior to 1994 were already severe, including the death penalty for some murders. More impactful was the two-strikes provision of the law, not advertised in the catchy three strikes and you're out language.[73]

The major differences between California's repeat offender law and other three strikes laws include a few provisions that dramatically increased California's law's application and dwarfed the frequency of use in other states.[74] Two provisions stand out most glaringly: although the law was aimed at felons who committed at least two violent felonies in the past, California included residential burglary in its list of qualifying felonies. While in theory residential burglary might become violent if a felon encountered a homeowner, as a statistical matter such confrontations are rare. Including burglary as a qualifying strike significantly expanded the population of prior felons who qualified for third strike punishments.[75]

Combine the inclusion of burglary as a qualifying felony with the definition of a third strike and one can understand why California's use of its law dwarfed other states. A felon with two prior felonies could be charged under the law if the current charge was any felony.[76] Some of the most egregious cases involved third felonies that seemed to be misdemeanor theft cases. But under California law, misdemeanor theft with a prior theft offense allowed the prosecutor to charge the crime as a felony.[77] Cases involving such so-called wobblers helped change public perceptions of the law; but that is getting ahead of the story.[78]

California's law included some other provisions that increased its whammy. That a felon committed a prior crime many years ago or as a juvenile was irrelevant. If a felon committed two felonies at the time of the current charges, the court could sentence the defendant to consecutive terms of imprisonment. At least as the law was written, while the prosecutor could "strike" (i.e., ignore) a prior felony, the sentencing judge could not do so.[79] Despite some ambiguity in the law's language, third strike prisoners were not entitled to good-time credits to secure early release. Limiting judges' discretion demonstrated Reynolds's hostility toward them. One more provision demonstrates the way that an offender might receive a minimum term well in excess of twenty-five years in prison: the law did not supersede other sentence-enhancement laws. And California has boatloads of such enhancements on the books.

Also, as indicated above, the Three Strikes label did not capture the law's broadest effect. Section 667(e) enhances punishment for some offenders on their second strikes. Pragmatically, the second-strike provision has had the greatest impact on California prison population. Early data make that point starkly: whereas other states had a few third-strike prisoners, by 1996 California had sentenced over twenty-six thousand felons under its Three Strikes Law. The comparison of California's Three Strikes Law to those in other states and the large increase in prison population suggests that Zimring and his coauthors were correct when they characterized California's law as the "largest penal experiment in American history."[80]

No wonder that in about a decade after passage of Three Strikes, a panel of three federal judges held that California was violating prisoners' constitutional rights to be free from cruel and unusual punishment: the net effect of prison overcrowding meant that the lack of adequate health care rendered incarceration inhumane.[81]

California's Three Strikes Law was and remains open to criticism as unprincipled and, at least in part, in conflict with stated justifications for punishment. In 1976, based on the misperception that rehabilitation did not work, California abandoned rehabilitation and, like other states, renewed a commitment to retribution.[82]

At times, Three Strikes' supporters seemed to claim that the law was retributive, for example, when they claimed that the law was aimed at murderers, rapists, and child molesters.[83] That is, the law seemed to be aimed at bad criminals, deserving of extreme punishment. But far more frequently, sentences under the law resulted inversely to an offender's culpability (the benchmark for retribution), especially in third-strike cases.[84]

Imagine two third-strike felons with similar prior felonies. In one instance, the offender's third felony is rape, at least in the 1990s an offense that would net the offender a six-year term of imprisonment. His sentence under Three Strikes would be twenty-five years to life in prison, absent any other enhancements. Compare an offender's punishment if his third strike was petty theft with a prior. Such an offender might be sentenced to a few months in jail but for Three Strikes. As enacted and *as enforced*, such an offender would be sentenced to twenty-five years to life. Any claim of retributive proportionality is unsustainable.[85]

Other similar anomalies exist under the law. As developed in a paper by Zimring, imagine two felons: one has committed prior theft offenses and finally commits a burglary. That offender does qualify for a third-strike punishment. But flip the crimes: an offender with two prior burglaries who now commits a theft is subject to a sentence of twenty-five years to life.[86] Such an example suggests a kind of perverse application of the law: commonly recognized is the fact that felons may "age" out of their peak crime years.[87] In this example, the offender receives the severe sanction despite committing a less serious offense, suggesting that the offender represents a less serious threat to public safety than many other offenders.

Examples of the law's odd application were not merely a matter of law school hypotheticals. Headline cases began arising around the state: a felon received his third-strike sentence for stealing a piece of pizza.[88] Offenders received similar twenty-five-years-to-life sentences for small-time drug offenses. A case that ended up in the Supreme Court involved a longtime drug addict who, on two occasions, stole videotapes. Because he had prior theft offenses, the offender's petty thefts were "wobblers," and the district attorney charged the thefts as qualifying third strikes. As a result, a drug addict in his late thirties received two third-strike sentences. The minimum twenty-five-year sentences were to be served consecutively, resulting in a fifty-year minimum sentence.[89]

Proponents of the law responded to criticisms with various explanations. For example, they focused on an offender's past conduct and suggested that the defendant continued to represent a risk. When confronted with the reality that most third-strike cases involved nonviolent third strikes, often drug offenses, proponents claimed that the law was working. They relied on a dramatic downturn in California's crime rates that they attributed to passage and application of the law.[90]

Even if the law lacked a coherent theory, proponents could maintain public support if the law worked well. Proponents relied on the idea that small numbers of felons committed the largest number of crimes. Thus, by incapacitating such offenders, crime rates would drop.[91]

Whether the law as applied in the early days was sweeping up those offenders is questionable. So many of the early third-strike defendants appeared to be petty criminals, not the high-rate offenders said to be the law's primary targets.[92] Another problem with the claim that the law was responsible for the drop in crime was a simple reality: most of the third-strike defendants would have been sentenced to terms of imprisonment. That is, it was not the especially long term of imprisonment that caused the decline in crime rates.[93]

Proponents shifted the argument from incapacitation to deterrence. Secretary of State Bill Jones, one of the law's early champions, cited a study conducted by the *Sacramento Bee*. According to the *Bee* report, inmates were talking only about the risks of receiving a sentence under the new law. He also pointed to reports that parolees were leaving the state because of the law.[94]

Unlike theoretical arguments about retributive theory, claims about deterrence are subject to empirical analysis. To date, the study done by Zimring and his coauthors remains the best work examining the question of whether Three Strikes' deterrent effect caused the steep crime decline in California.[95] Their data suggest that deterrence could not explain most of the decline in crime rates. For example, crime rates declined across the board, not just among targeted offenders. The authors left open the possibility that the law produced a "trace" amount of deterrence, perhaps 1 to 2 percent of the drop in crime.[96]

Proponents of the law made other claims that are worth considering in assessing benefits from the law. In 1998, California attorney general Dan Lungren's office published a report touting the law's benefits. The report observed that "California has experienced its largest overall drop in crime over any for-year period in history with double digit drops in every major crime category between 1994 and 1997."[97]

Obviously, such a drop in crime was worth celebrating. But was it brought about by Three Strikes, which also promised to cost the state a great deal? One important detail implied in the report was that Three Strikes was the reason for the crime decline. It compared aggregate crime data from 1990–93 with data from 1994–97. Crime rates were rising during the earlier period and began the sharp decline in 1994, the year that Three Strikes became law.[98]

That narrative is powerful but, at best, unintentionally misleading. By aggregating the data from 1990–93, the report could claim that Three Strikes caused the downturn. But that crime downturn began in 1993. Any claim that Three Strikes caused it to drop more sharply is also contradicted by the data. Crime rates began a rate of decline in 1993 that continued at the same downward rate.[99]

Other problems existed for the Three Strikes' good-news narrative. Comparing crimes in cities around the state contradicts the narrative. A city-by-city comparison should demonstrate sharper declining crime rates in cities where the district attorney's office invoked Three Strikes more often than cities not relying heavily on Three Strikes. That did not happen. San Francisco, a city where the law was invoked infrequently, had a sharper decline in crime rates than did San Diego, where the law was invoked frequently.[100] Notably, "[S]tudies that have found counties within California that were aggressive in enforcing Three Strikes 'had no greater declines in crime than did counties that used it far more sparingly.' In fact, crime dropped 21.3% in the six counties that have been the most lenient in enforcing Three Strikes, while the toughest counties experienced only a 12.7% drop in their crime rates."[101] Three Strikes' advocates also proudly compared the decline in crime rates in California with those in other states. Jones pointed to the fact that California's crime rates in 1994 declined 4.9 percent, compared to a national decline of only 2 percent, as more good news.[102]

Unpacking those data undercut Jones's argument. New York, a state without a budget-busting Three Strikes Law, led the nation in declining crime rates.[103] Criminologists offered several explanations for declining crime rates, not simplistically claiming a single cause like California's law. They could point to several factors contributing to the decline: "a strong economy, a decreasing number of people in their crime-prone years, and fewer turf battles among crack cocaine dealers."[104] Lost in the argument about declining crime rates was the fact that similar or greater rates of decline could be achieved with far less expensive alternatives to Three Strikes.[105]

Also at issue in the debate surrounding Three Strikes was the extent of the savings brought about by reduced crime rates when victims' costs were compared to increased prison costs. Mentioned above, Philip Romero, Governor Wilson's chief economist, prepared a report claiming that Three Strikes would save the state billions of dollars: "He determined the cost of crime by adding out-of-pocket expenses, monetary value of pain and suffering, and costs of crime prevention."[106] By Romero's rosiest calculation, a year of incarceration for each felon would result in 150 fewer crimes from being committed, leading to an annual savings of between $302,000 and $515,00, amounts far in excess of the cost of warehousing a felon for each year.[107]

More serious commentators, not politicians, suggest that such estimates are, at best, optimistic or, more candidly, wildly inaccurate. The RAND Corporation prepared a report in 1994 that estimated savings at only $20,000 to $40,000 per year, less than the cost of a year in prison for a felon.[108] Using a more realistic number of crimes prevented than the 150 figure chosen by Romero led to a much more sobering comparison of the cost of Three Strikes versus the savings it produced: two prominent criminologists estimated savings of between $3,500 and $7,000 per year. The title of Professor Zimring's article, *The Voodoo Economics of California Crime*, suggests an expert's view of Romero's assessment. Using Romero's methodology, according to Zimring, California's increased use of prison sentences in the 1980s should have brought its crime rate to zero.[109]

Three Strikes' supporters ignored indisputable consequences of the law's severe minimum sentences. For example, even if the law resulted in sentencing violent offenders, they would be incarcerated longer than necessary to protect the public. Well established is the fact that violent crime is "a young man's game," to quote former judge Richard Posner.[110] That is, by their late twenties, offenders "age out" of violent crime. Thus, even if an offender receives a third-strike sentence in his mid-twenties, he will remain in prison long after he no longer represents a serious threat to the public.[111] A second fact that was largely ignored by the law's supporters was that the law would dramatically increase the number of elderly prisoners and that the cost of warehousing them rises exponentially. Simply put, older prisoners need a great deal of health care, often not easily provided within the prison system.[112] A third fact conveniently ignored by Three Strikes' supporters was that violent offenders already faced extremely long sentences for their crimes: a murderer, for example, might be subject to the death penalty or to life in prison.[113]

Within less than a decade after passage of the law, data confirmed many claims by the law's opponents. Zimring and his coauthors' study in *Punishment and Democracy* reported that Three Strikes was not protecting Californians from violent crimes. The comparison of offenders committing third-strike offenses and non-third-strike offenses showed that "[t]he offenses charged at the current arrest is less likely to be a crime of violence for a third-strike defendant than for a defendant with no strikes at all."[114] Combine the inclusion of burglary as a qualifying felony with the law's original provision that made any felony a third strike and the results of who ended up in prison as a third-strike felon were not surprising: in effect, midrange offenders, not violent offenders, ended up with extremely long sentences. Further, most likely to qualify as a third-strike offender, an offender must have been convicted in the past and served prison time for the earlier offenses. Someone incarcerated in his mid-thirties, as indicated above, was likely phasing out of his violent criminal career and was likely to become a geriatric prisoner, which is extremely expensive to maintain with little benefit to the public.[115]

Three Strikes was hardly the only sentencing enhancement law in California. Mentioned earlier, California adopted another law backed by Reynolds requiring sentence enhancements when certain crimes were committed with a weapon.[116] Beyond that, the state has so many sentencing enhancements on the books that judges and lawyers need a computer program to sort them out.[117]

The VRM's participation has thus contributed to massive prison expenditures. The state has spent funds in excess of what it needed to protect the public from dangerous felons.[118]

Beyond the financial cost, the law has caused harm to many offenders and their families. Third-strike offenders whose offense was drug-related, a product of addiction, were sent away for years. One result, often below the radar, was that the law increased the number of children living in single-parent households.[119] Another result was the disproportionate impact on African Americans, who were targeted by the law more frequently than were white offenders.[120]

California may be moving toward a more coherent sentencing policy. But the road has not been smooth.

Mass Incarceration

After massive increases in prison populations nationwide, many states began rethinking the use of prison as the first resort. Reasons varied, but a primary one was the honest recognition that states could not afford to continue to incarcerate their way to safety. Critics from across a broad political spectrum recognized that mass incarceration was unsustainable. Especially as many Americans realized that the war on drugs was a failure, many states, often politically conservative states, adopted reforms to address the effects of generations of "tough-on-crime" laws.[121]

California was slow to the dance. The belief that Three Strikes was responsible for the state's declining crime rates created a powerful narrative for law-and-order conservatives. Many politicians, including many Democrats, had backed Three Strikes, at times with full-throated endorsements. For example, Democrat Gray Davis was able to defeat Republican attorney general Dan Lungren in the 1998 gubernatorial election, in part with support from the CCPOA.[122] In 1999, the California legislature passed a bill that would have authorized a study of Three Strikes to determine whether the law had delivered on its promises. Davis vetoed the bill.[123]

Despite strong support for Three Strikes among policy makers who had supported it, public support began to wane when voters realized what they had voted for. Headline cases like that involving the theft of a slice of pizza stunned members of the press and the public.[124] Other cases involved defendants found with small amounts of drugs[125] or petty theft charged as a felony. One such case, noted above, involved a drug addict in his late thirties who tried to shoplift videotapes on two separate occasions. His fifty-years-to-life sentence also generated similar national attention.[126] Some would admit voting for the law without understanding how it would be applied. But undoing Three Strikes has proven to be a daunting task.

Reynolds's distrust of the legislature led him to use the initiative process. The ballot initiative included a provision requiring a supermajority of the legislature to reform the law.[127] Even as California evolved from a purple to a blue state, finding that kind of support in the legislature was not going to happen. Resorting to the initiative process has produced mixed results.

In 2004, Three Strikes' opponents lined up donations from several prominent donors to qualify an initiative to reform the law. After initially supporting Three Strikes, Joe Klaas, Polly's grandfather, had reversed his support. He became a visible supporter of Proposition 66, which, arguably, would have brought the law into closer alignment to what voters originally thought they were voting for in 1994. For example, Proposition 66 would have required that the third felony be a serious or violent offense, which would eliminate cases like those that made headlines described above.[128]

Despite an early lead in the polls, the initiative failed. A late influx of cash from a wealthy donor whose sister was a murder victim (and who, five years later, would help get Marsy's Law passed in California)[129] and opposition from various high-profile politicians doomed the proposed changes. No one could have been surprised that former Republican governors Wilson and Deukmejian joined the opposition organized by then-governor Arnold Schwarzenegger. And given the politics of the day, no one should have been surprised that former governors Gray Davis and Jerry Brown (also a future governor) joined the Vote No on Proposition 66 campaign. The result was a reasonably close vote, with 52.7 percent of the voters opposing the reform.[130]

In 2006, former Republican Los Angeles district attorney Steve Cooley joined forces with prominent criminal defense lawyer Johnnie Cochran to amend the law. Not only would their efforts fail, but Cooley's willingness to support modest reforms to the law led to the California District Attorney Association's opposition to Cooley when he ran to be California's attorney general in 2010.[131]

Alongside efforts to change Three Strikes through the initiative process were efforts to effectuate change through the court system. For example, several defendants who received long prison terms challenged their sentences as in violation of the Eighth Amendment's prohibition against cruel and unusual punishment and, on occasion, the state constitutional prohibition against cruel or unusual punishment.[132] Virtually all of those challenges failed. Two seemingly strong cases made their way to the U.S. Supreme Court. Both failed by a 5–4 vote.[133]

Other judicial challenges had mixed results. For example, although seemingly contrary to the intent of the drafters, the California Supreme Court held that an offender could not get any good time credit to reduce a third-strike sentence.[134] One successful challenge involved a different aspect of the law: did a judge need the prosecutor to agree to the judge's decision to "strike" (ignore) a prior felony to eliminate the applicability of Three Strikes' provisions? The California Supreme Court found that the law gave judges that power and read the law to avoid a state constitutional separation of powers argument.[135]

Prior to 2012, voter initiatives suggested a more compassionate pro-defendant attitude among Californians. In 2000, voters approved Proposition 36, allowing some drug offenders to receive probation instead of incarceration.[136] In 2014, the voters passed Proposition 47, which reduced some low-level offenses from felonies to misdemeanors.[137] Finally, in 2012, the voters passed a new Proposition 36. The 2012 proposition changed Three Strikes in significant ways, most notably requiring that the third felony be a serious or violent felony. Each of these laws received support from large majorities of voters.[138] Despite opposition from Mike Reynolds and the California Republican Party, the 2012 Proposition 36 received support from 69.3 percent of voters, winning by a majority in every county.[139]

In 2019, the California legislature created the Committee on Revision of the Penal Code. The associated legislation required the committee to simplify and rationalize the state's substantive and procedural criminal law and directed the committee to study proposals made by law reform groups, including the American Law Institute, and by judges, other public officials, and members of the public. Most importantly, the committee was directed to make periodic recommendations to eliminate inequities in the law and to modernize the law.[140] Appointment of its chair signaled the hoped-for direction of the committee's recommendation. Michael Romano was the founder and has been the director of Stanford Law School's Three Strikes and Justice Advocacy projects since 2007.[141]

Despite Republican support elsewhere for sentencing reform, California Republicans showed little enthusiasm for SB 94. The Assembly voted in favor of the bill by a wide margin, 59–17, but with only one Republican joining the majority. In the California Senate, the vote in favor was 33–3, with five Republicans voting with the majority.[142]

Given the minimal support from Republicans, opposition to the committee has come from some predictable sources. Notably, the California District Attorneys Association, the CCPOA, and some victims' rights groups have criticized the legislation creating the committee and its recommendations.[143] For example, Glen Stailey, the current president of the CCPOA, has raised concerns about the potential negative impacts on public safety. The head of a victims' rights group, Nina Salarno, was quoted as saying that the committee's work puts Californians at risk.[144]

The committee's first report included ten recommendations, generally accepted as sound criminal justice policy. In many instances, other states have successfully adopted such laws. The recommendations included eliminating mandatory minimum sentences, shifting incarceration from state prison to county jail for some minor offenses, eliminating incarceration for some traffic violations, limiting gang affiliation as a basis for sentencing enhancement to only the most dangerous felonies, clarifying that the focus for parole eligibility should be on future serious or violent offenses, and allowing second-look sentencing by judges.[145] Some of the recommendations, notably reducing gang affiliation enhancement, should reduce racial disparities in sentencing.[146]

The legislature passed six of the committee's ten recommendations in its 2020 report. Among those recommendations were the following: eliminating mandatory minimum sentences for nonviolent drug offenses, limiting the prosecution's ability to present evidence of gang involvement until after a finding of guilt on the underlying offenses, and increasing the number of offenders who can have sentence enhancements removed retroactively.[147]

The committee's 2021 report's recommendations were even bolder than those in its first report.[148] The 2021 report included recommendations that have been successful elsewhere, including the use of evidence-based sentencing criteria and greater focus on rehabilitation. It also urged better reentry programs and diversion for the mentally ill. Coming full circle from the focus of this chapter, it recommended repeal of

Three Strikes.[149] In February 2022, efforts were underway to qualify a ballot initiative to repeal Three Strikes.[150] In a separate report, released at the end of 2021, the committee also recommended that California repeal its death penalty law.[151]

Also indicative of how far California has come since breaking free from the VRM's "success" in passing Three Strikes, the committee has relied on experts in the field as the basis for their recommendations.[152] This seems like a resounding defeat for the law-and-order wing of the VRM, the CCPOA, and the California District Attorneys Association. Of course, whether the state implements the committee's recommendations remains to be seen. Even with passage of some progressive reforms, the VRM's influence has not gone away. The next section turns to questions about the potential unraveling of progressive reforms.

Unraveling Reforms?

During the 1990s, several states created successful sentencing commissions. While not all commissions are created equal, some states achieved success in reducing reliance on incarceration without endangering the public. Often, sentencing commissions served as buffers to prevent increased terms of imprisonment based on a crime du jour. For example, some states enacted provisions that require a legislator demanding longer prison sentences to include a financial impact statement or a revenue source to pay for the impact on the prison system. Successful commission states brought coherence to the system at the outset. Specifically, some commissions have allocated available resources to ensure their use to limit the most serious crimes. The typical commission has resources to collect data to determine best practices.[153] The buffer from the political process tends to stabilize the system without risking public safety.[154]

Not all states have adopted such measures, which create a buffer between the politics of the moment and sound sentencing policy. They may lack a sentencing commission, or their legislation may lack restraint on the political process. (Even states that have in place legislation requiring the legislature to explain funding for new punishments can unravel that legislation.) California is a case study in how an unrestrained legislature can, even in times of concern about overuse of incarceration, overreact to the crime du jour.

California has worked backward by comparison to states that have adopted a commission model. As indicated above, California began moving away from Three Strikes and its broader reliance on prison as a one-size-fits-all approach in fits and starts. Motivated in part by the three-judge panel's decision that found the state's prison health care system in violation of the Eighth Amendment's prohibition against cruel and unusual punishment, voters' change in attitudes about the war on drugs and greater sense of security as crime rates decline, and a general move to the left politically, California has reduced its prison population and is moving toward greater rationality in its criminal justice policies. Many of the state's reforms demonstrate repudiation of the VRM. But as explored here, the VRM's influence remains a reality. Further, absent a coherent scheme in place that limits or slows the legislature from enhancing sentences, California remains under the sway of the VRM. A few examples demonstrate the continuing risks to rational sentencing policy.

In 2017, the California legislature repealed statutory provisions that resulted in three-year enhancements for each prior conviction of certain drug laws.[155] That came at the same time as the legislature broadened a judge's discretion to "strike" some enhancements that resulted when an offender used a gun in commission of the crime charged.[156] Both reflect the new mood in California described above.

Contemporaneously, the legislature also increased penalties for crimes involving fentanyl. That statute includes an increase in punishment for distribution of a certain amount of the drug, allowing sentencing of ten years to life in prison. That term of imprisonment increases to twenty years to life in prison if a death or serious bodily injury results from the use of the drug.[157]

What might be objectionable about such a result? California has needed sentencing reform for many reasons. Among those reasons is that the legislature has added enhancements based on the headline crime of the day. In fact, enhancements became so numerous and complex that lawyers and judges needed a computer program to determine the correct sentence. That has led to a significant number of reversals on appeal, based on a judge's erroneous determination of a sentence.[158] Beyond that, the driving force behind AB 3105 was yet again news headlines.[159] Instances involving use and sale of the drug seem to present similar issues to other drug offenses. The state seemed to recognize with passage of SB 180 the need to rethink the pathway from drugs to long prison sentences. One might have thought that a similar approach would be warranted for fentanyl as well, especially given current concerns about racial disparities in drug enforcement.[160]

The provision dealing with deaths resulting from fentanyl also suggests overreaction. Traditional homicide crimes cover many deaths that result from providing a toxic substance to a decedent. Adding a homicide crime to the penal code may be more form than substance if the elements are the same as those for second-degree murder or involuntary manslaughter.[161] But unclear in the language of the statute is whether an offender must satisfy the mens rea elements of those crimes. For second-degree murder, for example, a prosecutor must show that the offender has subjective awareness that their conduct creates a high risk of death or serious bodily injury. AB 3105's language is unclear whether a prosecutor must show that the offender knew that the drug contained fentanyl or even that the offender knew of the risk of death created by the drug's use.[162]

Organizations that benefit from criminality and incarceration have not gone away. The CCPOA has signaled its opposition to California's Committee on Reform of the Penal Code.[163] The victims' rights group may have lost some appeal in recent years but remains active in opposing many meaningful reforms.[164] California has a powerful statewide district attorneys association that has lined up in opposition to many progressive reforms. While some prosecutors have tried to emulate progressive prosecutors in other states, the California District Attorneys Association does not seem to have done much to join the trend.[165]

While progressive reforms have advanced in states like California, partly in reaction to the overuse of incarceration, worth considering is whether those reforms will take hold. Consider rising crime rates, including homicide rates, throughout the nation. Placing blame on progressive policies is a proven strategy for many politicians, even if the facts do not support those claims.[166] While a national consensus seemed to presage lasting reforms, our divided politics do not bode well.

Whatever lesson one might draw from the unraveling of laws like Three Strikes, I cannot get free of a nagging question: are we one headline case, involving a victim like Kimber Reynolds or Polly Klaas, away from a resurgence of the VRM's influence?[167]

8

What Should We Do if We Really Want to Help Victims?

As so often is the case in a deeply divided nation, the debate about victims' rights can be rancorous. Advocates on opposite sides of the debate may demonize their opponents.[1] Too often the debate seems premised on a zero-sum game between good and evil, between victims and victimizers. That is unfortunate. Despite the seeming gulf between Victims' Rights Movement advocates and their critics, critics of many of the VRM's initiatives no doubt share the grief of victims and their families.[2]

This chapter asks two related questions: what can we do to prevent victimhood, and what should we do if we really want to help victims?[3] It begins with a discussion about the mass murder at the Sandy Hook Elementary School, including a question about how to count the number of victims of that mass shooting. It then turns to the typical post-mass-shooting debate: gun rights supporters contend that the remedy is expanded mental health care, not additional gun regulations as demanded by grieving families.[4] Along the way, this chapter discusses the extent to which gun rights supporters have it right: we would be better served by having a first-rate health care system, with meaningful access to mental health care services. Indeed, this chapter argues, not only would victims be better off after they become victims in a society with a robust health care system, but also that expanded health care would result in far fewer victims. Anyone who knows about the life circumstances of many murderers knows a core truth: victimizers were often subjected to severe cruelty in their own lives.[5]

While one might agree with gun rights advocates' claim that we need expanded access to mental health care, this chapter questions many gun rights advocates' commitment to expanded mental health care. For example, many states where gun rights are sacred refused to expand health care under the Affordable Care Act.[6] Further, some killers, including Adam Lanza, the Sandy Hook shooter, received mental health care but killed anyway. Despite the NRA's mantra that the way to stop a bad person with a gun is to arm good people, far more families suffer grief from their loved one's suicides or accidental death than might be saved by expanding gun ownership. Easy access to firearms makes suicide far more likely than situations where individuals bent on suicide lack that access.[7]

Not only after mass killings are there calls for stronger gun regulations, but the majority of Americans routinely agree that gun control laws are needed.[8] Given the strong support for laws limiting gun rights, one might wonder why legislatures do not respond with meaningful gun laws. This chapter turns to that question. Initially, one part of the answer is clear: the NRA and gun rights organizations have had an outsized influence on American politics. But more importantly, even if legislative logjams were broken because of a recognition of the suffering caused by easy access to weapons, the Supreme Court's decisions holding that the Second Amendment created a personal right to possess weapons for self-defense limits the ability of the federal and state governments to limit gun possession. The chapter closes with a short discussion of the lawsuit brought by parents of children killed at Sandy Hook against Remington,[9] the manufacturer of the weapon that Adam Lanza used in his mass shooting. Settlement of that lawsuit suggests that states intent on regulating gun use may have a limited avenue to hold gun manufacturers responsible for gun violence. But, as concluded in that section, the suit against Remington leaves open more questions than it answers, including whether the Supreme Court might find that such suits violate an expanded reading of the Second Amendment.

Counting Victims

Chapter 3 focused on victimhood, including the differing definitions of who qualifies as a victim. That chapter did not attempt to provide a model definition for reasons explained in more detail here. To get at that point, this section asks how many victims died as a result of the Sandy Hook shooting.

When then-president Barack Obama eulogized the victims on the anniversary of the Sandy Hook shooting, he referred to twenty-six victims. As quoted in a 2014 *New Yorker* article, Obama referred to "six dedicated school workers and twenty beautiful children."[10] The local firehouse has twenty-six stars on its roof. Similarly, then-governor of Connecticut

Dannel Malloy asked churches to ring their bells twenty-six times.[11] According to current governor Ned Lamont's web page, that remains the number of officially recognized victims.[12]

Initially, however, some local churches tolled their bells twenty-eight times in recognition of the total number of lives that were lost. Pressure mounted to exclude Nancy Lanza, Adam's mother. Some argued that her indulgence of her son made her an accomplice of his violence. That argument is premised on the fact that she encouraged her son to learn to shoot and provided him with money to buy his own weapon.[13] Some faulted her for her failure to confront her son when she discovered violent images that he drew not long before his shooting spree.[14]

Others put Nancy Lanza in a more sympathetic light. In an article offering a detailed discussion of Adam's family's efforts to address his various mental health conditions, Andrew Solomon described her as a woman who gave up her career and much of her life beyond taking care of her son in an effort to get him needed care. Her efforts on his behalf included providing homeschooling when Adam found school attendance excruciating.[15] Shot before he went on his rampage, Nancy could qualify as a crime victim. That might mean that there were twenty-seven victims.

What about the early impulse of some churches to toll their bells twenty-eight times? Clearly, under existing statutes, Adam (who committed suicide) did not qualify as a victim. Many observers trying to figure out Adam's motivations wondered what could have caused his violent outburst. While on the autism spectrum, Adam was not diagnosed as schizophrenic. Nor was there evidence of child abuse. He had difficulty adjusting to middle school and was often subjected to bullying. Despite the characterization of Adam as pure evil, a judgment made by some members of the public, such a tidy explanation is hard to sustain if one reads the accounts of Adam's struggles with mental illness and the failure of the mental health care system to provide relief from his suffering.[16]

None of the statutes defining "victim" would include the person who was the shooter. That is so despite the fact that he suffered mental illness that almost certainly led to his suicide.[17] While a suicide does not fit within statutory definitions of who qualifies as a victim, family members and individuals who know others who are suicidal or who commit suicide recognize the pain that those individuals experience. The act of suicide often leaves the person's family and loved ones in grief. Their grief can be as real as the pain experienced by a murder victim's family.

Observers remain unclear what caused Adam's mental illness. For example, they do not know if Adam was the victim of some form of abuse. Researchers do know about victimizers more generally. Anyone who has worked on a death penalty case knows that an important part of preparing a capital defendant's case is developing the killer's full psychological profile. The correlation between an offender's abuse as a child and violence committed by that offender is robust.[18] Research into mass killers' backgrounds demonstrates the correlation between mental illness and extreme acts of violence.[19] Often, in capital cases, psychological evidence of the offender's abuse is so powerful that juries refuse to impose the death penalty. As recounted in *End of Its Rope: How Killing the Death Penalty Can Revive Criminal Justice*, attorneys' efforts in the Aurora, Colorado, mass shooting saved James Holmes from the death penalty despite ample evidence of careful planning.[20]

Also consider child sexual abuse cases. Such cases evoke universal condemnation, as they should. Victimizers seem unworthy of compassion. The VRM has led efforts to eliminate statutes of limitations in such cases, in part out of a strongly felt condemnation for such offenders. But what is often missed in such cases is that pedophiles were often victims themselves.[21] Seen in that light, dividing victims and victimizers tidily into two camps is simplistic. As a result, this discussion proceeds without defining victimhood, other than to suggest that churches in Connecticut that rang their bells twenty-eight times had it right.

Cases like these raise hard questions: should an affluent society provide adequate mental health care to prevent such violence and other kinds of abuse? Beyond an adequate mental health care system, would a robust health care system also reduce victimization? And should the law limit access to weapons to prevent such violence on self and others? Those questions are part of the discussion throughout the rest of this chapter.

Access to Mental Health Care

Watch the debate after reports of another mass shooting in the United States. A significant majority of Americans call for greater gun control measures, a reexamination of U.S. gun culture, and a challenge to the National Rifle Association's extraordinary control over legislatures around the country.[22] The NRA and other extreme gun rights advocates predictably claim that the problem is a lack of adequate mental health care.[23] Beyond that, they claim that basic freedoms are under attack and that more guns are the answer to gun violence.[24] Despite evidence to the contrary, the mantra of many gun rights advocates is that "the quickest way to stop a bad guy with a gun, is a good guy with a gun."[25]

Evidence suggests that the NRA has part of the answer to gun violence right: better health care contributes to reducing crime. That is the focus of this section.

The link between poor health and rising crime rates is well documented. Data consistently demonstrate a strong correlation between violent crime and intoxication. Similarly, research supports the commonly accepted view that substance users and addicts commit income-generating crimes to finance their substance use habits. Less well recognized is that involvement in an illegal drug market can expose one to an increased risk of criminal offense and victimization.[26]

The statistics are quite revealing: one study found that 52 percent of inmates charged with violent crimes reported being under the influence of alcohol or drugs during their crimes. Close to 40 percent of those charged with property crimes were also high. Involvement in drug trafficking notoriously increases the risk of violence, as evidenced by turf wars during the crack cocaine epidemic.[27]

As many Americans realized as they watched prison populations soar during the war on drugs, aggressive law enforcement efforts often do not work in eliminating drugs. Demand for drugs is too inelastic to respond to the arrest and incarceration of those involved in the drug trade. As Frank Zimring and Gordon Hawkins demonstrated in *Incapacitation: Penal Confinement and the Restraint of Crime*, incarcerating someone involved in drug trafficking made little difference in reducing crime because the arrested offender was easily replaced, for example, by another gang member.[28]

Policy makers from across a broad political spectrum recognized the failure of the war on drugs. Happily, alternatives to incarceration have worked in many cases, as demonstrated during the long decline in crime rates. Notably, substance abuse treatment has been an effective alternative to reducing crime because medical treatment alleviates addiction. In one longitudinal study, 40 to 60 percent of the clients who received recovery/rehabilitation-oriented substance use disorder treatment were continuously abstinent from substance use, and an additional 15 to 30 percent had not resumed abuse or dependent use at follow-up one year after treatment.[29]

Less certain, but still probable, is that an expanded mental health care system would reduce crime. Many studies indicate that large percentages of prison and jail inmates suffer from mental illness. As reported in 2018, half of state and federal prisoners and two-thirds of jail inmates are in serious psychological distress or have a history of mental illness.[30]

A separate question from whether many prisoners are mentally ill is whether expanded mental health care coverage reduces crime. One empirical study found that an increase in the availability of mental health offices within a given area led to reductions in violent crime, including fewer murders, aggravated assaults, and robberies.[31] More evidence of crime reduction through expanded health care services was found in the examination of the impact of expanded Medicaid benefits.

One of the first studies directly analyzing public health care effects on crime rates involved examining the changes that occurred after eligibility for state Medicaid Health Insurance Flexibility and Accountability (HIFA) waivers was broadened to apply to nontraditional populations, such as low-income, childless adults. Researchers found that expanded benefits reduced crime, particularly robbery, aggravated assault, and larceny. The authors suggested that the availability of care resulted in lower crime rates because of the correlation between substance abuse and violence. The study concluded that a 10 percent increase in treatment rates at a cost of $1.6 billion would lead to a savings of $2.9 to $5.1 billion.[32]

Jacob Vogler, a researcher from the University of Illinois, published the most thorough study on the effects of public health insurance expansion and its relationship on crime rates. Vogler assessed the causal relationship between access to health care and crime following the expansion of Medicaid coverage after the Affordable Care Act in 2015. The fact that states could opt in or out of expanded coverage provided a controlled study of the effects of expanded coverage. Vogler used state-level crime data from the Federal Bureau of Investigation Uniform Crime Reports for the years 2009 through 2018 to test his hypothesis that the Affordable Care Act expansions did cause crime rates to decrease. Vogler found significant reductions in reported violent crime rates that ranged from 4.8 percent to 5.7 percent.[33] Other findings included a reduction in burglaries that ranged between 2.5 percent and 4.4 percent. He estimated savings of about $4 billion, an amount greater than the cost of expanded Medicaid coverage.[34]

Yet another study confirming the benefits of health care coverage focused on the effects of young men "aging out of" Medicaid when they turned twenty-one. Comparing young men who had coverage but lost it upon turning twenty-one and those who retained coverage, researcher Elisa Jácome found that the young men who lost coverage were 15 percent more likely to be incarcerated than the control group. Even more significant, she found that young men who lost mental health care coverage were 22 percent more likely to have been incarcerated than young men in the control group. She concluded that Medicaid provided a safety net for low-income men that curtailed criminal activity, more than justifying the cost, especially when compared with the cost of traditional law enforcement and incarceration.[35]

Studies like these may explain part of the rising crime rates during the COVID-19 pandemic. Murder rates, for example, rose by nearly a third in 2020.[36] During the pandemic, access to health care became even more of a challenge than it had been prepandemic, a crisis that has occurred worldwide.[37] The United States has suffered the same shortage of mental health care providers, with especially bad consequences for financially deprived communities.[38]

These data support the adoption of a far more robust national health care system, including expanded access to mental health care. One might expect questions about funding such a system. But based on some estimates, the annual cost of crime borne by victims is in the hundreds of billions of dollars annually.[39] Even assuming some imprecision in such data, they suggest that investing in health care makes economic sense.

Investing in health care helps not only those receiving health care but also their potential victims. Reducing victimhood, of course, should be a top priority, if not the top priority, for policy makers. Providing adequate care, consistent with studies cited in this section, would reduce criminal conduct, leading to fewer victims. Also, once a person becomes a victim today, the care she receives depends on the state in which she lives and the adequacy of victim compensation funds.[40] A national health care system would be available to all without regard to state-by-state variation in coverage. It would also mean that a person who might suffer trauma as a result of crime but not qualify under narrow statutory definitions of who qualifies as a victim could receive necessary care.[41]

This approach is better than what the VRM has given victims today. Victims get to participate in the criminal justice process, which does not undo the harm suffered. They may qualify for some health care benefits and may get restitution. While some of those benefits were worth pursuing, the VRM has held sway for the past half century and not wholeheartedly backed a remedy (a first-class health care system) that would do far more for victims.

Given what seems like a sound economic investment and given the calls of groups like the NRA for expanded mental health care after mass shootings, one needs to ask why the United States has not achieved that expanded coverage. The next section asks about the NRA's commitment to expanded mental health care.

The NRA's Commitment to Mental Health Care Reform

The NRA's claim that a better mental health care (and better general health care) system would reduce gun violence is correct. But do the NRA and its followers' actions follow their rhetoric? Here, the answer is almost certainly not.

The web page for the NRA's Institute for Legislative Action (NRA-ILA) states that the organization has urged the federal government to address mental illness and violence.[42] That group attempts to portray itself as committed to reasonable reforms. A close reading, however, suggests that its commitment is not that deep. Any efforts at reform, according to the NRA-ILA, must not intrude on Americans' constitutional rights, but its view of the scope of the Second Amendment is extreme.[43] Its willingness to limit access to weapons goes only so far as preventing those adjudicated to be "mentally defective" or committed to a mental institution from getting weapons.[44]

Various commentators suggest that the NRA is not committed to meaningful reform. The National Alliance on Mental Illness (NAMI) responded to the NRA's statements about mentally ill killers like Adam Lanza by calling into question the NRA's commitment to mental health care reform.[45] The NAMI statement argued that the NRA's position about mental health care demonizes mentally ill individuals. The NRA's solution of committing mentally ill people, according to USA Today's editorial board, would be "wildly infeasible, legally impossible and hopelessly expensive."[46]

NAMI's statement asked critical questions about the NRA's rhetorical response. In effect, it asked whether the NRA had done anything to advance glaring mental health care needs in the United States. The inadequacy of the mental health care system in the United States is reflected in a tragic reality: mentally ill individuals are more likely to have encounters with the police than they are to get mental health care.[47] NAMI's statement asked, "Is the NRA doing anything to protect Medicaid, advocate for acute inpatient beds, more assertive community treatment (ACT) teams, or more supportive housing programs for people living with mental illness?" NAMI's message about the NRA's stand was clear: "Talk is cheap."[48]

More evidence of the NRA's lack of commitment to meaningful mental health care reform is visible around the country. Many states where the NRA's support is greatest rejected federal assistance to expand Medicaid as part of the Affordable Care Act.[49] As discussed in the previous section, expanded health care contributes to reducing crime. Further, recent studies suggest that life expectancy rates in strong NRA states have gone down while they have increased in bluer states. Among explanations for the changes in life expectancy are pro-gun-rights laws and poor health care systems.[50]

Yet another example of the NRA's lack of commitment to addressing gun violence by individuals suffering from mental illness was highlighted in a news story from Georgia shortly after the NRA's claimed commitment deal with mentally ill individuals after the Sandy Hook Elementary School shootings. As reported in the Atlanta Journal-

Constitution, the NRA was simultaneously pressuring the Georgia legislature to ensure gun rights for many mentally ill individuals. At root,
one could see the attempted focus on mental illness as a diversion from
the harm caused by firearms.[51] Thus, the NRA has attempted to strike
a note of reasonableness but fights enactment of the kinds of reforms
needed to keep guns out of the hands of individuals who represent a risk
of violence to themselves and others.

There is a more fundamental flaw in the NRA's position on protecting
victims. The next section turns to the real cost of gun violence.

Expanded Mental Health Care Does Not Go Far Enough

Without doubt, expanded health care is part of any meaningful solution
to reduce the number of victims in the United States. But this section
argues that the VRM should not stop there but also work for meaningful
gun restrictions.

Think back to Adam Lanza's situation. Suffering from severe mental
illness, he, unlike many Americans, received first-class mental health
care. As recounted in an article in the *New Yorker*, his parents sought
help for his various health care issues when he was quite young. Symptoms began to appear in preschool and continued throughout his life.
The article recites his parents' efforts to get him care, including taking
him to such distinguished facilities as Yale's Child Study Center. Nothing prevented his killing rampage. As his father said, "Here we are near
New York, one of the best locations for mental health-care, and nobody
saw this."[52]

Acts of unfathomable violence in the United States produce calls for
legislation to restrict access to weapons. As indicated earlier, gun rights
advocates rely on standard arguments, including their mantra that "guns
don't kill people, people do."[53] They contend that "the quickest way to
stop a bad guy with a gun, is a good guy with a gun."[54] Belief in such
dogma is almost messianic.[55] Also, as well documented, despite large
percentages of Americans who support various gun control measures,
gun rights advocates retain outsized influence in the political arena,
making even modest reforms difficult.[56] The spate of mass shootings
during 2022 did lead to the enactment of gun control legislation. But as

widely reported, the bill fell far short of reforms deemed necessary to reduce access to automatic weapons.[57]

Researchers have tested the proposition that more guns can reduce crime and save lives. An occasional study supports the position of gun rights advocates. John Lott Jr. is the most prominent scholar whose research suggests that access to weapons reduces crime rates.[58] He has written and lectured extensively on the subject and argues that gun control measures are based on several myths.[59] Further, Lott has argued, based on one study that he conducted, that right-to-carry laws reduce crime rates.[60]

Lott is the most prominent scholar who supports gun rights, but he is not alone. For example, the late James Q. Wilson, prominent criminologist, then a member of the board of the National Research Council, dissented from a report questioning Lott's conclusion that right-to-carry laws were responsible for a reduction in crime rates.[61]

Many scholars question Lott's conclusions or support the argument that gun control reduces violent crime and death from gun violence. Some, like Harvard professor of health policy David Hemenway, have published papers rebutting Lott's contentions.[62] Hemenway argued that Lott failed to consider other variables that might explain the changes in crime rates observed by Lott. A Stanford Law Review article by law professors Ian Ayres and John Donohue argued that Lott's study included coding errors and systematic bias, eroding confidence in its finds.[63] One can find other critics and supporters of Lott's work.[64] Further, empirical data support the opposite view: gun owners are more likely to be injured by their own weapon than they are to use their weapon successfully to defend themselves.[65]

Not surprisingly given the division among scholars described above, the RAND Corporation published a review of existing literature dealing with the effect of conceal-carry laws on violent crime, updated in 2020. Reviewing studies like Lott's and others, the RAND report concluded that the data are inconclusive.[66]

Similar problems exist with data from Europe, where gun violence is much lower than in the United States. One study that examined data from twenty-seven developed countries around the world concluded that the number of guns per capita was a predictor of firearm-related deaths in that country. The authors stated that their study debunked the widely asserted claim that guns make a nation safer.[67] A study of continental European countries excluding Turkey and Russia was more tentative in its conclusions. After reviewing empirical studies of the correlation between availability of firearms and criminal forms of violence, the authors reported that the studies varied in outcomes.[68]

Frank Zimring, one of the leading academic empiricists, sees the question of access to weapons and victimization as clear. His research over several decades has led inevitably to one conclusion: "Does the availability of guns increase the death rate from assault? Of course, it does. . . . Trying to reduce death totals without discussing guns belies logic."[69] His coauthored 1997 study reported in *Crime Is Not the Problem: Lethal Violence in America* concluded that while crime rates in the United States were comparable to or lower than rates in other developed countries, the United States led (and continues to lead) in lethal violence. Permissive gun laws and the sheer volume of guns are responsible for the lethal violence in the United States. Higher caliber weapons and higher capacity assault weapons increase lethal violence.[70] The results were replicated in other studies as well.[71] No doubt, this reality explains why almost 80 percent of homicides in the United States in 2020 involved a firearm.[72]

As Zimring argues, logic seems to point in one direction: access to weapons leads to more lethal violence. Guns are more effective at killing another person than are other weapons like knives; large caliber weapons are more lethal than smaller caliber ones.

The premise that access to weapons leads to more victims is supported by comparative data: in the United States, gun deaths vary widely from state to state. In 2020, Mississippi led the nation with 28.6 gun-related deaths per 100,000 residents, followed by other states where gun rights advocates hold great political clout: Louisiana (26.3), Wyoming (25.9), Missouri (23.9), and Alabama (23.6). Compare those data to statistics from states at the low end, all states where gun rights advocates have less political clout: New York (5.3), Rhode Island (5.1), New Jersey (5.0), Massachusetts (3.7), and Hawaii (3.4).[73]

Women are special targets of gun violence. According to the Giffords Law Center to Prevent Gun Violence, women are five times more likely to be killed by an intimate partner who has access to a firearm than by one who does not have such access.[74]

A recent study conducted by researchers at Stanford University supports the gun control position. Notably, the report concluded that people living with gun owners are seven times more likely to be killed by an intimate partner or spouse than by anyone else. Consistent with other studies, the overwhelming percentage (84 percent) of those killed were women. Further, a person living in a home with a gun owner was twice as likely to be a homicide victim than someone who lived in a home where no one owned a weapon.[75] The study is consistent with earlier studies as well.[76] Gun ownership seems far more dangerous to owners and their cohabitants than to intruders, directly in conflict with the NRA's message.[77]

More data suggest the strong correlation between availability of firearms in the United States and death: in 2016 the United States suffered 10.6 gun-related deaths per 100,000. Compare that to France (2.7), Canada (2.1), Australia (1.0), Germany (0.9), and Spain (0.6).[78]

Given the passionate belief of gun right advocates, conversations about expanded gun rights and the effect of crime rates may go nowhere. Gun rights advocates adhere to the idea that more guns prevent crime and increase the chances that a good guy with a gun can stop a bad guy with a gun. So according to that narrative, concern for victims is not advanced by limiting access to weapons. Much of the preceding evidence suggests otherwise.

What is harder for gun rights advocates to ignore is the role of guns in suicides. According to the Pew Research Center, in 2020, 54 percent of gun-related deaths were suicides. Gun-related murders accounted for 43 percent of the total. The rest of the cases involved accidents or police shootings (presumably justified killings), with a small number where the nature of the gun death was undetermined. Not only are most gun-related deaths suicides, but also most suicides involve firearms. As Pew reported, the 53 percent figure for 2020 is consistent with data over time.[79]

Mental illness may lead to suicide. Often, mentally ill individuals have been victims themselves, surely deserving our empathy. Families of suicide victims also suffer from the loss of a loved one. Their suffering resembles the suffering of crime victims. One can only ask rhetorically why victims' rights advocates would not want to extend relief to them as well as crime victims.

One needs to ask, only if rhetorically, what is stopping victims' rights advocates from joining efforts to enact gun control measures. Here, one sees division within the VRM. Organizations like Brady: United Against Gun Violence, created after John Hinckley Jr.'s unsuccessful shooting of President Reagan, which also resulted in serious injuries to James Brady, advance a variety of bills to regulate guns, often bills that seem to have overwhelming public support.[80] Some victims' rights organizations support laws like the Brady Bill, the 1993 law mandating background checks for some weapons purchases and a five-day waiting period for others.[81] The law-and-order wing of the VRM is decidedly on the other side of the debate.

As indicated above, the NRA advertises itself as a victims' rights organization.[82] Its positions on specific victims' rights efforts can put it at odds with other VRM organizations. Notable in recent years was its effort to prevent Congress from reauthorizing the Violence Against Women Act in 2019. At issue was a provision expanding law enforcement's ability to take weapons away from domestic abusers.[83] The Stanford study discussed above demonstrates why taking weapons from domestic abusers is so important if the goal is saving lives: women are victimized by gun-owning spouses or significant others at alarming rates. As indicated in the Stanford study, its findings are consistent with earlier studies as well.[84]

Dating back to the beginnings of the VRM, similar divisions existed. As discussed in chapter 1, Frank Carrington, the leading figure in the movement's law-and-order wing, advocated for expanded gun rights. Further, the NRA is not the only organization supporting gun rights that advertises itself as a victims' rights organization.[85]

Nonetheless, many Americans, including many who consider themselves victims' rights advocates, back gun regulations. Surely, meaningful regulation of firearms should be a part of the VRM's reform agenda. The next section turns to the increasingly difficult challenge that reformers face and are likely to continue to face into the identifiable future.

The Unreality of Gun Regulation

In the aftermath of the Sandy Hook Elementary School shootings, the United States seemed poised to enact some significant gun regulations.

Congress, for example, seemed ready to enact the Assault Weapons Ban of 2013, yet the bill failed by a vote of 60–40 in the Senate. Even West Virginia senator Joe Manchin and Pennsylvania senator Pat Toomey's bipartisan bill to expand background checks failed to get enough votes to get past a filibuster.[86] Another bill would have restricted the sale of "large capacity feeding devices." That too failed.[87] The NRA offered its solution: more armed guards in schools.[88] Some state legislatures have been more receptive to gun regulations.[89] (As an aside, many states have granted gun rights that are far more expansive than those required by the Court's reading of the Second Amendment.[90] The effect of those laws beyond state borders poses problems discussed below.)[91]

In addition to success in some states, gun control advocates can point to the success of the parents of some of the Sandy Hook victims in suing Remington Arms, the company that made and advertised the automatic weapon used by Adam Lanza. Some gun control advocates see the $73 million settlement between the families and Remington's insurance companies as a significant step forward in achieving gun control reform.[92] As one parent of a murdered child said, "[T]he resolution does provide a measure of accountability in an industry that has thus far operated with impunity."[93]

Most attempts to use the courts to regulate the industry have failed because of a bill passed during President George W. Bush's term in office. The 2005 Protection of Lawful Commerce in Arms Act (PLCAA) overrides many state laws and grants the industry broad immunity from civil liability.[94] The exception that the Sandy Hook families relied on is a narrow provision in the statute that allows suits if a manufacturer "knowingly violated a State or Federal statute applicable to the sale or marketing of the product."[95]

Relying on the limited exemption from immunity, the families focused on aspects of Remington's advertising that touted the weapon as a sign of manhood. The families contended that the advertisements inspired Lanza. As a result of the settlement, one can only speculate whether a jury would have agreed with them or with Remington, which contended that it did not target at-risk youth or that the families could not show that Lanza was motivated by its ads.[96] The settlement also avoided any industrywide claim that the families' theory of the case violated the Second Amendment to the Constitution.[97] Hope that the

Remington settlement might presage a new era of gun manufacturers' accountability may be unrealistic.

Avid gun rights advocates have pressed for an expanded reading of the Second Amendment.[98] With the addition of three Trump appointees to the Supreme Court, they may have their hopes fulfilled by the current Supreme Court, despite a heavily disputed interpretation of the Second Amendment.

In 2008, in *District of Columbia v. Heller*, for the first time in history the Supreme Court found that the Second Amendment to the Constitution created a personal right to bear arms for the purpose of self-defense.[99] While its meaning has been subject to considerable debate, *United States v. Miller* was the only major Supreme Court decision relevant to the meaning of the Second Amendment. It held that only weapons that have a reasonable relationship to a well-regulated militia are free from governmental regulation.[100] Gun control advocates read that holding to support the view that the Second Amendment assured states' ability to set up militias, not to create an individual right to bear arms.

Writing for a closely divided Court, Justice Scalia rejected that reading of *Miller* and found that the Second Amendment created a personal right to bear arms. His opinion was a tour de force of historical analysis. Reportedly, he saw this as the crowning achievement of his view of originalism.[101] As an aside, many historians dispute his interpretation of the Second Amendment's original meaning.[102] More important for this discussion was section III of his opinion, suggesting many limitations to a broad reading of the amendment.[103]

While Justice Scalia's opinion was over 17,000 words, section III's 538 words suggest numerous limitations to a right that, according to Justice Scalia, was like most other constitutional rights, subject to limitations. That section is worth a more detailed reading, but after noting that the Court was not engaging in a full interpretation of the amendment's scope, Justice Scalia suggested significant limitations of the amendment's scope. For example, "[N]othing in our opinion should be taken to cast doubt on longstanding prohibitions on the possession of firearms by felons and the mentally ill, or laws forbidding the carrying of firearms in sensitive places such as schools and government buildings, or laws imposing conditions and qualifications on the commercial sale of arms. We also recognize another important limitation on the right to keep and carry arms. *Miller* said, as we have explained, that the sorts of weapons protected were those 'in common use at the time.'"[104] Some commentators speculate that Justice Scalia needed to spell out such limitations to secure Justice Kennedy's vote.[105]

Given Justice Scalia's extensive historical explanation of the fundamental nature of the Second Amendment right to bear arms, the Court's decision two years later in *McDonald v. Chicago* was not surprising: the Second Amendment is a limitation on state power as well as a limitation on the federal government.[106]

Between 2010 and 2022, the Court avoided addressing many issues that arose in lower court adjudication. Most lower court challenges have failed. The NRA has begun a campaign to reverse that trend, by arguing that lower court judges treat the Second Amendment as a second-class right.[107] Until recently, only Justice Thomas took up the NRA's cause.[108]

With the addition of Trump's three appointments, Justice Thomas, the NRA, and other gun rights supporters are about to change the Court's commitment to Second Amendment rights. That is in evidence with the Court's 2022 decision in *New York State Rifle & Pistol Association, Inc. v. Bruen*.[109]

At issue in *Bruen* was a long-standing New York gun safety law that limited a gun owner's ability to obtain a license to carry a concealed weapon in public. The Court extended the Second Amendment right found in *Heller*, where the Court found that the right existed to own a weapon in one's home. The right exists outside the home as well. That conclusion was based on the Second Amendment's language, which indicates that one has a right not only to keep but also to bear arms. Writing for the majority, Justice Thomas echoed the NRA's mantra that the Second Amendment should not be a second-class constitutional right.[110]

Bruen's narrow holding was that New York's law granted state officials too much discretion in deciding whether a person has a need to carry a concealed weapon in public. The Court suggested that other gun safety regulations, including some laws limiting concealed weapons and requiring background checks, would meet constitutional muster.[111] At a minimum, courts will now have to define the line between too much and acceptable discretion.

Justice Thomas and concurring justices attempted to reassure the public that *Heller*'s dicta that states could still limit guns in "sensitive places" was still intact. Naming a few, justices pointed to polling places, schools, and courthouses.[112] Notably, Chief Justice Roberts and Justice Kavanaugh concurred, underscoring that they believe that gun laws meet the constitutional standard as long as the state's criteria are objective.[113] Given that Roberts and Kavanaugh were part of a 6–3 majority, presumably litigants defending gun regulations will appeal to their views as decisive.

One can only guess at how sweeping *Bruen's* holding will be. As indicated, gun control advocates can urge that state regulations are objective or that they regulate weapons in sensitive places. In that sense, *Bruen* did not sweep broadly. From a different perspective, *Bruen* signals a sharp turn from the past, even since *Heller*, making sensible gun legislation more difficult.

Since *Heller*, lower courts have frequently upheld gun regulations. Even if the law regulated conduct within the Second Amendment, courts balanced a state's interest in regulation against gun owners' rights.[114] Justice Thomas seemingly has upped the ante for states hoping to regulate guns. According to Thomas, "the government must affirmatively prove that its firearm regulation is part of the historical tradition."[115]

One can only speculate how active the Court will be in striking down laws regulating guns. At a minimum, the majority is tone deaf: as Justice Breyer observed in his dissent, by late June 2022 the United States had already witnessed 277 mass shootings.[116] Given that commitment to gun rights, one needs to ask how far the Court will go. For example, what about the right of a person to carry a weapon from a state with strong gun rights laws into another state that imposes stringent limitations on weapons?[117]

Reading the Second Amendment as broadly as gun rights advocates are urging is deeply troubling. States where gun regulations are in place may lose much of their authority to regulate weapons.

Consider again the optimism expressed by some gun control advocates about the settlement in the Remington case. As indicated, some gun rights advocates question the constitutionality of the provision of the PLCAA allowing a limited ability to sue gun manufacturers.[118]

Victims' rights advocates should be deeply concerned about this state of affairs. Some victims' rights advocates are avid gun rights supporters. But many organizations and individuals who have coalesced around victims' rights are not. Avid gun rights advocates may not be persuaded by the many studies demonstrating increased suffering caused by firearms. The rest of us should be deeply concerned if we are truly committed to helping victims. Ready availability of firearms leads to more deaths and to more grieving families, whether of crime victims or suicides.

Conclusion

Depending on when one asserts that the VRM began, the movement is in its sixth or seventh decade. As developed in chapter 2, the VRM has accomplishments to celebrate. But most of this book has focused on the movement's excesses or, as argued in this chapter, its failures to be more daring in its aspirations.

Some victims benefit from access to victim compensation funds that provide health care and some funds to make up for lost income. Despite continuing criticism of the system's treatment of sexual assault victims, few are subjected to the humiliation that many experienced before the VRM lobbied for greater sensitivities toward and protections for sexual assault victims.

By contrast to generally applauded accomplishments, the VRM's agenda has led to many undesirable results. As argued in chapter 3, encouraging individuals to see themselves as victims may be psychologically inappropriate. Chapter 6's discussion of victim impact statements raises similar concerns about what many see as a false promise: participation at criminal sentencing does not lead to "closure."

Also, as discussed in chapters 6 and 7, the VRM's agenda has often led to unnecessarily long prison sentences and contributed to racially discriminatory sentences, including death sentences. Such excessive punishment not only is expensive but also creates a different set of victims: families of those incarcerated well beyond society's need for self-protection.

This book has also focused on the VRM's challenge to basic criminal norms. For example, chapter 5 examined the risk posed by statutes that abandon statutes of limitations in various kinds of cases, including some sexual assault cases. Chapter 6's discussion of victim impact statements also raises concerns about introducing facts that may lead to longer sentences in ways entirely unrelated to an offender's culpability.

Apart from these and related criticisms, this book has argued that the United States can do better if the nation is committed to helping victims. A robust national health care system would provide victims with predictable care following crimes committed against them. Further, such a robust system would also prevent some individuals from becoming victimizers. Data are clear: many criminals were themselves victims, often of unspeakable cruelty.

Even with a robust system in place, many individuals will suffer unnecessarily without meaningful gun reforms. Too much data point in that direction. To quote Zimring and Hawkins, "crime is not the problem," lethal violence is. Access to firearms increases the risk of death or serious bodily injury. Despite the NRA's mantra that the way to stop a bad guy with a gun is for a good guy to have a gun, and despite some competing studies on the effect of gun ownership and deterrence of crime, the weight of authority suggests that Americans are less safe than residents of countries that limit access to weapons.

Finally, more firearm deaths are from suicides than from criminal violence. The United States could help those suffering from depression or other mental illness that makes them suicidal and families of suicide victims if the nation supported meaningful gun regulations. Sadly, this book ends on a sour note: even with some erosion of the NRA's clout and despite strong sentiment in favor of many gun regulation proposals, national gun regulation seems like a pipedream. Many liberal states have imposed some significant limitations on gun rights, but the Supreme Court's hard shift to the right since the Court's decisions in *Heller* and *McDonald* presage a Court intent on striking down many of those reform measures. For many individuals, the results will be tragic.

ACKNOWLEDGMENTS

In June 2021, I wrote to Clara Platter, my acquisitions editor at NYU Press, to ask her questions about technical submission requirements. My email included a brief description of the project. Even before seeing sample chapters, her response was enthusiastic. Throughout the process she has been a passionate supporter of this project. Her support has been invaluable.

The rest of the NYU Press staff have been great to work with as well. Veronica Knutson has been fun to interact with. Thanks to Martin Coleman, and to Lia Hagen, Mary Beth Jarrad, Michelle Duran, and Sydney Garcia in marketing and publicity. Joseph Dahm's skillful editing has helped greatly as well.

Several friends and colleagues have provided support for this project as well. In 2019, I received an invitation to participate in a symposium in honor of my friend and Criminal Law Professor Stephen Schulhofer. I ended up writing an article about the Victims' Rights Movement and realized that much of my work over more than twenty years was about the excesses of the movement. As my dedication indicates, Steve's friendship and his work have been invaluable in helping me develop as a criminal law scholar.

Several friends have provided insight into my project. My friend and former colleague Joshua Dressler has provided support throughout the process, including making significant suggestions about the first draft of the book. I also benefitted from comments by my colleague Professor Nadia Banteka and my friends Dr. Patrick Browning and Professor Michael Hoffheimer. Professor Susan Bandes's articles and email exchanges have been invaluable in shaping my understanding of many of the excesses of the Victims' Rights Movement.

Associate Dean Marybeth Moylan's decision to reduce my teaching load during the spring 2022 semester was instrumental in helping me finish my first draft well in advance of my deadline. McGeorge's Dean

Michael Hunter Schwartz and Associate Dean for Scholarship Frank Gevurtz deserve a shout-out for providing meaningful support for my scholarship.

Finally, several research assistants provided invaluable help with this book. Mikayla (Anderson) Steele, Sierra Horton, Vivian Lee, Marcie Murtha, James Filling, and Kyndall Banales not only provided wonderful and timely research assistance but were a joy to work with. Many of my friends, now retired, often ask why I have not done so as well. I am quick to explain that working with young people like my research assistants is too much fun for me to think about retirement anytime soon. Working with this wonderful group of assistants makes me even less likely to retire than I would have been without their help!

NOTES

INTRODUCTION

1 See Paul Cassell, "Crime Victims' Rights," *Utah Law Faculty Scholarship* 33 (2017): 4–6, https://dc.law.utah.edu.

2 Bruce Shapiro, "Victims & Vengeance: Why the Victims' Rights Amendment Is a Bad Idea," *Nation*, February 10, 1997, 12, www.sweetcommunication.com.au.

3 See Frank Carrington, *The Victims* (New York: Arlington House, 1975), 80. Carrington argues that the Warren Court went beyond the scope of fundamental fairness at the expense of exposing law-abiding citizens to increased crime.

4 See Raphael Ginsberg, "Victims Deserve the Best: Victims' Rights and the Decline of the Liberal Consensus" (PhD diss., University of North Carolina at Chapel Hill, 2013), 77–87.

5 Despite leading in the polls, Democratic candidate Michael Dukakis never recovered after Bush's Willie Horton ad, involving a prisoner who received early release during Dukakis's term as governor of Massachusetts. See Doug Criss, "This Is the 30-Year-Old Willie Horton Ad Everybody Is Talking about Today," *CNN*, November 1, 2018, www.cnn.com.

6 Aya Gruber, *The Feminist War on Crime: The Unexpected Role of Women's Liberation in Mass Incarceration* (Oakland: University of California Press, 2020), 147. For those who are too young to remember that 1988 election campaign, when Dukakis was the governor of Massachusetts, Horton, a state prisoner, received a work release from prison and committed a violent rape, assault, and armed robbery.

7 Gruber, *Feminist War on Crime*, 147.

8 Gruber, *Feminist War on Crime*, 149.

9 For example, even liberal Willie Brown, the speaker of the California Assembly for many years, joined forces with Republican governor Pete Wilson to pass California's Three Strikes Law. See Franklin Zimring, Gordon Hawkins, and Sam Kamin, *Punishment and Democracy: Three Strikes and You're Out in California* (New York: Oxford University Press, 2001), 12. The legislation passed the Assembly on a vote of 63–9 and passed the Senate on a vote of 29–7. Assembly Final History, 1993–94 Cal. Reg. Sess., 260 (October 6, 1994). A parallel initiative, Proposition 184, was approved by 71.85 percent of the electorate. Statement of Vote, General Elections, November 8, 1994, 107.

10 Susan Estrich, *Real Rape* (Cambridge, MA: Harvard University Press, 1987), 15–16.

11 President's Task Force on Victims of Crime, "Final Report" (1982), 64, https://ovc.ojp.gov.

12 Susan Bandes, for example, analyzes the intersection of emotion and the law in the context of victim impact statements and how they "evoke not merely sympathy, pity, and compassion for the victim, but also a complex set of emotions directed toward the defendant, including hatred, fear, racial animus, vindictiveness, undifferentiated vengeance, and the desire to purge collective anger." Susan Bandes, "Empathy, Narrative, and Victim Impact Statements," *University of Chicago Law Review* 63, no. 2 (1996): 395, https://chicagounbound.uchicago.edu. See also Markus Dirk Dubber, *Victims in the War on Crime: The Use and Abuse of Victims' Rights* (New York: New York University Press, 2020), 154–55. Dubber discusses the harmful tendencies of victimological and criminological essentialism, i.e., labeling victims as victims and offenders as offenders: "The act of offending reveals the offender's true nature as a source of danger, as a (super) predator. At the same time, the nonact of being offended reveals the victim's true nature, as a target of danger, as a (super) prey. [T]he offender and the victim both are stripped of their human nature, their personhood."

13 See generally Michael Vitiello, "The Victim Impact Statements: Skewing Criminal Justice Away from First Principles," *NYU Annual Survey of American Law* 76, no. 2 (2021), https://scholarlycommons.pacific.edu.

14 See Michael Vitiello, "Introducing the Warren Court's Criminal Procedure Revolution: A 50-Year Retrospective," *University of the Pacific Law Review* 51, no. 4 (2020): 629–31, https://scholarlycommons.pacific.edu; see also Jeff Shesol, "Opening the Door to a Conservative Court," *New York Times*, June 22, 2016, www.nytimes.com.

15 See Ginsberg, "Victims Deserve the Best," 58–61.

16 Ginsberg, "Victims Deserve the Best," 27–28, 40; Bandes, "Empathy, Narrative, and Victim Impact Statements," 398.

17 Marie Gottschalk, *The Prison and the Gallows: The Politics of Mass Incarceration in America* (Cambridge: Cambridge University Press, 2006), 1–6.

18 James Forman Jr., *Locking Up Our Own: Crime and Punishment in Black America* (New York: Farrar, Straus and Giroux, 2017), 6–13.

19 Cal. Const. art. I, § 28.

20 Washington, Minnesota, and even Texas are examples of states where substantial prison reforms have taken place. See Michael Vitiello, "Alternatives to Incarceration: Why Is California Lagging Behind?," *Georgia State Law Journal* 28, no. 4 (2012): 1286–94, https://core.ac.uk.

21 See, e.g., Hana Callaghan, "End the Statute of Limitations" (Markkula Center for Applied Ethics, August 27, 2018), www.scu.edu; see also Jenny Singer, "Statutes of Limitations Put an Expiration Date on Prosecuting Sexual Assault: In the #MeToo Era, Survivors Want Them Eliminated," *Glamour*, January 7, 2020, www.glamour.com.

22 Gruber, *Feminist War on Crime*, 86–87.

23 The House Judiciary Subcommittee on Constitution and Civil Justice proposed a Victims' Rights Amendment on May 1, 2015. The committee proposed a previous, nearly identical amendment in 2003 as well. H.R.J. Res. 45, 114th Cong. (2015).

24 Gruber, *Feminist War on Crime*, 7–9.

25 See Cassell, "Crime Victims' Rights," 20–21. Cassell considers a variety of recommended crime victims' rights measures to be placed in the U.S. Constitution.

26 Paul G. Cassell and Margaret Garvin, "Protecting Crime Victims in State Constitutions: The Example of the New Marsy's Law for Florida," *Journal of Criminal Law and Criminology* 110, no. 2 (Spring 2020): 103, https://scholarlycommons.law.northwestern.edu.

27 See chapter 2, *infra*.

1. A BRIEF HISTORY OF THE VICTIMS' RIGHTS MOVEMENT

1 Paul Cassell, "Crime Victims' Rights," *Utah Law Faculty Scholarship* 33 (2017): 4–6, https://dc.law.utah.edu/cgi/viewcontent.cgi?article=1032&context=scholarship.

2 Cassell, "Crime Victims' Rights," 5.

3 Paul G. Cassell and Margaret Garvin, "Protecting Crime Victims in State Constitutions: The Example of the New Marsy's Law for Florida," *Journal of Criminal Law and Criminology* 110, no. 2 (Spring 2020): 99, https://scholarlycommons.law.northwestern.edu.

4 Steven Derene, Steve Walker, and John Stein, "History of the Crime Victims' Rights Movement in the United States" (Participant Manual Module 2, National Victim Assistance Academy: Foundational Level Training Office of Victims of Crime Training & Technical Assistance Center, 2022), 2–21, www.ovcttac.gov.

5 See, for example, the placement of the infamous Three Strikes bill on California's November 1994 ballot via an initiative that required 365,000 voter signatures. Joe Domanick, *Cruel Justice: Three Strikes and the Politics of Crime in America's Golden State* (Berkeley: University of California Press, 2004), 108.

6 See, for example, the murder of eighteen-year-old Kimber Reynolds in 1992, which was the catalyst for the Three Strikes movement—and subsequent legislation—in California. George Skelton, "A Father's Crusade Born from Pain," *Los Angeles Times*, December 9, 1993, www.latimes.com; see also Aya Gruber, *The Feminist War on Crime: The Unexpected Role of Women's Liberation in Mass Incarceration* (Oakland: University of California Press, 2020), 110, et seq.

7 See Daniel Okrent, *Last Call: The Rise and Fall of Prohibition* (New York: Scribner, 2011), 1–4, 12–23.

8 Okrent, *Last Call*, 85–87, 100–106.

9 Okrent, *Last Call*, 86–87.

10 See generally Okrent, *Last Call*, 355, et seq.

11 Prohibition lasted for only thirteen years in the United States. The VRM has lasted for over fifty years. It remains a force in American politics even as some aspects of the movement have begun to unravel.

12 The NRA benefitted by focusing attention on criminals rather than on reducing access to weapons when perpetrators used firearms to commit violent crimes. Domanick, *Cruel Justice*, 108.

13 For years, the CCPOA could boast one legislative victory after another, leading to longer sentences and more lucrative jobs for its members. Domanick, *Cruel Justice*, 114; see also Michael Vitiello, "Alternatives to Incarceration: Why Is California Lagging Behind?," *Georgia State Law Journal* 28, no. 4 (2012): 1304–5, https://core.ac.uk.

14 Gruber, *Feminist War on Crime*, 113–14.

15 Michael Vitiello, "Introducing the Warren Court's Criminal Procedure Revolution: A 50-Year Retrospective," *University of the Pacific Law Review* 51, no. 4 (2020): 626, https://scholarlycommons.pacific.edu.

16 Richard Nixon, "1968 Republican Acceptance Speech" (speech, Miami Beach, FL, August 8, 1968), American Presidency Project, www.presidency.ucsb.edu.

17 Nixon, "1968 Republican Acceptance Speech."

18 Warren Weaver, "Agnew Deplores 'Permissiveness.' Says His Political Mission Is to Arouse a Desire for National Self-Discipline," *New York Times*, September 26, 1970, www.nytimes.com.

19 Don Irwin, "Crime Victim Rights of Concern to Powell," *Los Angeles Times*, October 22, 1971. Powell's use of the term "forgotten men," ignoring forgotten women, is ironic; for years, women have been among the most vocal supporters of the VRM and are often victims of violence, including domestic violence.

20 *Furman v. Georgia*, 408 U.S. 238 (1972).

21 *To Abolish the Death Penalty Under All Laws of the United States: Hearings on H.R. 3243, H.R. 193, H.R. 17796, Before the House of Representatives Judiciary Subcommittee*, 92nd Cong. 15, 17 (1972) (statement of Frank Carrington).

22 Office for Victims of Crime, "2021 National Crime Victims' Rights Week Resource Guide: Landmarks in Victims' Rights and Services" (2021), 3, https://ovc.ojp.gov (hereafter "Landmarks in Victims' Rights and Services").

23 "Landmarks in Victims' Rights and Services," 3.

24 U.S. Department of Justice, *New Directions from the Field: Victims' Rights and Services for the 21st Century* (Washington, DC: U.S. Department of Justice, Office of Justice Programs, 1998), 10–11, www.ncjrs.gov.

25 U.S. Department of Justice, *New Directions from the Field*, 15–17.

26 For an overview of state constitutional amendments regarding victims' rights, see Cassell and Garvin, "Protecting Crime Victims in State Constitutions," 100–105.

27 The law-and-order branch of the VRM remains powerful today. It is supported by district attorney associations, prison guard unions, and the National Rifle Association, for example. Carrington's intellectual heir is professor and former federal district court judge Paul Cassell, the leading victims' rights advocate in the legal academy. As such, this book makes frequent reference to his work.

28 "Landmarks in Victims' Rights and Services," 2.

29 National Organization for Victim Assistance, "Who We Are" (2022), www. trynova.org.

30 National Organization for Victim Assistance, "Who We Are."

31 Marlene Young and John Stein, "The History of the Crime Victims' Movement in the United States" (Office for Victims of Crime, December 2004), www.ncjrs.gov.

32 Young and Stein, "History of the Crime Victims' Movement."

33 History.com Editors, "MADD Founder's Daughter Killed by Drunk Driver," *History*, November 13, 2009, www.history.com; "MADD Struggles to Remain Relevant," *Washington Times*, August 6, 2002, www.washingtontimes.com. As an aside, Lightner left the organization five years later in protest over its increasingly strident prohibitionist positions. Lightner complained that the neo-prohibitionist positions were inconsistent with her focus on drunk driving as the issue.

34 Maryland Crime Victims' Resource Center, "About MCVRC" (2022), www.mdcri-mevictims.org.

35 See generally *America's Most Wanted*, created by Michael Linder and Stephen Chao, featuring John Walsh, aired on Fox and Lifetime. Walsh was an executive producer and the host of the program for over twenty years. See also Gruber, *Feminist War on Crime*, 110–12.

36 "Landmarks in Victims' Rights and Services," 1.

37 History.com Editors, "Man Charged in Murder of Megan Kanka," *History*, November 13, 2009, www.history.com.

38 Cal. Penal Code § 290.46.

39 "Megan's Law Resources by State," *FindLaw*, February 4, 2019, www.findlaw.com.

40 Greg Allen, "Sex Offenders Forced to Live under Miami Bridge," *NPR*, May 20, 2009, www.npr.org.

41 "California Proposition 83, Jessica's Law Sex Offender Penalties and Restrictions Initiative (2006)," *Ballotpedia*, https://ballotpedia.org.

42 Cassell and Garvin, "Protecting Crime Victims in State Constitutions," 107.

43 Cassell and Garvin, "Protecting Crime Victims in State Constitutions," 107.

44 California Department of Corrections and Rehabilitation, "Marsy's Law" (2022), www.cdcr.ca.gov.

45 California Department of Corrections and Rehabilitation, "Marsy's Law."

46 Human Rights Watch, "No Easy Answers: Sex Offender Laws in the US" (September 11, 2007), www.hrw.org. For another thoughtful discussion on the limits of registries, see Eli Lehrer, "Rethinking Sex-Offender Registries," *National Affairs*, Winter 2016, www.nationalaffairs.com.

47 See Lehrer, "Rethinking Sex-Offender Registries." Patty Wetterling, whose son Jacob Wetterling was abducted in 1989 and never found, lobbied to have the state of Minnesota establish the nation's first-ever public sex-offender registry. In 1994, President Clinton signed the Jacob Wetterling Crimes Against Children and Sexually Violent Offender Registration Act, which required all states to create their own registries.

48 See Human Rights Watch, "No Easy Answers." "Registrants and their families have been hounded from their homes, had rocks thrown through their home windows, and feces left on their front doorsteps. They have been assaulted, stabbed, and had their homes burned by neighbors or strangers who discovered their status as a previously convicted sex offender. At least four registrants have been targeted and killed (two in 2006 and two in 2005) by strangers who found their names and addresses through online registries. Other registrants have been driven to suicide, including a teenager who was required to register after he had exposed himself to girls on their way to gym class. Violence directed at registrants has injured others. The children of sex offenders have been harassed by their peers at school, and wives and girlfriends of offenders have been ostracized from social networks and at their jobs."

49 See Lehrer, "Rethinking Sex-Offender Registries." Lehrer reports that the restrictive nature of many laws forbid "sex offenders from living anywhere near schools or daycare centers, which often requires them to live far outside any city or reasonably dense suburb. Many are even barred from homeless shelters."

50 E.g., Craig Reinarman, "The Social Construction of an Alcohol Problem: The Case of Mothers against Drunk Drivers and Social Control in the 1980s," *Theory and Society* 17, no. 1 (January 1988): 96–97. Outraged from the loss of her daughter and "what she perceived as the extraordinary leniency with which DUI offenses were routinely handled," Candy Lightner founded Mothers Against Drunk Driving (MADD) in August 1980 to lobby for tougher drunk driving laws in California; Dan Morain, "Column One: A Father's Bittersweet Crusade: Mike Reynolds Vowed That His Murdered Daughter Would Not Die in Vain," *Los Angeles Times*, March 7, 1994, www.latimes.com. Mike Reynolds, whose daughter Kimber Reynolds was shot to death after two parolees attempted to steal her purse, proposed the infamous Three Strikes Law to target habitual criminals; Sarah Stillman, "The List: When Juveniles Are Found Guilty of Sexual Misconduct, the Sex-Offender Registry Can Be a Life Sentence," *New Yorker*, March 6, 2016, www.newyorker.com. After Jacob Wetterling was abducted, his mother, Patty Wetterling, fought for "the first federal mandate that all states create a database of people convicted of violent sex crimes or crimes against children." This later became known as the Jacob Wetterling Act. This act "marked the first in a series of sex-registry laws" and led to the passage of the nation's most sweeping law, the Adam Walsh Act. Promulgated by the father of six-year-old Adam Walsh, who was abducted inside a shopping mall and beheaded, this law broadened the scope of the sex-offender registry and threatened jurisdictions with withholding federal funds if they refused to comply. None of them was involved in the movement before crimes were committed against their children.

51 Jewelle Taylor Gibbs and Teiahsha Bankhead, *Preserving Privilege: California's Politics, Propositions, and People of Color* (Westport, CT: Praeger, 2001), 57. Gibbs and Bankhead characterize the NRA's support of the Three Strikes initiative as an attempt to rehabilitate its reputation among voters in western states: "Through

advocating harsher penalties for the victims of crime, the NRA used an effective strategy of diverting attention away from the public's easy access to guns, which are the weapons of choice for most criminals."

52 Domanick, *Cruel Justice*, 109, 114–15; Joshua Page, *The Toughest Beat: Politics, Punishment, and the Prison Officers Union in California* (Oxford: Oxford University Press, 2013), 112.

53 Vitiello, "Alternatives to Incarceration," 1304–8.

54 Gruber, *Feminist War on Crime*, 19.

55 Quoted in Olivia B. Waxman, "The Surprisingly Complex Link between Prohibition and Women's Rights," *Time*, January 16, 2019, https://time.com.

56 Waxman, "Surprisingly Complex Link between Prohibition and Women's Rights."

57 There is a danger in speaking of the Women's Movement with regard to its positions on criminal justice matters. In perhaps the best discussion of feminism and the war on crime, Professor Aya Gruber discusses not only changes within the movement that occurred over time but also class and racial differences within the movement. For example, poor, often minority, women view domestic violence laws, often mandating arrest for abusers, differently from their more financially secure feminist colleagues. See Gruber, *Feminist War on Crime*.

58 Derene, Walker, and Stein, "History of the Crime Victims' Rights Movement in the United States," 2–8.

59 Susan Estrich, *Real Rape* (Cambridge, MA: Harvard University Press, 1987), 15–16.

60 Gruber, *Feminist War on Crime*, 44, 15. "The other strand of TBTN was the radical movement that emerged on the West Coast. Less concerned about random sexual or nonsexual attacks at night, these protesters directed their efforts against hardcore pornography, considering it a glorification and cause of violent rape and prostitution. . . . Feminist efforts to ban pornography in the late 1970s and early 1980s sparked the infamous 'sex wars' where antiporn feminists and sex-positive scholars clashed fiercely over the meaning of pornography to women." Perhaps the most notable antipornography radical feminists are Andrea Dworkin and Catharine MacKinnon, who proposed the enactment of "antipornography civil rights ordinances" that would treat pornography as a civil rights issue. See Andrea Dworkin and Catharine MacKinnon, *Civil Rights: A New Day for Women's Equality* (Minneapolis: Organizing Against Pornography, 1988).

61 Gruber, *Feminist War on Crime*, 44.

62 Susan Miller, *Against Our Will: Men, Women, and Rape* (New York: Simon & Schuster, 1975), 377; Andrea Parrot and Laurie Bechhofer, *Acquaintance Rape: The Hidden Crime* (New York: Wiley, 1991), 318; Note, "Recent Statutory Development in the Definition of Forcible Rape," *Virginia Law Review* 61 (1975): 1500.

63 Gruber, *Feminist War on Crime*, 98–99.

64 *State in Int. of M.T.S.*, 129 N.J. 422, 433, 609 A.2d 1266, 1271 (1992), quoting Cynthia Ann Wicktom, "Focusing on the Offender's Forceful Conduct: A Proposal for the Redefinition of Rape Laws," *George Washington Law Review* 56 (1988): 403.

65 *State in Int. of M.T.S.*, 129 N.J. at 436.

66 *State in Int. of M.T.S.*, 129 N.J. at 436.

67 Gruber, *Feminist War on Crime*, 131.

68 Gruber, *Feminist War on Crime*, 45.

69 Gruber, *Feminist War on Crime*, 44. One area where the NRA and some feminists coalesced was around stand-your-ground laws, promoted by the NRA as a way to protect women on the street. "The duty to retreat had been imposed by the system and essentially if someone had tried to drag a woman into an alley to rape her, the wom[a]n—even though she might be licensed to carry concealed and ready to protect herself, the law would not allow her to do so. It required her to try to get away and run and be chased down by the perpetrator before she could then use force to protect herself." Center for Individual Freedom, "Former NRA President Exposes the Lies and Misinformation Aimed at Florida's 'Castle Doctrine' Law" (November 3, 2005), www.cfif.org.

70 Gruber, *Feminist War on Crime*, 102.

71 Gruber, *Feminist War on Crime*, 102. As discussed more fully in chapter 3, even the definition of "victim" is controversial. As Professor Gruber argues at 101–5, often the law-and-order right identified victims as idealized white women. Some feminists participated in the VRM even though many minority women victims, often suffering from financial need, were not well served by the punitive approach of the right wing. Nor did they benefit from its emphasis on "family values."

72 Gruber, *Feminist War on Crime*, 109.

73 Gruber, *Feminist War on Crime*, 110.

74 Gruber, *Feminist War on Crime*, 112. Gruber provides examples of children who have faced the consequences of such broadly written prohibitions: "There is Charla, who was placed on the registry at age ten for pulling a boy's pants down at school and whose photo still appears online under the banner 'Protect Your Child from Sex Offenders.' There is Anthony, convicted under 'statutory rape' laws for consensual sex as a teenager. Years later, the conditions of his sex offender status prohibited him from living with his newborn daughter, and his violations of those conditions landed him a ten-year sentence." See also Frank Zimring, *An American Travesty: Legal Responses to Adolescent Sexual Offending* (Chicago: University of Chicago Press, 2004), 143–59. Zimring details the way in which the many sex offender registration laws "pose a potential disaster for youth welfare and the interests of juvenile justice." Finally, for an example of an extreme punishment imposed on a juvenile offender, see the case of Genarlow Wilson. See Alberto Cadoppi and Michael Vitiello, "A Kiss Is Just a Kiss, or Is It? A Comparative Look at Italian and American Sex Crimes," *Seton Hall Law Review* 40, no. 1 (2010): 218–19.

75 Gruber, *Feminist War on Crime*, 111; Lehrer, "Rethinking Sex-Offender Registries."

76 Zimring, *American Travesty*, 147–48.

77 Gruber, *Feminist War on Crime*, 113–14. "[T]he relationship between feminism and child predator panic is not so easily dismissed. In the 1970s, it was feminists, not conservatives, who spotlighted child sexual abuse and lobbied for legislative change."

78 Gruber, *Feminist War on Crime*, 7–10.
79 Carrie Johnson, "Life without Parole for 'Felony Murder': Pa. Case Targets Sentencing Law," *NPR*, February 4, 2021, www.npr.org; Cheryl Corley, "Juvenile Justice Groups Say Felony Murder Charges Harm Children, Young Adults," *NPR*, November 14, 2019, www.npr.org.
80 "MADD Struggles to Remain Relevant."
81 Madeleine Baran and Jennifer Vogel, "Sex-Offender Registries: How the Wetterling Abduction Changed the Country," *American Public Media Reports*, October 4, 2016, www.apmreports.org.
82 Sarah Stillman, "The List," *New Yorker*, March 14, 2016, www.newyorker.com.
83 Stillman, "The List."
84 Baran and Vogel, "Sex-Offender Registries."
85 Gruber, *Feminist War on Crime*, 113.

2. WHAT THE VICTIMS' RIGHTS MOVEMENT GETS RIGHT

 1 One cannot help grieving along with families who, for example, lose a child to violence. Perhaps the most famous example is the brutal kidnapping and murder of Adam Walsh, whose father remains prominent in the Victims' Rights Movement. See "40 Years Later, Adam Walsh's Abduction and Murder Not Forgotten in South Florida," *NBC 6 South Florida*, July 27, 2021, www.nbcmiami.com. Mothers Against Drunk Driving provides a similar example. Candy Lightner, one of its cofounders, became involved in the VRM after a drunk driver killed her thirteen-year-old daughter. See "Candy Lightner of Madd (Mothers Against Drunk Driving)," *Alcohol Problems and Solutions*, January 16, 2022, www.alcoholproblemsandsolutions.org.
 2 Steven Derene, Steve Walker, and John Stein, "History of the Crime Victims' Rights Movement in the United States" (Participant Manual Module 2, National Victim Assistance Academy: Foundational Level Training, Office of Victims of Crime Training and Technical Assistance Center, 2022), 2–21, www.ovcttac.gov.
 3 For example, Chief Justice Rehnquist, author of *Payne v. Tennessee*, 501 U.S. 808 (1991), probably the most important Supreme Court case advancing the VRM agenda, wrote the 5–4 decision in *United States v. Morrison*, 529 U.S. 598 (2000), striking down the act as a violation of the Commerce Clause.
 4 Not only the NRA but also law enforcement groups opposed the Brady Bill. See Richard E. Gardner and Stephen P. Halbrook, "NRA and Law Enforcement Opposition to the Brady Act: From Congress to the District Courts," *Journal of Civil Rights and Economic Development* 10, no. 1 (Fall 1994), https://scholarship.law.stjohns.edu.
 5 One topic not covered in this chapter is restorative justice. While some VRM members support such measures, they remain limited in their scope. Other books have dealt with such programs in depth. See Danielle Sered, *Until We Reckon: Violence, Mass Incarceration, and a Road to Repair* (New York: New Press, 2019).

6 Peggy M. Tobolowsky, *Crime Victim Rights and Remedies* (Durham, NC: Carolina Academic Press, 2001), 4–5.

7 Yue Ma, "Exploring the Origins of Public Prosecution," *International Criminal Justice Review* 18, no. 2 (June 2008): 196, https://journals.sagepub.com (explaining how the changed perception of crime led to the shift to public prosecutions on the European continent).

8 Kenneth W. Simmons, "The Crime/Tort Distinction: Legal Doctrine and Normative Perspectives," *Widener Law Journal* 17, no. 3 (2008): 729, https://scholarship.law.uci.edu.

9 Tobolowsky, *Crime Victim Rights and Remedies*, 6; see Paul G. Cassell, "Treating Crime Victims Fairly: Integrating Victims into the Federal Rules of Criminal Procedures," *Utah Law Review* 2007, no. 4 (2007): 865, https://heinonline.org ("Victims' advocates argued that the criminal justice system had become preoccupied with defendants' rights to the exclusion of considering the legitimate interests of crime victims").

10 Tobolowsky, *Crime Victim Rights and Remedies*, 9 (e.g., President Ronald Reagan's Task Force on Victims of Crime).

11 See Tobolowsky, *Crime Victim Rights and Remedies*, 56 (explaining how the President's Task Force recommendations explicitly provide for an opportunity for the victim to be notified of the resolution of a case).

12 See Lynne Henderson, "Revisiting Victim's Rights," *Utah Law Review* 1999, no. 2 (1999): 397, https://scholars.law.unlv.edu ("Obviously, everyone should be given equal dignity and respect").

13 Maryland Crime Victims' Resource Center, "History of Victims' Rights in America" (2022), www.mdcrimevictims.org (providing a timeline of advancements in the VRM).

14 "What Rights Do California Crime Victims Have Post-Conviction?," *Justice 4 Crime Victims*, June 13, 2020, www.justice4crimevictims.com.

15 Pretrial Justice Center for Courts, "Victims' Rights" (National Center for State Courts, 2022), www.ncsc.org.

16 Crime Victims' Rights Act, 18 U.S.C. § 3771(a) (2004).

17 Cal. Const. art. I, § 28(b).

18 Office for Victims of Crime, "2021 National Crime Victims' Rights Week Resource Guide: Landmarks in Victims' Rights and Services" (September 2021), https://ovc.ojp.gov.

19 Examples include the Walsh family's involvement in passing the 1984 Missing Children's Assistance Act as well as Candace Lightner's efforts as a cofounder of Mothers Against Drunk Driving to further the ends of the VRM. See *America's Most Wanted*, created by Michael Linder and Stephen Chao, featuring John Walsh, aired on Fox and Lifetime; History.com Editors, "MADD Founder's Daughter Killed by Drunk Driver," *History*, November 13, 2009, www.history.com.

20 MADD, "Our History" (2022), www.madd.org.

21 Editorial Staff, "Effectiveness of Mothers Against Drunk Driving" (American Addiction Centers, August 31, 2020), www.alcohol.org.

22 See chapter 6, *infra.*

23 Steven Grossman, "Hot Crimes: A Study in Excess," *Creighton Law Review* 45, no. 1 (2011): 55, https://scholarworks.law.ubalt.edu.

24 Susan Estrich, *Real Rape* (Cambridge, MA: Harvard University Press, 1987), 9.

25 "Qualitative evidence indicates that some law enforcement agencies still deny the seriousness of rape. Victims of rape are asked to explain why they did not resist their attack and have to deny complicity." Kenneth J. Meier and Jill Nicholson-Crotty, "Gender, Representative Bureaucracy, and Law Enforcement: The Case of Sexual Assault," *Public Administration Review* 66, no. 6 (2006): 854.

26 Rebecca Campbell and Patricia Y. Martin, "Services for Sexual Assault Survivors: The Role of Rape Crisis Centers," in *Sourcebook on Violence Against Women,* ed. Claire M. Renzetti, Jeffrey L. Edleson, and Raquel K. Bergen (Thousand Oaks, CA: Sage, 2017), 227–41 (noting the ways in which rape crisis centers benefit survivors); Aya Gruber, *The Feminist War on Crime: The Unexpected Role of Women's Liberation in Mass Incarceration* (Oakland: University of California Press, 2020), 126, 137 (noting that date rape has become increasingly acknowledged and the presence of laws that prevent, without proper justification, the use of the victim's previous sexual behavior from being used as evidence); Lalenya Weintraub Siegel, "The Marital Rape Exemption: Evolution to Extinction," *Cleveland State Law Review* 43, no. 2 (1995): 367–69, https://engagedscholarship.csuohio.edu (noting that marital rape is now a crime in many jurisdictions).

27 See City of San Diego, "Sexual Assault" (2022), www.sandiego.gov.

28 International Association of Chiefs of Police, "Trauma Informed Sexual Assault Investigations" (2022), www.theiacp.org.

29 Margo Kaplan, "Reconciling #MeToo and Criminal Justice," *Ohio State Journal of Criminal Law* 17, no. 2 (Spring 2020): 367–68, https://heinonline.org.

30 American Law Institute, "Model Penal Code: Sexual Assault and Related Offenses" (2022), www.ali.org.

31 Washington Coalition of Sexual Assault Programs, "History of the Movement" (2022), www.wcsap.org.

32 Stacy Lee, "Crime Victim Awareness and Assistance through the Decades" (National Institute of Justice, June 9, 2019), https://nij.ojp.gov. See also Gruber, *Feminist War on Crime,* 113 ("'[Professor Leigh Beinen] observed, 'When feminists began to lobby for changes in the rape laws in the 1970s, recharacterizing sex offenses involving children became a powerful and persuasive component of both the practical and the political arguments for redefining all sex offenses and for changing the criminal justice system's response to sex crimes generally'").

33 See *Barbe v. McBride,* 521 F.3d 443 (4th Circuit 2008) (holding that the state violated the defendant's Sixth Amendment rights in not allowing the defense to cross-examine the prosecution's expert witness with regard to the victim's previ-

ous sexual abuse); see also *Lewis v. Wilkinson*, 307 F.3d 413 (6th Circuit 2002) (holding that the state violated the defendant's Sixth Amendment rights in not allowing the defense to introduce the victim's diary detailing previous sexual encounters).

34 See Tobolowsky, *Crime Victim Rights and Remedies*, 3.

35 U.S. Federal Government, Benefits, "State Crime Victims Compensation" (2022), www.benefits.gov.

36 CalVCB, State of California, "For Victims" (2022), https://victims.ca.gov.

37 CalVCB, State of California, "For Victims."

38 Andrew LaMar, "California Victim Compensation Board Awards $13 Million in Grants to Trauma Recovery Centers" (CalVCB, May 20, 2021), https://victims. ca.gov.

39 See Tobolowsky, *Crime Victim Rights and Remedies*, 202–3.

40 Lisa N. Sacco, "The Crime Victims Fund: Federal Support for Victims of Crime" (Congressional Research Service, April 2, 2020), https://crsreports.congress.gov.

41 In 2019, the California legislature passed Senate Bill 94, which created the Committee on Revision of the Penal Code within the California Law Review Commission. Public Safety: Omnibus, S. Bill 94, 2019–2020 Reg. Sess., chap. 25, Cal. Stat. The broad-brush approach in this discussion also ignores the complex questions that have arisen when courts have had to interpret state constitutional or statutory provisions. Leading victims' rights scholars' treatise on the subject elaborates on legal issues addressing almost every aspect of victims' rights legislation. A cursory inspection of the table of contents gives a sampling of the kinds of issues that need to be resolved. For example, who qualifies as a victim? How does the relevant law define a "crime"? How have courts interpreted a victim's right to notification? What happens if a victim is not given adequate notice?

42 Tobolowsky, *Crime Victim Rights and Remedies*, 159–64.

43 Tobolowsky, *Crime Victim Rights and Remedies*, 133–36.

44 Tobolowsky, *Crime Victim Rights and Remedies*, 127–31.

45 Dana A. Waterman, "A Defendant's Ability to Pay: The Key to Unlocking the Door of Restitution Debt," *Iowa Law Review* 106, no. 1 (November 2020): 455–82, https://ilr.law.uiowa.edu.

46 See Tobolowsky, *Crime Victim Rights and Remedies*, 181.

47 USC Suzanne Dworak-Peck School of Social Work, "Ensuring Financial Stability for Ex-Convicts Reduces Rates of Recidivism" (October 3, 2019), https://dworak-peck.usc.edu.

3. VICTIMHOOD, DEMAGOGUERY, AND MENTAL HEALTH

1 See Liz Kelly, Shaila Burton, and Linda Regan, "Beyond Victim or Survivor: Sexual Violence, Identity and Feminist Theory and Practice," in *Sexualizing the Social: Power and the Organization of Sexuality*, ed. Lisa Adkins and Vicki Merchant (New York: St. Martin's, 1996), 77–101; Alletta Brenner, "Resisting Simple Dichotomies: Critiquing Narratives of Victims, Perpetrators, and Harm in Femi-

nist Theories of Rape," *Harvard Journal of Law and Gender* 36, no. 2 (Summer 2013): 503–68.

2 Joe Ferullo, "Thanks, Trump—Republicans' Victim Mentality Intensifies, Despite Reality," *Hill*, January 31, 2021, https://thehill.com.

3 I use the term "Conservative Movement" because that is how the movement describes itself. As I have argued elsewhere, the movement is not "conservative" in any traditional sense of that word. Instead, it is dominated by economic libertarians on the far right. Michael Vitiello, "Trump's Legacy: The Long-Term Risks to American Democracy," *Lewis & Clark Law Review* 26, no. 2 (2022): 467–529.

4 Steve Benen, "'We're All Victims': Trump Pushes Persecution Complex to Supporters," *MSNBC*, December 7, 2020, www.msnbc.com; Alan D. Blotcky, "Donald Trump's Pathology of Victimhood: It's Dangerous For His Own Party—and the Rest of Us," *Salon*, August 30, 2020, www.salon.com; Chris Cillizza, "Donald Trump's Victimhood Complex," *CNN*, October 31, 2018, www.cnn.com.

5 Martin Pengelly, "Josh Hawley Finds New Publisher after Simon & Schuster Cancels Book," *Guardian*, January 18, 2021, www.theguardian.com; Ferullo, "Thanks, Trump."

6 Mia Jankowicz, "Marjorie Taylor Greene Said That She's the Victim of Democrat Bullying When Questioned about Her Hounding of AOC," *Insider*, May 15, 2021, www.businessinsider.com.

7 Ashton Pittman, "Gov. Reeves Claims Critical Race Theory 'Humiliates' White People at Bill Signing," *Mississippi Free Press*, March 14, 2022, www.mississippi-freepress.org; Charles C. Bolton, "The Last Stand of Massive Resistance: Mississippi Public School Integration, 1970," *Mississippi History Now*, February 2009, www.mshistorynow.mdah.ms.gov.

8 Robert B. Horwitz, "Politics as Victimhood, Victimhood as Politics," *Journal of Policy History* 30, no. 3 (2018): 553.

9 Horwitz, "Politics as Victimhood," 554.

10 Horwitz, "Politics as Victimhood," 564.

11 "Foremost in the pantheon of true victims were those individuals who had been pushed aside or cut in front of, castigated, censored, and punished in other ways by affirmative action and minority preferences, political correctness, hate-speech codes, and similar manifestations of injurious victim politics. These individuals— often members of the groups that constituted the norm of American society, and often conservatives—were the victims of victimhood." Horwitz, "Politics as Victimhood," 564.

12 Horwitz, "Politics as Victimhood," 563.

13 Horwitz, "Politics as Victimhood," 557.

14 Evgenia Peretz, "Dinesh D'Souza's Life after Conviction," *Vanity Fair*, May 2015, www.vanityfair.com.

15 Martha Minow, "Surviving Victim Talk," *UCLA Law Review* 40, no. 6 (August 1993): 1412.

16 Horwitz, "Politics as Victimhood," 570.

17 "Wall Street bankers see themselves as misjudged victims of fatuous, irresponsible anti-capitalist reformers; evangelical Christians understand themselves as victims of an insolent, triumphant secular humanism; African Americans see themselves as victims of unrelenting, eternal white racism; Tea Party adherents and Trump supporters view themselves as victims of big government and smug self-serving elites. These examples hardly exhaust contemporary claims of victimhood. Trans-gendered people see themselves as victims of biological norming; many straight people see themselves as victims of the gay activist agenda. The list could go on, for the performance of victimhood is how we now do politics." Horwitz, "Politics as Victimhood," 570.

18 Miles T. Armaly and Adam Enders, "'Why Me?' The Role of Perceived Victim-hood in American Politics," *Political Behavior* (2021): 4.

19 Armaly and Enders, "'Why Me?,'" 4.

20 Minow, "Surviving Victim Talk," 1414.

21 As Spiro Agnew said, "[The] rights of the accused have become more important than the rights of victims in our courtrooms." Warren Weaver, "Agnew Deplores 'Permissiveness.' Says His Political Mission Is to Arouse a Desire for National Self-Discipline," *New York Times*, September 26, 1970, www.nytimes.com.

22 Nicholas Fandos and Katie Glueck, "Cuomo Portrays Himself as a Victim in a Six-Figure TV Ad Blitz," *New York Times*, February 28, 2022, www.nytimes.com.

23 Jessica Kwong, "Bill Clinton Is a Sexual Predator, Not a Victim, Most Americans Say in New Poll," *Newsweek*, June 11, 2016, www.newsweek.com.

24 Experts have broken victimhood down into three forms: (1) legal, (2) sociocul-tural, and (3) self-defined. Legal victims are those who have experienced a "crimi-nal injustice." Sociocultural victimhood is generally experienced by groups who have been "systemically mistreated." Self-defined victims are those who perceive themselves as victims, whether or not they actually experienced any genuine form of victimization. Armaly and Enders, "'Why Me?,'" 3.

25 Eric W. Dolan, "Egocentric Victimhood Is Linked to Support for Trump, Study Finds," *PsyPost*, January 18, 2021, www.psypost.org.

26 Armaly and Enders, "'Why Me?,'" 5.

27 Armaly and Enders, "'Why Me?,'" 7.

28 Armaly and Enders, "'Why Me?,'" 23.

29 Dolan, "Egocentric Victimhood Is Linked to Support for Trump, Study Finds."

30 Horwitz, "Politics as Victimhood," 573.

31 Aya Gruber, *The Feminist War on Crime: The Unexpected Role of Women's Libera-tion in Mass Incarceration* (Oakland: University of California Press, 2020), 96.

32 Gruber, *Feminist War on Crime*, 96.

33 See *Jacobellis v. Ohio*, 378 U.S. 184, 197 (1964) (Stewart, J. concurring). Here is the context for the oft-quoted line: "I shall not today attempt further to define the kinds of material I understand to be embraced within that shorthand description; and perhaps I could never succeed in intelligibly doing so. But I know it when I see it, and the motion picture involved in this case is not that."

34 Peggy M. Tobolowsky, *Crime Victim Rights and Remedies* (Durham, NC: Carolina Academic Press, 2001), 14–16; Douglas E. Beloof, Paul G. Cassell, Meg Garvin, and Steven J. Twist, *Victims in Criminal Procedure*, 4th ed. (Durham, NC: Carolina Academic Press, 2018), 45–109.

35 Tobolowsky, *Crime Victim Rights and Remedies*, 14–16; Beloof et al., *Victims in Criminal Procedure*, 45–109.

36 Crime Victims' Rights Act, 18 U.S.C 3771(e) (2004).

37 Cal. Const. art. I, § 28(c).

38 Mass Stat. 258B § 1 (1984).

39 MI Comp. Laws Ann. Section 780.826 (1985).

40 *Knapp v. Martone*, 823 P.2d 685 (Ariz. 1992).

41 *Beck v. Commonwealth*, 484 S.E.2d 898 (Virginia 1997).

42 Beloof et al., *Victims in Criminal Procedure*, 75–76.

43 *In re Roser*, 684 N.E.2d 749 (Ohio Ct. of Claims) (finding that an Ohio resident shot by an unknown man in Michigan was entitled to Ohio's victim compensation fund); *In re Cooper*, 593 N.E.2d 506 (Ohio Ct. of Claims) (finding that an Ohio resident whose wife was murdered while they were both living in California was entitled to Ohio's victim compensation even though he could still apply to California's victim compensation fund since he had not received any money from California's fund).

44 "While the [] judge has broad latitude to control cross-examination, giving controverted evidence to the factfinder with no opportunity for the accused to examine or cross-examine witnesses or in any way to rebut that evidence in front of the [jury] is unprecedented in our legal system, and cannot be reconciled with due process." *United States v. Bess*, 75 M.J. 70, 75 (2016).

45 *In re McNulty*, 597 F.3d 344, 346–53 (6th Cir. 2010) (employee's $6.3 million restitution request was denied because he was not directly affected by his employer's antitrust violations—despite being fired for failing to abide by antitrust protocols and being blackballed in the industry—and therefore was not a victim); *United States v. Hunter*, 2008 WL 53125 (D. Utah 2008) (holding that the decedent's parents were not entitled to victim restitution or to a victim impact statement because the defendant's act of selling a gun to a minor was too attenuated from the minor's act of shooting the decedent).

46 More often than not, without expert testimony to illustrate the defendant's perspective as a woman with battered woman's syndrome and thus demonstrate that the defendant acted reasonably given her circumstances, a claim for self-defense would fail to exonerate her, especially if she killed her husband while he was sleeping or otherwise nonconfrontational. Lenore E. A. Walker, "Battered Women Syndrome and Self-Defense," *Notre Dame Journal of Law, Ethics & Public Policy* 6, no. 2 (1992): 323–26.

47 Christie Thompson and Taylor Elizabeth Eldridge, "Treatment Denied: The Mental Health Crisis in Federal Prisons," *Marshall Project*, November 21, 2018, www.themarshallproject.org; Christine Herman, "Most Inmates with Mental Illness Still Wait for Decent Care," *NPR*, February 3, 2019, www.npr.org.

48 Tobolowsky, *Crime Victim Rights and Remedies*, 17, 153.

49 Anthony A. Braga, Rod K. Brunson, and Kevin M. Drakulich, "Race, Place, and Effective Policing," *Annual Review of Sociology* 45 (July 2019): 538–40.

50 Gruber, *Feminist War on Crime*, 87.

51 Scott Barry Kaufman, "Unraveling the Mindset of Victimhood," *Scientific American*, June 29, 2020, www.scientificamerican.com.

52 Kaufman, "Unraveling the Mindset of Victimhood."

53 Kaufman, "Unraveling the Mindset of Victimhood."

54 Kaufman, "Unraveling the Mindset of Victimhood."

55 Kaufman, "Unraveling the Mindset of Victimhood."

56 "What if we all learned at a young age that our traumas don't have to define us? That it's possible to have experienced a trauma and for victimhood to not form the core of our identity? That it's even possible to grow from trauma, to become a better person, to use the experiences we've had in our lives toward working to instill hope and possibility to others who were in a similar situation? What if we all learned that it's possible to have healthy pride for an in-group without having out-group hate? That if you expect kindness from others, it pays to be kind to yourself? That no one is entitled to anything, but we all are worthy of being treated as human?" Kaufman, "Unraveling the Mindset of Victimhood."

57 Kaufman, "Unraveling the Mindset of Victimhood."

58 Viktor Frankl, *Man's Search for Meaning* (1946; Boston: Beacon, 2006).

59 "Martin Seligman," *Pursuit of Happiness* (2022), www.pursuit-of-happiness.org; Peter Gibbon, "Martin Seligman and the Rise of Positive Psychology," *Humanities* 41, no. 3 (Summer 2020), www.neh.gov.

60 Carol S. Dweck, *Mindset: Changing the Way You Think to Fulfill Your Promise* (New York: Ballantine Books, 2006), 57.

61 Gruber, *Feminist War on Crime*, 96.

62 Minow, "Surviving Victim Talk," 1433.

63 Gruber, *Feminist War on Crime*, 100.

64 Dan Brennan, "What Is a Victim Mentality?," *WebMD*, February 3, 2022, www.webmd.com.

65 "Justice for Whom?: The Dangers of the Growing Victims' Rights Movement," *Harvard Civil Rights–Civil Liberties Law Review*, November 27, 2018, https://harvardcrcl.org.

66 "Restorative or transformative models of justice are being developed because there is a need for a more positive process than the criminal justice system. And these models are being developed as alternatives to the courtroom because the courtroom precludes the emotional catharsis or reconciliation that parties crave. Victims' rights should not be expanded within the courtroom. Instead, energy should be redirected to developing more appropriate forums for victim and survivor participation, forums that do not rely on the coercion of the state and the threat of incarceration to achieve restorative outcomes. Otherwise, the victims'

rights movement will threaten the court's commitment to the core principle of innocent until proven guilty." "Justice for Whom?"

67 Lara Bazelon and Bruce A. Green, "Victims' Rights from a Restorative Perspective," *Ohio State Journal of Criminal Law* 17 (2020): 18–22, https://ir.lawnet. fordham.edu.

68 Bazelon and Green, "Victims' Rights from a Restorative Perspective," 21.

69 "Any process built on the assumption that victims are a monolithic group who all want and need to see the offender convicted and harshly punished is deeply flawed." Bazelon and Green, "Victims' Rights from a Restorative Perspective," 28.

70 Bazelon and Green, "Victims' Rights from a Restorative Perspective," 29.

71 Danielle Sered, *Until We Reckon: Violence, Mass Incarceration, and a Road to Repair* (New York: New Press, 2019), 135–41. Restorative justice aims to include all relevant parties in a dialogue and an eventual agreement centered around the harm that has occurred and how it can be repaired; the focus is on repairing the harm and not on the state's reassertion of authority over a broken rule. It is a much more individualized approach that empowers the harmed party by giving them a governing role in deciding how the justice process plays out.

72 "Regardless of the type of violence in question, U.S. justice systems typically rely on incarceration as the single blunt instrument in their toolbox." Sered, *Until We Reckon*, 12.

73 Stephen D. Sugarman, "Tort Reform through Damages Law Reform: An American Perspective," *Sydney Law Review* 27, no. 3 (September 2005): 507–24, www. law.berkeley.edu. For an example of the mildly frivolous aspects of pain and suffering damages, see Greg Coleman Law, "Why Is It Important to Keep a Personal Injury Journal?" (May 17, 2019), www.gregcolemanlaw.com.

74 See chapter 6, *infra*.

75 Michael Vitiello, "Brock Turner: Sorting through the Noise," *University of the Pacific Law Review* 49, no. 3 (January 2018): 642, https://scholarlycommons.pacific. edu.

76 Vitiello, "Brock Turner," 642.

77 Elena Kadvany, "Woman Testifies in Brock Turner Trial," *Palo Alto Online*, March 21, 2016, www.paloaltoonline.com.

78 Maia Szalavitz, "The Story of the Stanford Rape Is Also the Story of a Drug Overdose," *Vice*, June 16, 2016, www.vice.com.

79 Emily Bazelon, "Why the Stanford Rape Trial Actually Represents Progress," *New York Times*, June 9, 2016, www.nytimes.com.

80 Callie Marie Rennison, "I'm the Professor Who Made Brock Turner the 'Textbook Definition' of a Rapist," *Vox*, November 17, 2017, www.vox.com ("The two dropped charges were rape of an intoxicated person and rape of an unconscious person").

81 Rennison, "I'm the Professor."

82 "A recall effort . . . was announced . . . in a sexual assault case . . . that ignited public outrage after the defendant was sentenced to a mere six months in jail and his father complained that his son's life had been ruined for '20 minutes of action' fu-

eled by alcohol and promiscuity." Liam Stack, "Light Sentence for Brock Turner in Stanford Rape Case Draws Outrage," *New York Times*, June 6, 2016, www.nytimes. com.

83 See Cal. R. Ct. 4.411.5.

84 Brandon Garrett and John Monahan, "Assessing Risk: The Use of Risk Assessment in Sentencing," *Judicature* 103, no. 2 (Summer 2019), https://judicature.duke.edu.

85 Vitiello, "Brock Turner," 642.

86 Probation Report, *People v. Turner*, No. B1577162 (Cal. Super. Ct. June 2, 2016), 8, www.documentcloud.org.

87 Vitiello, "Brock Turner," 644.

88 Probation Report, *People v. Turner*, 6.

89 Vitiello, "Brock Turner," 641.

90 Vitiello, "Brock Turner," 637.

91 Vitiello, "Brock Turner," 637.

92 Ellie Kaufman, "Brock Turner Registers as Sex Offender in Ohio," *CNN*, September 6, 2016, www.cnn.com.

93 Katie J. M. Baker, "Here's the Powerful Letter the Stanford Victim Read to Her Attacker," *Buzzfeed News*, June 3, 2016, www.buzzfeednews.com.

94 Baker, "Here's the Powerful Letter."

95 Gruber, *Feminist War on Crime*, 179.

96 Baker, "Here's the Powerful Letter."

97 Gruber, *Feminist War on Crime*, 180.

98 Gruber, *Feminist War on Crime*, 180.

99 Humane Justice, *Collateral Damage* (Independently published, 2020), 115.

100 Maura Dolan, "Vandalism, Threats, Broken Friendships: The Heated Campaign to Recall Judge in Brock Turner Case," *Los Angeles Times*, June 3, 2018, www.latimes. com (reporting on Dauber's leadership in the recall of Judge Persky); Wiemond Wu, Comment, "Crocodiles in the Judge's Bathtub: Why California Should End Unregulated Judicial Recall," *University of the Pacific Law Review* 49, no. 3 (January 2018): 716, https://scholarlycommons.pacific.edu (Michele Dauber stated that the "'recall is the only realistic way to remove Judge Persky from office'").

101 See Aishwarya Kumar, "From Survivor to Activist, Chanel Miller is Taking Toxic Sports Culture to Task," *ESPN*, March 30, 2020, www.espn.com.

102 E.g., Amanda Holpuch, "Stanford Students Launch Tribute to Sexual Assault Survivor Chanel Miller," *Guardian*, September 27, 2019, www.theguardian.com (launching the Dear Visitor project, which would project excerpts of Miller's victim impact statement near the site where the assault occurred, in recognition of Miller's newfound status as the poster child of American rape culture).

103 See generally Wu, "Crocodiles in the Judge's Bathtub" (explaining that the media attention enabled California voters to utilize the judicial recall process against Judge Persky).

104 In California, it is a crime to commit sexual acts with persons who are so intoxicated that they cannot resist, i.e., say no. Cal. Penal Code § 261(a)(3). However,

"in about forty jurisdictions, criminal prohibitions of sexual assault of intoxicated victims cover only cases where the victim was surreptitiously duped after the actor intentionally administered him or her intoxicants, including rape-facilitating drugs, in order to accomplish intercourse." Michal Buchhandler-Raphael, "The Conundrum of Voluntary Intoxication and Sex," *Brooklyn Law Review* 82, no. 3 (January 2017): 1051, https://brooklynworks.brooklaw.edu. In these jurisdictions, the law might not have considered Miller to be a victim since she was voluntarily intoxicated.

105 Rahila Gupta, "'Victim' vs 'Survivor': Feminism and Language," *Open Democracy*, June 16, 2014, www.opendemocracy.net.

106 Frankl, *Man's Search for Meaning*, 82–87; Lewina O. Lee et al., "Optimism Is Associated with Exceptional Longevity in 2 Epidemiologic Cohorts of Men and Women," *Proceedings of the National Academy of Sciences* 116, no. 37 (July 2019): 18357–62.

107 Y. Joel Wong et. al., "Does Gratitude Writing Improve the Mental Health of Psychotherapy Clients? Evidence from a Randomized Controlled Trial," *Psychotherapy Research* 28, no. 2 (May 2016): 1–11; Nathaniel M. Lambert, Frank D. Fincham, and Tyler F. Stillman, "Gratitude and Depressive Symptoms: The Role of Positive Reframing and Positive Emotion," *Cognition and Emotion* 26, no. 4 (2012): 615–33; "Giving Thanks Can Make You Happier" (Harvard Health Publishing, August 14, 2021), www.health.harvard.edu; Martin E. P. Seligman, Tracy A. Steen, Nansook Park, and Christopher Peterson, "Positive Psychology Progress: Empirical Validation of Interventions," *American Psychology* 60, no. 5 (July–August 2005): 410–12.

108 Vitiello, "Brock Turner," 642.

109 Humane Justice, *Collateral Damage*, 293.

110 As an aside, commentators have argued that the criminal justice system is not well designed for defendants to accept responsibility for the harm that they have caused. Various aspects of the system, like the Fifth Amendment right to remain silent and guilt beyond a reasonable doubt, permit defendants never to address their victims. See, e.g., Aya Gruber, "When We Breathe: Re-envisioning Safety and Justice in a Post-Floyd Era," *Ohio State Journal of Criminal Law* 18, no. 2 (Spring 2021): 693–707, https://kb.osu.edu. Supporters of restorative justice make that point in arguing that by comparison, defendants must acknowledge the harm that they cause as part of that process. Sered, *Until We Reckon*, 97–106.

111 Humane Justice, *Collateral Damage*, 294.

112 Humane Justice, *Collateral Damage*, 115.

113 Jori Finkel, "Chanel Miller's Secret Source of Strength," *New York Times*, August 5, 2020, www.nytimes.com.

114 Megan Garber, "The Paradox at the Heart of 'Know My Name,'" *Atlantic*, October 2, 2019, www.theatlantic.com; Chanel Miller, *Know My Name: A Memoir* (New York: Viking, 2019).

115 Mike C. Materni, "Criminal Punishment and the Pursuit of Justice," *British Journal of American Legal Studies* 2, no. 1 (Spring 2013): 266, https://bcuassets.blob.

core.windows.net. Of course, other scholars, such as Herbert Morris, believe that "protective retribution" serves as a way to show respect for the wrongdoer and to ultimately entitle the person to be free of stigma. Herbert Morris, "Persons and Punishment," *The Monist* 52, no. 4 (October 1968): 500–501.

116 Becky Beaupre Gillespie, "The Trouble with Anger and Forgiveness" (University of Chicago Law School, May 23, 2016, www.law.uchicago.edu; Martha C. Nussbaum, *Anger and Forgiveness: Resentment, Generosity, Justice* (New York: Oxford University Press, 2016).

117 Alexander Pope, "An Essay on Criticism: Part 2" (Poetry Foundation, 2022), www.poetryfoundation.org.

118 "Unfortunately, after reading the defendant's report, I am severely disappointed and feel that he has failed to exhibit sincere remorse or responsibility for his conduct. . . . Someone who cannot take full accountability for his actions does not deserve a mitigating sentence." Baker, "Here's the Powerful Letter."

119 "Your attorney is not your scapegoat, he represents you." Baker, "Here's the Powerful Letter."

120 "[T]he criminal process denies the victim an opportunity to pursue a form of justice—restorative justice—that may be more important to her than the retributive justice achieved by traditional criminal adjudications." Bazelon and Greene, "Victims' Rights from a Restorative Perspective," 23; see also Sered, *Until We Reckon*, 92–93.

121 "Intoxication can negate the required mental state of a specific intent crime, such as attempted rape." *People v. Bradslaw*, 233 Cal.App.4th 1239 (2015).

122 "If a defendant entertains a reasonable and bona fide belief that a prosecutrix voluntarily consented . . . to engage in sexual intercourse, it is apparent he does not possess the wrongful intent that is a prerequisite . . . to a conviction of . . . rape by means of force or threat." *People v. Mayberry*, 15 Cal.3d 143 (1975).

123 See chapter 6, *infra*.

4. THE WARREN COURT'S CRIMINAL PROCEDURE REVOLUTION AND ITS INSPIRATION FOR THE VICTIMS' RIGHTS MOVEMENT

1 Raphael Ginsberg, "Mighty Crime Victims: Victims' Rights and Neoliberalism in the American Conjuncture," *Cultural Studies* 28, no. 5–6 (March 2014): 919.

2 Paul G. Cassell, "In Defense of Victim Impact Statements," *Ohio State Journal of Criminal Law* 6, no. 2 (Spring 2009): 612, https://papers.ssrn.com.

3 Raphael Ginsberg, "Victims Deserve the Best: Victims' Rights and the Decline of the Liberal Consensus" (PhD diss., University of North Carolina at Chapel Hill, 2013), 68.

4 See Frank Carrington, *The Victims* (New York: Arlington House, 1975), 8. Carrington criticizes Justice Brennan's position against the death penalty by arguing that criminal defendants are afforded human dignity through constitutional protections at the expense of denying human dignity to crime victims.

5 Ginsberg, "Victims Deserve the Best," 60; Arthur J. Goldberg, "Warren Court and Its Critics, the Supreme Court History Project: The Warren Court 1962–1969," *Santa Clara Law Review* 20, no. 3 (1980): 831–39, https://digitalcommons.law.scu.edu.

6 Michael Vitiello, "Introducing the Warren Court's Criminal Procedure Revolution: A 50-Year Retrospective," *University of the Pacific Law Review* 51, no. 4 (2020): 626, https://scholarlycommons.pacific.edu.

7 Vitiello, "Introducing the Warren Court's Criminal Procedure Revolution," 625.

8 *Dickerson v. United States*, 530 U.S. 428, 432 (2000).

9 *Gideon v. Wainwright*, 372 U.S. 335 (1963).

10 Paul G. Cassell, "Treating Crime Victims Fairly: Integrating Victims into the Federal Rules of Criminal Procedures," *Utah Law Review* 2007, no. 4 (2007): 894–95, https://papers.ssrn.com (arguing that the Advisory Committee drafted rules in favor of criminal defendants at the expense of victim's rights).

11 Ginsberg, "Victims Deserve the Best," 7.

12 *Mapp v. Ohio*, 367 U.S. 643 (1961).

13 Carrington, *Victims*, 3.

14 Carrington, *Victims*, 102–15 (arguing that *Miranda* led to the elimination of voluntary confessions through case studies); William W. Berry, "Magnifying *Miranda*," *Texas Tech Law Review* 50 (2017): 100, https://papers.ssrn.com; Paul G. Cassell, "All Benefits, No Costs: The Grand Illusion of *Miranda*'s Defenders," *Northwestern University Law Review* 90, no. 3 (Spring 1996): 1087–89, https://papers.ssrn.com.

15 Vitiello, "Introducing the Warren Court's Criminal Procedure Revolution," 626 (quoting Kevin J. McMahon, *Nixon's Court: His Challenge to Judicial Liberalism and its Political Consequences* [Chicago: University of Chicago Press, 2011], 41–43).

16 "Americans for Effective Law Enforcement (AELE)," *Law Crossing*, 2021, www.lawcrossing.com/.

17 Ginsberg, "Victims Deserve the Best," 56.

18 Vitiello, "Introducing the Warren Court's Criminal Procedure Revolution," 625.

19 Vitiello, "Introducing the Warren Court's Criminal Procedure Revolution," 626.

20 Vitiello, "Introducing the Warren Court's Criminal Procedure Revolution," 626.

21 Vitiello, "Introducing the Warren Court's Criminal Procedure Revolution," 626–27.

22 Vitiello, "Introducing the Warren Court's Criminal Procedure Revolution," 627; Charles M. Lamb, "Making of a Chief Justice Warren Burger on Criminal Procedure 1956–1969," *Cornell Law Review* 60, no. 5 (June 1975): 744–45, http://scholarship.law.cornell.edu.

23 "A History of Conflict in High Court Appointments," *NPR*, July 6, 2005, www.npr.org.

24 Linda Greenhouse, "Documents Reveal the Evolution of a Justice," *New York Times*, March 4, 2004, www.nytimes.com.

25 John W. Dean, *The Untold Story of the Nixon Appointment That Redefined the Supreme Court* (New York: Simon & Schuster, 2001) (reporting on President

Nixon's appointment of William Rehnquist to replace Justice Harlan); "The Nation: Nixon's Court: Its Making and Its Meaning," *Time*, November 1, 1971, http://
content.time.com; John A. Stookey and S. Sidney Ulmer, "Nixon's Legacy to the
Supreme Court: A Statistical Analysis of Judicial Behavior," *Florida State University Law Review* 3, no. 3 (Summer 1975): 332, https://ir.law.fsu.edu.

26 Jerold H. Israel, "Criminal Procedure, the Burger Court, and the Legacy of the
Warren Court," *Michigan Law Review* 75, no. 7 (June 1977): 1324, https://reposi-
tory.law.umich.edu; Lewis F. Powell, "Stare Decisis and Judicial Restraint," *Washington and Lee Law Review* 47, no. 2 (Spring 1990): 284, https://repository.law.
umich.edu.

27 Michael Vitiello, "Arnold Loewy, Ernesto Miranda, Earl Warren, and Donald
Trump: Confessions and the Fifth Amendment," *Texas Tech Law Review* 52 (Fall
2019): 70, https://scholarlycommons.pacific.edu (citing *Miranda v. Arizona*, 384
U.S. 436, 462–63 [1966]).

28 Omnibus Crime Control and Safe Streets Act of 1968, 18 U.S.C. §3501 (1990).

29 Paul G. Cassell, "The Paths Not Taken: The Supreme Court's Failures in *Dickerson*," *Michigan Law Review* 99, no. 5 (March 2001): 910, https://repository.law.
umich.edu (inferring that *Miranda*'s application in habeas proceedings is predi-
cated on the contention that *Miranda* is of constitutional origin); Eric D. Miller,
"Should Courts Consider 18 U.S.C. § 3501 Sua Sponte?," *University of Chicago Law
Review* 65, no. 3 (Summer 1998): 1037–38, https://chicagounbound.uchicago.edu
(referencing the *Miranda* Court's stance that the case's issues were of "constitutional dimensions").

30 Miller, "Should Courts Consider 18 U.S.C. § 3501 Sua Sponte?," 1039.

31 Vitiello, "Arnold Loewy, Ernesto Miranda, Earl Warren, and Donald Trump," 74
(describing the Court's gradual gutting of *Miranda*'s core protections in subsequent case law).

32 *Brewer v. Williams*, 430 U.S. 387 (1977).

33 Yale Kamisar, "Brewer v. Williams, Massiah and Miranda: What Is 'Interrogation'?
When Does It Matter?," *Georgetown Law Journal* 67 (1978): 3–4, https://repository.
law.umich.edu (explaining that the Court did not need to consider whether the
"Christian burial speech" constituted police "interrogation" pursuant to *Miranda*
because Justice Stewart resolved *Brewer* as a Sixth Amendment constitutional
violation case).

34 Paul G. Cassell, "The Statute That Time Forgot: 18 U.S.C. § 3501 and the Over-
hauling of Miranda," *Iowa Law Review* 85 (October 1999): 241–43, https://papers.
ssrn.com (arguing that § 3501 is a valid exercise of Congress's power to override nonconstitutional procedures because the *Miranda* Court concluded that
Miranda could be overruled if other procedures, such as § 3501, were proposed);
Yale Kamisar, "Foreword: From Miranda to § 3501 to Dickerson To . . . ," *Michigan
Law Review* 99, no. 5 (March 2001): 881 (criticizing the Fourth Circuit's affirmance
of § 3501 because the statute merely echoes remnants of the outdated pre-*Miranda*
voluntariness test), https://repository.law.umich.edu/articles/347/; Cassell, "Paths

Not Taken," 926 (Professor Cassell responding to Professor Kamisar's discussion on the Court's legal determinations about the constitutionality of § 3501 as incomplete because he does not mention Congress's factual determinations about the underlying harm to law enforcement).

35 Yale Kamisar, "The Miranda Case Fifty Years Later," *Boston University Law Review* 97, no. 3 (2017): 1295, https://repository.law.umich.edu; e.g., *Lego v. Twomey*, 404 U.S. 477 (1972) (holding the state merely had to prove by a preponderance of the evidence standard that a suspect waived his *Miranda* rights); *Harris v. New York*, 401 U.S. 222 (1971) (holding a statement made by a defendant may still be used to impeach his testimony at trial despite the police failing to give his *Miranda* warning).

36 *Edwards v. Arizona*, 451 U.S. 477, 481–82 (1981).

37 Vitiello, "Arnold Loewy, Ernesto Miranda, Earl Warren, and Donald Trump," 74 (describing the Court's gradual gutting of *Miranda*'s core protections in subsequent case law). See also Michael Vitiello, "*Miranda* Is Dead, Long Live *Miranda*," *Texas Tech Law Review* 54, no. 1 (2022), https://scholarlycommons.pacific.edu.

38 *Dickerson v. United States*, 530 U.S. 428, 438 (2000); Kamisar, "Foreword," 888–89 (describing Chief Justice Rehnquist's surprise upholding of *Miranda* on constitutional grounds).

39 See M. K. B. Darmer, "Scalian Skepticism and the Sixth Amendment in the Twilight of the Rehnquist Court," *University of San Francisco Law Review* 43 (Fall 2008): 347, https://repository.usfca.edu.

40 See Kamisar, "Foreword"; see also Vitiello, "Introducing the Warren Court's Criminal Procedure Revolution," 628–29.

41 See Paul Cassell and Amos N. Guiora, "Point/Counterpoint on the Miranda Decision: Should It Be Replaced or Retained?," *Utah Bar Journal* 31, no. 5 (2018): 20, https://papers.ssrn.com (arguing that enforcing *Miranda* leads to a miscarriage of justice by suppressing the truth and setting the criminal loose in the community without punishment).

42 Scott W. Howe, "Moving Beyond Miranda: Concessions for Confessions," *Northwestern Law Review* 110, no. 4 (June 2016): 908, https://scholarlycommons.law.northwestern.edu (discussing various limitations imposed on *Miranda*, such as the very warning that the *Miranda* Court deemed to be mandatory as confusing, misleading, and overall detrimental to criminal defendants); see Earl M. Maltz, *The Coming of the Nixon Court: The 1972 Term and the Transformation of Constitutional Law* (Lawrence: University Press of Kansas, 2016).

43 Carrington, *Victims*, 86 (applying the exclusionary rule to show that physical evidence obtained as a result of an illegal arrest or search and seizure bars the introduction of such evidence into trial and leading to the truth of the matter suppressed).

44 U.S. Const. amend. IV; "In considering this question, then, we must never forget that it is a *constitution* we are expounding." *McCulloch v. Maryland*, 17 U.S. 316, 407 (1819) (holding that the Constitution was broadly drafted on purpose to

ensure longevity and understanding from the public); Laurence H. Tribe, "Approaches to Constitutional Analysis," in *American Constitutional Law* (New York: Foundation Press, 1978), 22; American Constitution Society for Law and Policy, "It Is a Constitution We Are Expounding" (2009), www.acslaw.org.

45 *Weeks v. United States*, 232 U.S. 383, 393 (1914).

46 *Wolf v. People of the State of Colorado*, 338 U.S. 25, 1360–61 (1949).

47 *Mapp v. Ohio*, 367 U.S. 643, 654–55 (1961).

48 *Mapp*, 367 U.S. at 644–45.

49 "Mapp v. Ohio (1961)," The Papers of Justice Tom C. Clark, Tarlton Law Library, updated May 27, 2020, https://tarlton.law.utexas.edu.

50 "Mapp v. Ohio (1961)"; see also Donald F. Tibbs, "The Start of a Revolution: *Mapp v. Ohio* and the Warren Court's Fourth Amendment Case That Almost Wasn't," *Stetson Law Review* 49, no. 3 (2020): 505 (noting that the exclusionary rule, as part of the Fourth and Fourteenth amendments, is consistent with the Constitution after showing the irony of a federal prosecutor's inability to use illegally obtained evidence while a state attorney across the street can make use of such evidence), www2.stetson.edu.

51 Robert M. Bloom and David H. Fentin, "'A More Majestic Conception': The Importance of Judicial Integrity in Preserving the Exclusionary Rule," *University of Pennsylvania Journal of Constitutional Law* 13, no. 1 (2010): 54, https://scholarship. law.upenn.edu (reiterating Justice Clark's decision to apply the exclusionary rule as a remedy for Fourth Amendment violations to carry out the "true administration of justice").

52 "Mapp v. Ohio (1961)."

53 See Jerold H. Israel, "Gideon v. Wainwright: The Art of Overruling," *Supreme Court Review* 1963 (1963): 221 (discussing the "lessons of experience" test as a covert method judges use to overrule precedent).

54 See Warren E. Burger, "Who Will Watch the Watchman?," *American University Law Review* 14, no. 1 (December 1964): 1–23.

55 *Stone v. Powell*, 428 U.S. 465, 500 (1976) (Burger, J., concurring).

56 See *Linkletter v. Walker*, 381 U.S. 618, 636–37 (1965) (holding that the exclusionary rule is the only effective deterrent to illegal police action while stating that retroactive application of *Mapp* would affect judicial integrity without explaining why).

57 See *United States v. Calandra*, 414 U.S. 338, 351 (1974) (explaining that a prosecutor would unlikely request an indictment where a conviction could not be obtained due to the exclusionary rule).

58 *United States v. Janis*, 428 U.S. 433, 454 (1976).

59 *Stone*, 428 U.S. at 481–82.

60 *United States v. Leon*, 468 U.S. 897, 923n23 (1984).

61 *Herring v. United States*, 555 U.S. 135, 144 (2009).

62 *Herring*, 555 U.S. at 144.

63 Craig M. Bradley, "Is the Exclusionary Rule Dead?," *Journal of Criminal Law and Criminology* 102, no. 1 (Winter 2012): 11, https://scholarlycommons.law.northwest-

ern.edu (comparing the *Davis* Court's discussion of whether or not "negligence" is enough to invoke the exclusionary rule is virtually the same as the unadopted dictum from *Herring*).

64 Samuel Walker, *Taming the System: The Control of Discretion in Criminal Justice* (New York: Oxford University Press, 1993), 49–50.

65 See Richard A. Oppel Jr., Derrick Bryson Taylor, and Nicholas Bogel-Burroughs, "What to Know about Breonna Taylor's Death," *New York Times*, April 26, 2021, www.nytimes.com. Overly aggressive policing led to a shootout that caused Ms. Taylor's death. By most news accounts, she was innocent of criminal conduct and a victim of police violence.

66 Burger, "Who Will Watch the Watchman?," 10 (proposing the vast reduction or possible elimination of the exclusionary rule would best serve society and the administration of justice).

67 See generally Israel, "Gideon v. Wainwright" (discussing different methods the Court has used to justify and purportedly overrule precedent). The Court has also narrowed the application of the exclusionary rule by increasing the requirements for a defendant to demonstrate standing to object to a search. For example, in *United States v. Payner*, 447 U.S. 727 (1980), the Court found that the defendant could not object to a search that federal officers knew was flagrantly illegal because his property was not searched by the agents.

68 For example, Carrington cited the Warren Court's holding in *United States v. Wade*, 388 U.S. 218 (1967) and *Gilbert v. California*, 388 U.S. 263 (1967) as similar examples of judicial overreach that would frustrate legitimate law enforcement interests. See Carrington, *Victims*, 116 (positing that *Wade-Gilbert* led to a direct suppression of the truth if police officers were not allowed to have crime victims pick a suspect from a lineup without an attorney present). Those cases found that post-indictment lineups were sufficiently important to require the presence of Sixth Amendment counsel to prevent misidentification. Almost from its beginning, the Burger Court effectively gutted those protections. For a fuller discussion, see Michael Vitiello, "The Warren Court's Eyewitness Identification Case Law: What If?," *University of the Pacific Law Review* 51, no. 4 (2020): 867–86, https://scholarlycommons.pacific.edu.

69 Indeed, cutting back on some Warren Court decisions has increased the chances for convicting innocent defendants. Vitiello, "Warren Court's Eyewitness Identification Case Law," 884 (questioning the Court's refusal to use better practices to avoid the conviction of innocent defendants in light of the Burger and Rehnquist Courts' erosion of the *Wade-Gilbert* protection).

70 Geoffrey R. Stone and David A. Strauss, *Democracy and Equality: The Enduring Constitutional Vision of the Warren Court* (New York: Oxford University Press, 2020).

71 The Court would later extend that right to a defendant charged with a misdemeanor if the defendant received a jail sentence. See *Scott v. Illinois*, 440 U.S. 367, 373 (1979) (establishing that the right to counsel is triggered by actual imprisonment).

72 *Powell v. Alabama*, 287 U.S. 45, 71 (1932).

73 See *Barron v. City of Baltimore*, 32 U.S. 243, 247 (1833) (reasoning that the amendments were designed to be a limitation on the federal government rather than on state constitutions).

74 See *Betts v. Brady*, 316 U.S. 455, 472 (1942) (holding that state courts have the power to appoint counsel to uphold the fundamental interest of fairness).

75 See *McNeal v. Culver*, 365 U.S. 109, 111 (1961) (holding that the Constitution required that an indigent, ignorant, mentally ill Black defendant have legal assistance who was originally denied right to counsel).

76 *Betts*, 316 U.S. at 476 (Black, J., dissenting).

77 Anthony Lewis, *Gideon's Trumpet* (New York: Random House, 1970), 48.

78 *Gideon*, 372 U.S. at 344–45.

79 Lewis, *Gideon's Trumpet*, 237.

80 See Carrington, *Victims*, 80 (acknowledging that the Warren Court did improve to a large extent the fundamental fairness of the criminal justice system).

81 "The Legacy of Gideon v. Wainwright" (U.S. Department of Justice Archives, updated October 24, 2018), www.justice.gov.

82 See American Bar Association, "ABA Resolution Endorsing a Civil Right to Counsel" (August 2006), www.americanbar.org (unanimously adopting a resolution urging "federal, state, and territorial governments" to provide legal counsel for low-income defendants involved in civil matters); see also American Bar Association, "Basic Principles of a Civil Right to Counsel" (August 2010), www.americanbar.org (providing guidance on the basic principles of a right to counsel in the civil context to supplement the government's initiative in providing counsel to all people found in the 2006 report).

83 Mary Sue Backus and Paul Marcus, "The Right to Counsel in Criminal Cases: Still a National Crisis?," *George Washington Law Review* 86, no. 6 (November 2006): 1589–99, https://scholarship.law.wm.edu (discussing legislative reform in various states aimed at addressing the shortcomings of public defender offices); David Carroll, "Right to Counsel Services in the 50 States," Indiana Government, March 2017, www.in.gov (describing California's highly regarded programs involving private attorneys representing indigent defendants); see Sarah Breitenbach, "Right to an Attorney? Not Always in Some States" (Pew Charitable Trusts, April 11, 2016), www.pewtrusts.org (discussing Miami's effort to deploy public defenders for misdemeanor cases while public defender offices in other states struggle to find enough public defenders for more serious felony cases).

84 See U.S. Department of Justice, "Contracting for Indigent Defense Services: A Special Report" (April 2000), www.ojp.gov (outlining the different types of contracts the government enters into with private attorneys); cf. Eve Brensike Primus, "Defense Counsel and Public Defence," in *Reforming Criminal Justice: Pretrial and Trial Processes*, ed. Erik Luna (Phoenix: Arizona State University, 2017), 121–45, https://repository.law.umich.edu (discussing how contract systems still exacerbate the public defender shortage issue).

85 John H. Blume and Rebecca K. Helm, "The Unexonerated: Factually Innocent Defendants Who Plead Guilty," *Cornell Law Review* 100, no. 1 (November 2014): 159–61, https://scholarship.law.cornell.edu (describing how prosecutors created a coercive Alford plea bargain in order to lead the West Memphis Three to plead guilty to the murders of three young boys, despite new DNA evidence weighing against the conviction of the three defendants).

86 See Primus, "Defense Counsel and Public Defence," 123–26 (outlining the consequences of underfunding public defenders).

87 National Association of Criminal Defense Lawyers, "The Trial Penalty: The Sixth Amendment Right to Trial on the Verge of Extinction and How to Save It" (July 2018), 5, www.nacdl.org.

88 Emily Yoffe, "Innocence Is Irrelevant," *Atlantic*, September 2017, www.theatlantic.com (reporting that of the $200 billion spent on all criminal justice activities by state and local governments in 2008, only 2 percent was expended on indigent defendants); see also *Missouri v. Frye*, 566 U.S. 134, 144 (2012) (quoting Robert E. Scott and William J. Stuntz, "Plea Bargaining as Contract," *Yale Law Journal* 101, no. 8 [June 1992]: 1912).

89 Jed S. Bakoff, "Why Innocent People Plead Guilty," *New York Review of Books*, November 20, 2014 (discussing how young, unintelligent, or risk-averse defendants will often provide false confessions to avoid interrogations); see also Blume and Helm, "Unexonerated," 17 (hypothesizing three reasons why innocent defendants plead guilty).

90 See U.S. Department of Justice, "Investigation of the Ferguson Police Department" (March 2015), www.justice.gov (explaining how indigent defendants are disadvantaged by the confusing procedures in posting bond).

91 Blume and Helm, "Unexonerated," 17; Yoffe, "Innocence Is Irrelevant"; see *North Carolina v. Alford*, 400 U.S. 25 (1970) (creating the Alford plea).

92 U.S. Department of Justice, "Investigation of the Ferguson Police Department," 3; Michael Vitiello, "Marijuana Legalization, Racial Disparity, and the Hope for Reform," *Lewis & Clark Law Review* 23, no. 3 (2019): 806–7, https://docplayer.net (providing an example of how a marijuana offense can derail a defendant's life).

93 See U.S. Department of Justice, "Investigation of the Ferguson Police Department," 2; *Pierce v. City of Velda City*, No. 4:15-cv-570-HEA, 2015 WL 10013006 (E.D. Mo. June 3, 2015) (challenging the municipal court's practice of requiring cash or surety bonds in set amounts for municipal violations, regardless of the defendant's circumstances or ability to pay).

94 National Association of Criminal Defense Lawyers, "Public Defense Litigation" (NACDL Foundation for Criminal Justice, July 23, 2019), www.nacdl.org; see, e.g., *Hurrell-Harring v. State*, 930 N.E.2d 217 (N.Y. 2010); see also *Wilbur v. City of Mount Vernon*, No. C11-1100RSL, 989 F.Supp.2d 1122 (W.D. Wash. 2013).

95 See Tina Peng, "I'm a Public Defender. It's Impossible for Me to Do a Good Job Representing My Clients," *Washington Post*, September 3, 2015, www.washingtonpost.com (citing excessive caseloads as a major hindrance to adequately repre-

senting indigent clients); Andrew Cohen, "How Much Does a Public Defender Need to Know about a Client?," *Atlantic*, October 23, 2015, www.theatlantic.com (discussing how Terrence Miller was disadvantaged from the beginning when he met his court-appointed lawyer for the first time on the day of his trial); also, e.g., Kashmir Hill, "Imagine Being on Trial. With Exonerating Evidence Trapped on Your Phone," *New York Times*, November 22, 2019, www.nytimes.com (comparing the technology gap between prosecutors and public defenders and how lack of technological innovations affects their ability to carry out thorough investigations).

96 National Juvenile Defender Center, "Juvenile Defense Policy and Practice Career Resource Guide" (September 2015), 4, https://hls.harvard.edu (setting guidelines on best practices for representing juveniles).

97 E.g., *Allen v. Edwards*, No. 2017 CW 1581, 2018 WL 735362 (La. App. February 6, 2018) (citing systemic shortcomings leading to inadequate counsel disproportionately affecting African Americans).

98 National Association of Criminal Defense Lawyers, "Trial Penalty" (citing *Yarls v. Bunton*, 905 F.3d 905 [5th Cir. 2018]) (underfunding public defender services in Louisiana leading to public defenders refusing to take cases while hundreds of defendants wait in jail to be appointed an attorney).

99 Brandon L. Garrett, *End of Its Rope: How Killing the Death Penalty Can Revive Criminal Justice* (Cambridge, MA: Harvard University Press, 2017), 112–27.

100 Garrett, *End of Its Rope*, 106–31.

101 Garett, *End of Its Rope*, 51.

102 Garett, *End of Its Rope*, 110.

103 E.g., *Burdine v. State*, 719 S.W.2d 309 (Tex. Crim. App. 1986); see David R. Dow, "The State, the Death Penalty and Carl Johnson," *Boston College Law Review* 37, no. 4 (July 1996): 694–95, https://lawdigitalcommons.bc.edu; and e.g., Henry Weinstein, "A Sleeping Lawyer and a Ticket to Death Row," *Los Angeles Times*, July 15, 2000, www.latimes.com.

104 Weinstein, "Sleeping Lawyer."

105 See generally David C. Baldus, George Woodworth, and Charles A. Pulaski, *Equal Justice and the Death Penalty: A Legal and Empirical Analysis* (Boston: Northeastern University Press, 1990); see also Scott Phillips and Justin Marceau, "Whom the State Kills," *Harvard Civil Rights–Civil Liberties Law Review* 55, no. 2 (2020), https://harvardcrcl.org.

5. ELIMINATING AND EXTENDING STATUTES OF LIMITATIONS

1 See generally Mayo Moran, "Cardinal Sins: How the Catholic Church Sexual Abuse Crisis Changed Private Law," *Georgetown Journal of Gender and the Law* 21, no. 1 (2019): 101–3, www.law.georgetown.edu; Michael Rezendes, "Church Allowed Abuse by Priest for Years," *Boston Globe*, January 6, 2002, www.bostonglobe.com; see also Wade Goodwyn, "Boy Scouts of America Sexual Abuse Victims Seek Justice in Bankruptcy Court," *NPR*, November 13, 2020, www.npr.org.

2   Michael Vitiello, "Expanding Statutes of Limitations for Sex Crimes: Bad Public
    Policy," *Diritto Pubblico Comparato ed Europeo* 49, no. 4 (2022): 4093–128, www.
    dpceonline.it.

3   "Full Coverage: Harvey Weinstein Is Found Guilty of Rape," *New York Times*, Feb-
    ruary 4, 2020, www.nytimes.com. The *Times* lists several allegations against Wein-
    stein for which charges could not be filed because too much time had passed.
    See also Matt Giles and Nate Jones, "A Timeline of the Abuse Charges Against
    Bill Cosby," *Vulture*, December 30, 2015, www.vulture.com. *Vulture* reported only
    one accusation against Bill Cosby fell within the statute of limitations. See also
    Michael C. Dorf, "The Epstein Indictment and Statutes of Limitations," *Dorf on
    Law*, July 9, 2019, www.dorfonlaw.org.

4   Christian Menno, "Attorney General, DAs Join Fight for Child Sex Abuse Legisla-
    tion Reform," *Intelligencer*, updated October 12, 2008, www.theintell.com.

5   Office for Victims of Crime, "2021 National Crime Victims' Rights Week Resource
    Guide: Landmarks in Victims' Rights and Services" (2021), 17, 22, https://ovc.
    ojp.gov (noting that Presidents Bush and Obama signed into law legislation that
    limits or removes statutes of limitations in particular contexts).

6   See Lara Bazelon and Bruce A. Green, "Victims' Rights from a Restorative Per-
    spective," *Ohio State Journal of Criminal Law* 17 (2020): 307. The authors describe
    how the Victims' Rights Movement and the #MeToo Movement have led to
    reform, including New York's Child Victims Act, which extends the statute of
    limitations in sexual assault cases.

7   See Jenny Singer, "Statutes of Limitations Put an Expiration Date on Prosecuting
    Sexual Assault: In the #MeToo Era, Survivors Want Them Eliminated," *Glamour*,
    January 7, 2020, www.glamour.com.

8   Singer, "Statutes of Limitations"; see Jim Hopper, "How Reliable Are the Memo-
    ries of Sexual Assault Victims?," *Scientific American*, September 27, 2018, https://
    blogs.scientificamerican.com.

9   Michelle Mark, "The 'Ultimate Feminist' Defending Harvey Weinstein," *Insider*,
    February 5, 2020, www.insider.com. Mark reports on Harvey Weinstein's lead
    defense attorney, Donna Rotunno, who has defended men accused of sex crimes
    for over fifteen years and who (at the time) had lost only one of the forty sex
    crimes cases she had tried; see also Maureen O'Connor, "Who Would Defend
    Harvey Weinstein?," *Vanity Fair*, January 5, 2020, www.vanityfair.com. After
    Weinstein hired numerous "brand-name defense attorneys" who then quit (in-
    cluding the attorney, Jose Baez, who represented Casey Anthony), Weinstein's
    ultimate defense team at trial consisted of Rotunno and six other lawyers in-
    cluding retired judge Barry Kamins and Fox News legal analyst Arthur Aidala.
    See also Maryclaire Dale, "Bill Cosby Fighting $1M a Month Legal Bill in
    Arbitration," *AP News*, April 23, 2019, https://apnews.com. Bill Cosby hired the
    firm Quinn Emanuel Urquhart & Sullivan, which at one point had "28 lawyers
    working on 10 cases involving 14 accusers across the country as Cosby's legal
    woes snowballed."

10 See generally Charles Doyle, "Statutes of Limitation in Federal Criminal Cases: An Overview" (Congressional Research Service, November 14, 2017), https:// fas.org. Doyle offers general information about statutes of limitations in federal criminal cases, ranging from sex crimes to arson and immigration offenses.

11 "No person shall be prosecuted, tried, or punished for a violation of or conspiracy to violate Section 668 unless the indictment is returned or the information is filed within 20 years after the commission of the offense." 18 U.S.C. § 3294 (1994); "No person shall be prosecuted, tried, or punished for any non-capital offense under Section 81 [arson in the special maritime or territorial jurisdiction of the United States] or subsection (f), (h), or (i) of Section 844 [use of fire or explosives to commit a federal offense, and burning or bombing of federal property or property used in or in activities affecting interstate or foreign commerce] unless the indictment is found or the information is instituted not later than 10 years after the date on which the offense was committed." 18 U.S.C. § 3295 (1996).

12 18 U.S.C. § 3283 (2006).

13 See Ambrosio Rodriguez, "Why Is There No Statute of Limitations for Murder in California?," *Criminal Defense Blog, The Rodriguez Law Group*, May 4, 2018, www. aerlawgroup.com.

14 "Time Limits for Charges: State Criminal Statutes of Limitations," *FindLaw*, April 16, 2020, https://criminal.findlaw.com.

15 James Herbie DiFonzo, "In Praise of Statutes of Limitations in Sex Offense Cases," *Houston Law Review* 41, no. 4 (2004): 1212, https://scholarlycommons.law.hofstra.edu.

16 18 U.S.C. § 3290 (2000).

17 DiFonzo, "In Praise of Statutes of Limitations in Sex Offense Cases," 1213.

18 *Working Papers of the National Commission on Reform of Federal Criminal Laws* (Washington, DC: U.S. Government Printing Office, 1970), 281.

19 See generally Me Too, "History & Inception" (2022), https://metoomvmt.org.

20 See Hana Callaghan, "End the Statute of Limitations" (Markkula Center for Applied Ethics, August 27, 2018), www.scu.edu. Callaghan argues that ending or extending statutes of limitations for sex crimes may help abuse victims in the future.

21 Moran, "Cardinal Sins," 101–3.

22 Rezendes, "Church Allowed Abuse by Priest for Years"; see also Office of the Attorney General, Commonwealth of Pennsylvania, "Report I of the 40th Statewide Investigating Grand Jury" (2018), www.attorneygeneral.gov.

23 See, e.g., Laurie Goodstein and Monica Davey, "Catholic Church in Illinois Withheld Names of at Least 500 Priests Accused of Abuse, Attorney General Says," *New York Times*, December 19, 2018, www.nytimes.com. The dioceses publicly named only 185 of the 690 priests accused of abuse.

24 Richard Owen, "Pope Calls for Continuous Prayer to Rid Priesthood of Paedophilia," *Times*, January 7, 2008, www.bishop-accountability.org.

25 Office of the Attorney General, Commonwealth of Pennsylvania, "Report I of the 40th Statewide Investigating Grand Jury."

26 Office of the Attorney General, Commonwealth of Pennsylvania, "Report I of the 40th Statewide Investigating Grand Jury."

27 Claudia Lauer and Meghan Hoyer, "Almost 1,700 Priests and Clergy Accused of Sex Abuse are Unsupervised," *NBC News*, October 4, 2019, www.nbcnews.com.

28 Goodwyn, "Boy Scouts of America Sexual Abuse Victims."

29 See Eliana Dockterman, "These Men Say the Boy Scouts' Sex Abuse Problem Is Worse Than Anyone Knew," *Time*, June 1, 2010, https://time.com. Dockterman explains how the Boy Scout organization is in denial about claims of abuse despite the fact that tens of thousands of members have come forward alleging abuse.

30 See Colin Dwyer, "Harvey Weinstein Sentenced to 23 Years in Prison for Rape and Sexual Abuse," *NPR*, March 11, 2020, www.npr.org; see also "Full Coverage: Harvey Weinstein Is Found Guilty of Rape." The *Times* lists several allegations against Weinstein for which charges could not be filed because too much time had passed.

31 "Full Coverage: Harvey Weinstein Is Found Guilty of Rape"; Maria Puente, "Harvey Weinstein's Los Angeles Sex-Crimes Case Set for Trial in October," *USA Today*, June 10, 2022, www.usatoday.com.

32 Giles and Jones, "Timeline of the Abuse Charges Against Bill Cosby."

33 Mahita Gajanan, "Here's What to Know about the Sex Trafficking Case Against Jeffrey Epstein," *Time*, July 17, 2019, https://time.com; see also Dorf, "Epstein Indictment and Statutes of Limitations."

34 Bazelon and Green, "Victims' Rights from a Restorative Perspective."

35 See, e.g., Paul G. Cassell, "In Defense of Victim Impact Statements," *Ohio State Journal of Criminal Law* 6, no. 2 (Spring 2009): 621–23. Cassell suggests that victim impact statements can be therapeutic for victims. But see generally Susan A. Bandes, "Victims, 'Closure,' and the Sociology of Emotion," *Law and Contemporary Problems* 72, no. 2 (Spring 2009). Bandes critiques the closure rationale for victim impact statements.

36 Singer, "Statutes of Limitations."

37 Corsiglia McMahon & Allard Attorneys for Child Molestation Victims, "Changing the Statute of Limitations to Benefit Sex Abuse Victims" (2022), https://child-molestationattorneys.com.

38 Sean P. McIlmail Statutes of Limitations Research Institute at Child USA, "Child Sex Abuse Statute of Limitations Reform" (2021), https://childusa.org/sol/.

39 Hannah Giorgis, "The Biggest Deterrent to Reporting Child Sexual Abuse," *Atlantic*, June 26, 2019, www.theatlantic.com.

40 "[M]emories of highly stressful and traumatic experiences, at least their most central details, *don't* fade over time." Hopper, "How Reliable Are the Memories of Sexual Assault Victims?"; see also Singer, "Statutes of Limitations."

41 DiFonzo, "In Praise of Statutes of Limitations in Sex Offense Cases," 1221.

42 Cassell, "In Defense of Victim Impact Statements," 611–12.

43 Associated Press, "A Look at 15 States Making It Easier to Sue over Sex Abuse," *ABC News*, December 1, 2019, https://abcnews.go.com.

44 See chapter 8, discussing providing adequate health care to all Americans.

45 Bandes, "Victims, 'Closure,' and the Sociology of Emotion," 1.

46 See Susan Bandes, "Reply to Paul Cassell: What We Know about Victim Impact Statements," *Utah Law Review* 545 (1999): 552, https://core.ac.uk.

47 See, e.g., Loyola University Maryland Counseling Center, "Common Reactions to Sexual Assault" (2022), www.loyola.edu; see also National Institute of Mental Health, "Post-Traumatic Stress Disorder" (2022), www.nimh.nih.gov.

48 Interestingly, victims' rights advocates argue against the use of prior sexual conduct by women in rape cases on the grounds that cross-examination on prior sexual history is traumatizing. Yet, here, many of the same advocates would urge or even require victims to participate years after the sexual assault, potentially retraumatizing the victim.

49 See Michael Vitiello, "Punishing Sex Offenders: When Good Intentions Go Bad," *Arizona State Law Journal* 40 (2008): 668, *et seq*, https://scholarlycommons. pacific.edu; see also Elizabeth J. Letourneau et al., "No Check We Won't Write: A Report on the High Cost of Sex Offender Incarceration," *Sexual Abuse* (March 2022).

50 Vitiello, "Punishing Sex Offenders," 667.

51 Katharine K. Baker, "Once a Rapist? Motivational Evidence and Relevancy in Rape Law," *Harvard Law Review* 110, no. 3 (1997): 578–79.

52 "[T]hose persons who have committed crimes in the distant past and have not repeated their errors are apparently self-rehabilitated and as a result seem to offer little cause for fear as to their future conduct." Note, "The Statute of Limitations in Criminal Law: A Penetrable Barrier to Prosecution," *University of Pennsylvania Law Review* 102, no. 5 (1954): 634, https://scholarship.law.upenn.edu; see also Human Rights Watch, "No Easy Answers: Sex Offender Laws in the U.S." (September 11, 2007), www.hrw.org. Human Rights Watch reports lower-than-expected recidivism rates for sex offenders and discusses how some young offenders age out of their behavior.

53 See George Antunes and A. Lee Hunt, "The Deterrent Impact of Criminal Sanctions: Some Implications for Criminal Justice Policy," *Journal of Urban Law* 51 (1973): 145, https://scholarlycommons.law.northwestern.edu. The authors summarize studies that support this assertion. Valerie Wright, "Deterrence in Criminal Justice" (Sentencing Project, November 2010), www.sentencingproject.org. Wright indicates that studies support the concept that certainty of punishment is more important than severity.

54 See, e.g., *Roper v. Simmons*, 543 U.S. 551, 569–70 (2005) (highlighting the differences between juvenile and adult offenders), *Thompson v. Okla.*, 487 U.S. 815, 834–35 (1988) (prohibiting the execution of a fifteen-year-old and asserting that less culpability should attach to a crime committed by a juvenile because adolescents are less mature than adult offenders), and *Graham v. Fla.*, 560 U.S. 48, 82 (2010) (ruling the imposition of a life without parole sentence on juvenile offenders who did not commit homicide unconstitutional).

55 Singer, "Statutes of Limitations"; Hopper, "How Reliable Are the Memories of Sexual Assault Victims?"

56 Hopper, "How Reliable Are the Memories of Sexual Assault Victims?"

57 See generally Elizabeth Loftus, *Memory* (Ardsley, NY: Ardsley House, 1988), 37, 47; see also Elizabeth Loftus, *The Myth of Repressed Memory* (New York: St. Martin's, 1994), 8–19.

58 Loftus, *Memory*, 45–47.

59 Loftus, *Myth of Repressed Memory*, 45–65.

60 Loftus, *Myth of Repressed Memory*, 75–79.

61 Loftus, *Myth of Repressed Memory*, 90–101. Elizabeth Loftus, "Lost-in-the-Mall: Misrepresentations and Misunderstandings," *Ethics & Behavior* 9, no. 1 (1999): 5.

62 Donna Coker and Robert Weisberg, *Criminal Law Stories* (New York: Foundation Press, 2012), 199–204.

63 Aya Gruber, *The Feminist War on Crime: The Unexpected Role of Women's Liberation in Mass Incarceration* (Oakland: University of California Press, 2020), 159.

64 See, e.g., Andrew E. Taslitz, "Willfully Blinded: On Date Rape and Self-Deception," *Harvard Journal of Law and Gender* 28, no. 2 (Summer 2005): 381, https://papers.ssrn.com. Taslitz describes the psychological phenomenon of "self-deception" frequently occurring "when the alleged rapist consciously, but incorrectly, believes that he has the woman's consent when, at some less-than-fully conscious level, he knows otherwise."

65 *Commonwealth v. Berkowitz*, 415 Pa. Super. 505 (1992), order aff'd in part, vacated in part, 537 Pa. 143 (1994). Joshua Dressler and Stephen P. Garvey, *Criminal Law Cases and Materials*, 8th ed. (Saint Paul, MN: West, 2019), 449.

66 18 Pa. Stat. and Cons. Stat. § 3121 (2016).

67 *Berkowitz*, 537 Pa. at 146.

68 *Berkowitz*, 537 Pa. at 148.

69 *Berkowitz*, 537 Pa. at 149.

70 *Berkowitz*, 415 Pa. Super. at 511.

71 American Law Institute, "Model Penal Code: Sexual Assault and Related Offenses" (tentative draft no. 5, May 4, 2021), 256–67.

72 "[A] recent survey of the laws of the 53 most relevant U.S. jurisdictions . . . shows that 36 (68%) punish sexual penetration solely on the basis of the absence of consent. Of these, 12 do not define consent and accordingly may punish more or less conduct than would Section 213.6. The remaining 24 jurisdictions (67% of the 36 that punish penetration without consent) define consent in a way that imposes criminal sanctions for penetration in the absence of contextual consent or in the absence of a more specific form of agreement or permission." American Law Institute, "Model Penal Code," 268.

73 Singer, "Statutes of Limitations."

74 *Berkowitz*, 415 Pa. Super. at 511–12.

75 Loftus, *Memory*, 63–76.

76 Humane Justice, *Collateral Damage: A Candid Look at the Brock Turner Case and Recall of Judge Aaron Persky* (Self-Published, 2020), 123, *et seq.*

77 Loftus, *Myth of Repressed Memory*, 90–101.

78 "The requirement of proof beyond a reasonable doubt has this vital role in our criminal procedure for cogent reasons. The accused during a criminal prosecution has at stake interest of immense importance, both because of the possibility that he may lose his liberty upon conviction and because of the certainty that he would be stigmatized by the conviction. Accordingly, a society that values the good name and freedom of every individual should not condemn a man for commission of a crime when there is reasonable doubt about his guilt." *In re Winship*, 397 U.S. 358, 363–64 (1970).

79 See Clyde Haberman, "The Trial That Unleashed Hysteria over Child Abuse," *New York Times*, March 9, 2014, www.nytimes.com.

80 Haberman, "Trial That Unleashed Hysteria over Child Abuse."

81 Emma Bryce, "False Memories and False Confessions: The Psychology of Imagined Crimes," *Wired*, July 22, 2017, www.wired.co.uk.

82 *Cooper v. Brown*, 565 F. 3d 581, 582 (9th Cir. 2009) (Fletcher, J., dissenting).

83 See generally J. Patrick O'Connor, *Scapegoat: The Chino Hills Murders and the Framing of Kevin Cooper* (Rock Hill, SC: Strategic Media Books, 2012). See also *Cooper*, 565 F. 3d at 584–91 (Fletcher, J., dissenting).

84 *Cooper*, 565 F. 3d at 614.

85 Nicholas Kristof, "Is an Innocent Man Still Languishing on Death Row?," *New York Times*, January 23, 2021, www.nytimes.com.

86 *Cooper*, 565 F. 3d at 594–608 (Fletcher, J., dissenting).

87 See Brent Snook et al., "Let 'em Talk!: A Field Study of Police Questioning Practices of Suspects and Accused Persons," *Criminal Justice and Behavior* 39, no. 10 (2012): 1328–39.

88 See Snook et al., "Let 'em Talk!"

89 Some states extend or eliminate the statute of limitations in cases involving strangers when DNA evidence exists. Commentators have argued that DNA evidence is fallible for many reasons, including degradation of DNA samples over time. See, e.g., DiFonzo, "In Praise of Statutes of Limitations in Sex Offense Cases," 1232–33. The debate about such narrow provisions is beyond the scope of this discussion. Cases where DNA evidence exists present the best case for extending statutes of limitations, at least where courts can be confident about the quality of that evidence.

90 Prominent criminal law professor Franklin Zimring, among others, has lamented the rejection of expertise in the development of criminal justice policy. Franklin Zimring, Gordon Hawkins, and Sam Kamin, *Punishment and Democracy: Three Strikes and You're Out in California* (New York: Oxford University Press, 2001), 13. Unquestionably, the VRM relies on popular sentiment and repudiates experts' views. See, e.g., Raphael Ginsberg, "Victims Deserve the Best: Victims' Rights and the Decline of the Liberal Consensus" (PhD diss., University of North Carolina at

Chapel Hill, 2013), 10–11. Ginsberg describes the work of Frank Carrington, who laid the foundation of the VRM while rejecting scientific knowledge and expertise.

91 See, e.g., Michael Vitiello, "Brock Turner: Sorting through the Noise," *University of the Pacific Law Review* 49, no. 3 (2018): 634–38, https://scholarlycommons.pacific. edu. Headlines surrounding the Brock Turner case were, in many instances, not accurate reflections of the facts of the case.

92 See, e.g., Liam Stack, "Light Sentence for Brock Turner in Stanford Rape Case Draws Outrage," *New York Times*, June 6, 2016, www.nytimes.com; "Turner and his dad have both referred to the night of January 18th as being caused by 'binge drinking and promiscuity,' which is oblivious at best and malicious at worst. Both seem to think that it is Brock Turner's life that has truly been ruined, as he has watched his swimming career and academic future go down the drain because of this case." "The Brock Turner Rape Case: A Complete Injustice," *Brofessional*, June 7, 2016, https://thebrofessional.net.

93 See generally, Vitiello, "Brock Turner." For example, many members of the public believe that Turner raped his victim. The evidence did not support that "fact." Widely reported was the "fact" that Turner was committing his sexual assault behind a dumpster, creating a powerful image of an insensitive male treating his victim as garbage. Again, those were not the facts. He and the victim were found in front of a dumpster, visible to any passerby. Humane Justice, *Collateral Damage*, vi, 26.

94 See the "Counterarguments to VRM's Claims about Statutes of Limitations: Faulty Memory, Convicting Innocent Defendants" section above.

95 See the "Counterarguments to VRM's Claims about Statutes of Limitations: Serial Rapists and Culpability" section above.

96 See the "Counterarguments to VRM's Claims about Statutes of Limitations: Closure" section above.

97 See the "Counterarguments to VRM's Claims about Statutes of Limitations: Closure" section above.

98 See Equal Justice Initiative, "How to Save Billions of Dollars in Unnecessary Government Spending" (January 22, 2018), https://eji.org.

99 See chapter 8, discussing providing adequate health care to all Americans.

100 See generally Eliana Dockterman, "Can Bad Men Change? What It's Like Inside Sex Offender Therapy," *Time*, May 14, 2018, https://time.com; see also Kristan N. Russell and Shawn C. March, "Public Perceptions of Youth Who Commit Sexual Offense Is Skewed, Our Research Shows," *Juvenile Justice Information Exchange*, January 11, 2021, https://jjie.org.

101 See Susan Bandes, "Empathy, Narrative, and Victim Impact Statements," *University of Chicago Law Review* 63, no. 2 (1996): 361. Bandes analyzes the intersection of emotion and the law generally and, more specifically, in regard to victim impact statements.

102 See the "Pressure to Eliminate or Extend Statutes of Limitations in Sex Offense Cases" section above.

103 "The requirement of proof beyond a reasonable doubt has this vital role in our criminal procedure for cogent reasons. The accused during a criminal prosecution has at stake interest of immense importance, both because of the possibility that he may lose his liberty upon conviction and because of the certainty that he would be stigmatized by the conviction. Accordingly, a society that values the good name and freedom of every individual should not condemn a man for commission of a crime when there is reasonable doubt about his guilt." *In re Winship*, 397 U.S. 358, 363–64 (1970).

104 See the "Counterarguments to VRM's Claims about Statutes of Limitations" section above.

6. VICTIM IMPACT STATEMENTS AND AN ASSESSMENT OF THE VALUE OF A HUMAN LIFE

1 S. Rep. 108-191, 108th Cong. (2003) at 16–30.

2 See Paul G. Cassell, "Treating Crime Victims Fairly: Integrating Victims into the Federal Rules of Criminal Procedures," *Utah Law Review* 2007, no. 4 (2007): 866–70, https://papers.ssrn.com (providing a timeline of proposed and passed legislation supporting the Crime Victims' Rights Movement).

3 See generally Peggy M. Tobolowsky, Douglas E. Beloof, Mario T. Gaboury, Arrick L. Jackson and Ashley G. Blackburn, "Restitution," in *Crime Victim Rights and Remedies* (Durham, NC: Carolina Academic Press, 2016), 196.

4 Peggy M. Tobolowsky, *Crime Victim Rights and Remedies* (Durham, NC: Carolina Academic Press, 2001), 81.

5 Tobolowsky, *Crime Victim Rights and Remedies*, 84.

6 Tobolowsky, *Crime Victim Rights and Remedies*, 82.

7 President's Task Force on Victims of Crime, "Final Report" (1982), 76–78, https://ovc.ojp.gov.

8 President's Task Force on Victims of Crime, "Final Report," 76. As argued in chapter 3, Carrington's attack on the Court was almost certainly overstated at the time. Since then, any claim that the criminal justice system mollycoddles criminal defendants is a gross overstatement. See chapter 3.

9 Tobolowsky, *Crime Victim Rights and Remedies*, 21.

10 Tobolowsky, *Crime Victim Rights and Remedies*, 88–92 (discussing how state and federal courts have upheld the admissibility of victim impact evidence after the decision in *Payne v. Tennessee*, 501 U.S. 808 [1991]).

11 Tobolowsky, *Crime Victim Rights and Remedies*, 89 (reviewing courts' determinations that admission of victim impact evidence amounted to harmless error).

12 See Tobolowsky, *Crime Victim Rights and Remedies*, 84 (describing the various provisions of the federal Crime Victims' Rights Act of 2004).

13 See generally Tobolowsky, *Crime Victim Rights and Remedies*.

14 *Booth v. Maryland*, 482 U.S. 496 (1987).

15 *Booth*, 482 U.S. 496.

16 *Booth*, 482 U.S. at 504–5 (holding that considerations such as the victims' personal characteristics and impact on the victims' family are wholly irrelevant as to the defendant's blameworthiness and overall unfair to use considerations that the defendant personally is unaware of to determine whether the death penalty should be imposed).

17 *Furman v. Georgia*, 408 U.S. 238 (1972).

18 See *Gregg v. Georgia*, 428 U.S. 153 (1976) (creating the standard in evaluating proportionality challenges to the death penalty in a two-pronged test); cf. Linda E. Carter, Ellen S. Kretzberg, and Scott W. Howe, "The Death Penalty Debate," in *Understanding Capital Punishment Law* (Durham, NC: Carolina Academic Press, 2018), 16 ("Proponents of the death penalty argue that a defendant deserves death because he or she has taken a life").

19 *Booth*, 482 U.S. at 504 (quoting *Witherspoon v. Illinois*, 391 U.S. 510, 519 [1968]).

20 *Booth*, 502 (quoting *Zant v. Stephens*, 462 U.S. 862, 879 [1983] [emphasis omitted]).

21 *Booth*, 504–5 (reasoning that the jury can wrongly impose the death penalty based on factors that the defendant was not aware of at the time of the offense).

22 *Booth*, 506–7 (highlighting the difficulty of the defendant to rebut inflammatory evidence about the victim's personal characteristics).

23 *South Carolina v. Gathers*, 490 U.S. 805 (1989).

24 *Gathers*, 808.

25 *Gathers*, 810.

26 *Gathers*, 812 (holding that such evidence cannot provide any information relevant to the defendant's moral culpability).

27 Adam Liptak, "Souter's Exit Opens Door for a More Influential Justice," *New York Times*, May 7, 2009, www.nytimes.com.

28 *Payne*, 501 U.S. at 814–15.

29 *Payne*, 865 (Stevens, J., dissenting).

30 *Payne*, 808 (quoting *Booth*, 482 U.S. at 504–5).

31 *Payne*, 819.

32 *Payne*, 819.

33 See *Payne*, 825 (emphasizing that the victim's death represents a unique loss to society and to his family).

34 See Frank Carrington, *The Victims* (New York: Arlington House, 1975), 80 (acknowledging that the Warren Court did improve to a large extent the fundamental fairness of the criminal justice system with the *Gideon* decision).

35 *Payne*, 826 (emphasis added). If, as suggested by the lower court, a defendant seeks to introduce irrelevant evidence, one would have thought that the remedy was for the court to exclude such evidence. That is Rule 1 in the law of evidence, requiring a threshold showing of relevancy.

36 See Tobolowsky, *Crime Victim Rights and Remedies*, 92 (explaining how the *Booth* Court not precluding the potential use of victim impact information in noncapital sentencing proceedings allowed the *Payne* Court to hold that general admissibility of victim impact evidence is allowed for noncapital cases).

37 *Payne*, 825.

38 Tobolowsky, *Crime Victim Rights and Remedies*, 89–92.

39 "Although we have presumed that sentencing judges were able to sort out truly relevant, admissible evidence presented in the form of victim impact statements, to allow the introduction of victim testimony espousing the death penalty for consideration by a jury is reversible error." *State v. Lovelace*, 90 P.3d 298 (Idaho 2004).

40 Tobolowsky, *Crime Victim Rights and Remedies*, 86–96.

41 Tobolowsky, *Crime Victim Rights and Remedies*, 89.

42 At times, the debate about such evidence and other victims' rights claims becomes heated. For example, Professor Cassell has accused critics of victims' rights as believing that VRM supporters are "barbarians at the gate." Paul Cassell, "Barbarians at the Gates? A Reply to the Critics of the Victims' Rights Amendment," *Utah Law Review* 1999, no. 2 (1999): 479–543.

43 Paul Cassell, "In Defense of Victim Impact Statements," *Ohio State Journal of Criminal Law* 6, no. 2 (Spring 2009): 611–12.

44 See Douglas E. Beloof, Paul G. Cassell, Meg Garvin, and Steven J. Twist, *Victims in Criminal Procedure*, 4th ed. (Durham, NC: Carolina Academic Press, 2018).

45 See Beloof et al., *Victims in Criminal Procedure*, 600–604.

46 See Beloof et al., *Victims in Criminal Procedure*, 618–19 (providing an excerpt of Susan Antrobus's victim impact statement when her daughter, Vanessa Quinn, was murdered).

47 Cassell, "Barbarians at the Gates?," 488.

48 For additional examples of victim impact statements, see generally Cassell, "In Defense of Victim Impact Statements," 611–48.

49 Cassell, "In Defense of Victim Impact Statements," 630 (listing various individuals who have published statements about their own victimization or their family member's tragedy, who are all white except for some of the children who survived the Oklahoma City bombing); see also Cassel, "In Defense of Victim Impact Statements," 618–19 for the victim impact statement made by a white mother whose daughter was murdered.

50 *Payne*, 808.

51 *Payne*, 819 (citing Justice Scalia's example of two equally culpable bank robbers receiving different punishments based on the different amounts of harm inflicted); see also Michael Vitiello, "*Payne v. Tennessee*: A 'Stunning Ipse Dixit,'" *Notre Dame Journal of Law, Ethics & Public Policy* 8, no. 1 (1994): 176, https://scholarship.law.nd.edu.

52 *Payne*, 823.

53 *Payne*, 825.

54 See chapter 5.

55 Julyssa Lopez, "Judge Rosemarie Aquilina's 10 Most Powerful Quotes from the Nassar Hearings," *Glamour*, January 24, 2018, www.glamour.com.

56 Cassell, "In Defense of Victim Impact Statements," 622.

57 Lopez, "Judge Rosemarie Aquilina's 10 Most Powerful Quotes" (stating the possibility of victims declining to participate in order to break away from their victim identity).

58 Cassell, "In Defense of Victim Impact Statements," 623; see also U.S. Department of Justice, "What Is a Victim Impact Statement?" (updated December 14, 2020), www.justice.gov.

59 If VRM supporters are genuinely concerned that judges should not increase prison sentences, as some advocates state (see, e.g., Irvin Waller, *Less Law, More Order: The Truth about Reducing Crime* [Ontario: Manor House, 2006]), but still believe that victims achieve closure by addressing the defendant, they could support a rule that allows a victim impact statement after the judge has determined the appropriate system. I have not found support for such a limited rule in leading VRM advocates' writings, however.

60 Cassell, "In Defense of Victim Impact Statements," 623–24.

61 See Cassell, "In Defense of Victim Impact Statements," 624–25.

62 See Richard A. Bierschbach, "Allocution and the Purposes of Victim Participation under the CVRA," *Federal Sentencing Reporter* 19, no. 1 (October 2006): 44–48, https://papers.ssrn.com (advocating for the benefits of oral victim participation); see also U.S. Department of Justice, "What Is a Victim Impact Statement?"

63 "Even accepting the premise that 'death is different,' the question remains: how is the death penalty context different and in some way relevant to the admission of victim impact evidence?" Cassell, "In Defense of Victim Impact Statements," 628.

64 At times, justices have argued that "death is different," that is, that the Court's analysis changes depending on whether an offender faces the death penalty or merely a term of years in prison. See Michael Vitiello, "The Expanding Use of Genetic and Psychological Evidence: Finding Coherence in the Criminal Law," *Nevada Law Journal* 14, no. 3 (Summer 2014): 906, https://scholarlycommons.pacific.edu ("the death penalty must be proportional based on retributive grounds [only]"). Critics rightly argue that the distinction has more to do with efforts to limit the death penalty, justifying a willingness to abandon consistency in the name of narrowing the death penalty, than with principled analysis. See Simone Unwalla, "Death Is Different: Death Sentencing Is Not," *Philosophy, Politics and Economics Undergraduate Journal* 14, no. 2 (Spring 2019): 48, https://repository.upenn.edu ("*Woodson* and the other 1976 post-*Furman* decisions demonstrated, instead a developing prioritization of protecting moral mercy over maintaining moral consistency").

65 See *Booth*, 482 U.S. at 504.

66 Cassell, "In Defense of Victim Impact Statements," 629.

67 Tyler Grove, "Are All Prosecutorial Activities 'Inherently Governmental'?: Applying State Safeguards for Victim-Retained Private Prosecutions to Outsourced Prosecutions," *Public Contract Law Journal* 40, no. 4 (Summer 2011): 991, 1004–5.

68 Grove, "Are All Prosecutorial Activities 'Inherently Governmental'?"

69 For example, a court might decide that a defendant-manufacturer should be liable even without a showing of fault because the manufacturer is in a position

to spread the cost of harm to users of the product rather than burdening the innocent and injured plaintiff with the cost of injuries caused by the product.

70 Kenneth W. Simmons, "The Crime/Tort Distinction: Legal Doctrine and Normative Perspectives," *Widener Law Journal* 17, no. 3 (2008), https://scholarship.law.uci.edu.

71 I have not placed material from that article in quotations. While much of the material is from that article, I have also edited it to make it more directly relevant to the discussion in this chapter.

72 Michael Vitiello, "The Victim Impact Statements: Skewing Criminal Justice Away from First Principles," *NYU Annual Survey of American Law* 76, no. 2 (2021), https://scholarlycommons.pacific.edu.

73 18 PA. Const. Stat. § 3124.1 (2019).

74 See 18 PA. Const. Stat. §106(b)(2).

75 For example, what if a person did not signal the lack of consent in any manner and an act of intercourse took place? The harm occurred: the act of nonconsensual sex. But the offender had no reason to know that consent was not present.

76 See generally Sanford H. Kadish, Stephen J. Schulhofer, and Rachel E. Barkow, *Criminal Law and Its Processes: Cases and Materials*, 10th ed. (Frederick, MD: Wolters Kluwer, 2017) (containing chapters on the institutions and processes of criminal law, the justification of punishment, and the elements of just punishment).

77 See Kadish, Schulhofer, and Barkow, *Criminal Law and Its Processes*, 258.

78 See Kadish, Schulhofer, and Barkow, *Criminal Law and Its Processes*, 202.

79 See Kadish, Schulhofer, and Barkow, *Criminal Law and Its Processes*, 38.

80 See Joshua Dressler and Stephen Garvey, *Cases and Materials on Criminal Law*, 7th ed. (Saint Paul, MD: West, 2015), 113.

81 Dressler and Garvey, *Cases and Materials on Criminal Law*, 113.

82 See Kadish, Schulhofer, and Barkow, *Criminal Law and Its Processes*, 87.

83 *Staples v. United States*, 511 U.S. 600, 605 (1994); *Morissette v. United States*, 342 U.S. 246, 250 (1952) ("The contention that an injury can amount to a crime only when inflicted by intention is no provincial or transient notion").

84 *Staples*, 605 ("[W]e must construe the statute in light of the background rules of the common law . . . in which the requirement of some mens rea for a crime is firmly embedded").

85 See *Staples*, 616.

86 See *Harmelin v. Michigan*, 501 U.S. 957, 959–60 (1991) (Kennedy, J., concurring); *Solem v. Helm*, 463 U.S. 277, 292 (1983).

87 See Michael Vitiello, "Defining the Reasonable Person in the Criminal Law: Fighting the Lernaean Hydra," *Lewis & Clark Law Review* 14, no. 4 (Winter 2010): 1439–42, https://scholarlycommons.pacific.edu.

88 See Vitiello, "Defining the Reasonable Person in the Criminal Law."

89 Dressler and Garvey, *Cases and Materials on Criminal Law*, 157–58.

90 See Danielle Lenth, "Life, Liberty, and the Pursuit of Justice: A Comparative Legal Study of the Amanda Knox Case," *McGeorge Law Review* 45, no. 2 (2013): 347–82, https://scholarlycommons.pacific.edu; *In re Winship*, 397 U.S. 358, 363–64 (1970).

91 See *Winship*, 363–64.

92 See *Winship*, 372.

93 Dressler and Garvey, *Cases and Materials on Criminal Law*, 113–14.

94 Dressler and Garvey, *Cases and Materials on Criminal Law*, 113–14.

95 Dressler and Garvey, *Cases and Materials on Criminal Law*, 113–14.

96 Dressler and Garvey, *Cases and Materials on Criminal Law*, 113–14.

97 *Payne*, 501 U.S. at 819 (explaining that the level of harm inflicted on the victim is relevant in sentencing).

98 E.g., *People v. Conley*, 411 P.2d 911 (Cal. 1966).

99 See John L. Diamond, Lawrence C. Levine, and Anita Bernstein, *Understanding Torts*, 6th ed. (Durham, NC: Carolina Academic Press, 2018), 185–86; e.g., *Keegan v. Minneapolis & St. Louis R.R. Co.*, 78 N.W. 965, 965 (Minn. 1899) (holding that the fact that the railroad could not have reasonably anticipated the plaintiff's endocarditis is immaterial to the plaintiff's damages calculations); see also, e.g., *Bean v. Thomas*, 512 N.W. 2d 537 (Iowa, 1999) (applying the "thin skull plaintiff rule" to a victim who died of a heart attack after an automobile accident).

100 See American Law Institute, Model Penal Code § 2.02(3) (1985) ("When the culpability sufficient to establish a material element of an offense is not prescribed by law, such element is established if a person acts purposely, knowingly or recklessly"); Vitiello, "Defining the Reasonable Person in the Criminal Law," 1439 (discussing the Model Penal Code's reform of the criminal law to premise "criminal liability on an offender's culpable mental state").

101 *Regina v. Cunningham* [1957] 2 QB 396 (Eng.).

102 See *Cunningham*, 2 QB 396.

103 See *Cunningham*, 2 QB 396.

104 See *Cunningham*, 2 QB 396.

105 See *Cunningham*, 2 QB 396.

106 See *Cunningham*, 2 QB 396.

107 American Law Institute, Model Penal Code § 2.02 (1985) (providing that the code's recklessness standard, awareness of risk, is a higher culpability standard than that of negligence). Of course, disconnecting the culpability of the offender from the social harm is why almost all commentators rejected the felony murder rule. See "Felony Murder as a First Degree Offense: An Anachronism Retained," *Yale Law Journal* 66, no. 3 (January 1957): 432–33 (stating that the felony murder rule renders the existence of differing degrees of murder meaningless); Sanford H. Kadish, "Foreword: The Criminal Law and the Luck of the Draw," *Journal of Criminal Law and Criminology* 84, no. 4 (Winter 1994): 680 (arguing that the felony murder doctrine "does not serve the crime preventive purposes of the criminal law, and is not redeemed by any defensible normative principle").

108 See *Staples*, 511 U.S. at 617.

109 See *Staples*, 619.

110 See *Elonis v. United States*, 575 U.S. 723 (2015) ("We have repeatedly held that 'mere omission from a criminal enactment of any mention of criminal intent' should not be read 'as dispensing with it'").

111 See *Tison v. Arizona*, 481 U.S. 137, 157–58 (1987) (holding that reckless disregard for human life is the lowest mental state required before imposition of the death penalty).

112 See American Law Institute, Model Penal Code § 2.05.

113 See American Law Institute, Model Penal Code § 2.05.

114 See American Law Institute, Model Penal Code § 2.02(3).

115 See American Law Institute, Model Penal Code § 2.02(3); American Law Institute, Model Penal Code, § 2.02(2)(d) (requiring a gross deviation from the standard of care that a reasonable person would observe in the actor's situation); Vitiello, "Defining the Reasonable Person in the Criminal Law," 1439–42.

116 Vitiello, "Defining the Reasonable Person in the Criminal Law," 1439–41.

117 See, e.g., Alan C. Michaels, "Constitutional Innocence," *Harvard Law Review* 112, no. 4 (February 1999): 833, https://papers.ssrn.com.

118 Guyora Binder, "Making the Best of Felony Murder," *Boston University Law Review* 91, no. 2 (March 2011): 459, https://digitalcommons.law.buffalo.edu (recounting how a felon's "liability for murder did not depend on proof of awareness that his co-felons were armed" in *State v. Tesack*).

119 See Shobha L. Mahadev and Steven Drizin, "Felony Murder, Explained," *The Appeal*, March 4, 2021, https://theappeal.org.

120 Nelson E. Roth and Scott E. Sundby, "The Felony Murder Rule: A Doctrine at Constitutional Crossroads," *Cornell Law Review* 70, no. 3 (1984–85): 454, https://scholarship.law.cornell.edu ("The inapplicability of transferred intent to felony murder becomes evident when the crime's two different mens rea elements are examined: the intent to commit the felony and the culpability for the killing"); *People v. Dillon*, 668 P.2d 697, 734 (Cal. 1983) (Bird, C. J., concurring).

121 E.g., *People v. Dillon*, 719 (holding that considering the circumstances involving the seventeen-year-old defendant, a sentence of life imprisonment under the felony murder rule violated California's prohibition on cruel and unusual punishment); see also, e.g., *People v. Howard*, 104 P.3d 107, 110–11 (Cal. 2005); contra *People v. Stamp*, 2 Cal. App. 3d 203 (1969) (upholding the felony murder conviction when the victim died from a heart attack as a result of the fright he felt from the robbery).

122 The one notable exception is from Crump and Crump. See David Crump and Susan Waite Crump, "In Defense of the Felony Murder Doctrine," *Harvard Journal of Law and Public Policy* 8, no. 2 (Spring 1985): 359–98, https://heinonline.org.

123 Dressler and Garvey, *Cases and Materials on Criminal Law*, 345.

124 Cal. Legis. Serv. Ch. 1015 (SB 1437) (West 2018).

125 See Karl Vick and Josiah Bates, "Minneapolis Police Were Cleared in the Killing of Terrance Franklin. Franklin's Family Says a Video Proves He Was Executed—and Now the Case May Be Reopened," *Time*, June 25, 2021, https://time.com (". . . at the time [of Franklin's fatal shooting in 2014], [] settlements by the city and other agencies total[ed] $700,000").

126 See Johnathan Cardi, Valerie P. Hans, and Gregory Parks, "Do Black Injuries Matter? Implicit Bias and Jury Decision Making in Tort Cases," *Southern California Law Review* 93, no. 3 (March 2020) (for a full discussion of the issue), https://southerncalifornialawreview.com (citing Erik Girvan and Heather J. Marek, "Psychological and Structural Bias in Civil Jury Awards," *Journal of Aggression, Conflict, & Peace Resolution* 8 [2016]: 252–53); see also Jennifer B. Wriggins, "Torts, Race, and the Value of Injury, 1900–1949," *Howard Law Journal* 49, no. 1 (Fall 2005): 99–138, https://digitalcommons.mainelaw.maine.edu (questioning the application of statistical damages tables when such estimates historically excluded data about African Americans); e.g., *McMillan v. City of New York*, 253 F.R.D. 247 (E.D.N.Y. 2008) (holding that statistical evidence suggesting that a spinal-cord-injured African American was likely to survive fewer years than someone of a different race with similar injuries was inadmissible for computing life expectancy and damages).

127 Sanford H. Kadish, "Respect for Life and Regard for Rights in the Criminal Law," *California Law Review* 64, no. 4 (July 1976): 875 (explaining that the Model Penal Code meant to extend the defense of necessity to homicide cases "on the footing that the death of two persons is a greater evil than taking the life of one").

128 *Payne*, 501 U.S. at 823.

129 Cassell, "In Defense of Victim Impact Statements," 620 (justifying the admission of victim impact statements as a way for the judge to fully understand the extent of the victim's harm before sentencing).

130 *Payne*, 819.

131 Vitiello, "*Payne v. Tennessee*," 218–19 (citing multiple Model Penal Code sections to show that harm becomes relative in light of the offender's mental state).

132 Gideon Yaffe, "Criminal Attempts," *Yale Law Journal* 124, no. 1 (October 2014): 101 (synthesizing the debate between the "subjectivists," who form their argument on the mens rea elements of criminal attempt, and the "objectivists," who focus on the actus reus elements instead); Nick Zimmerman, "An Attempt-to-Almost-Attempt-to-Act," *Northern Illinois University Law Review* 20, no. 1 (Spring 2000): 220, https://commons.lib.niu.edu (". . . when 'inchoate' crimes . . . are enacted, the legislature implicitly creates an attempt of the same crime").

133 Paul H. Robinson and Jane A. Grall, "Element Analysis in Defining Criminal Liability: The Model Penal Code and Beyond," *Stanford Law Review* 35, no. 4 (April 1983): 745, https://scholarship.law.upenn.edu ("Th[e] [Model Penal Code's] reliance upon the defendant's [subjective] perspective assures that even impossible attempts will be punished").

134 See Vitiello, "*Payne v. Tennessee*," 219n344.

135 See Douglas E. Beloof, "The Third Wave of Crime Victims' Rights: Standing, Remedy, and Review," *Brigham Young University Law Review* 2005, no. 2 (2005): 255n65, https://digitalcommons.law.byu.edu (citing various works on what private individuals historically were able to do during court proceedings).

136 See Alan Vinegrad, Essay, "The Role of the Prosecutor: Serving the Interests of All the People," *Hofstra Law Review* 28, no. 4 (Summer 2000): 898, https://scholarly-commons.law.hofstra.edu.

137 Susan A. Bandes, "Closure in the Criminal Courtroom: The Birth and Strange Career of an Emotion," in *Research Handbook on Law and Emotion*, ed. Susan A. Bandes, Jody L. Madeira, Kathryn D. Temple, and Emily Kidd White (Northampton, MA: Edward Elgar, 2021), 102–3.

138 See Susan A. Bandes, "Victims, 'Closure,' and the Sociology of Emotion," *Law and Contemporary Problems* 72, no. 2 (Spring 2009): 11n62, https://scholarship.law.duke.edu (describing the argument in favor of victim impact statements as one that emphasizes the giving back of something to victims' families and friends that was previously taken by the defendant).

139 See Franklin E. Zimring, *The Contradictions of American Capital Punishment* (New York: Oxford University Press, 2003), 114 ("Prior to 1989, the term ['closure'] does not appear in death penalty stories in the United States").

140 Bandes, "Closure in the Criminal Courtroom," 103.

141 Susan A. Bandes, "Share Your Grief but Not Your Anger: Victims and the Expression of Emotion in Criminal Justice," in *Emotional Expression: Philosophical, Psychological, and Legal Perspectives*, ed. Catherine Abell and Joel Smith (Cambridge: Cambridge University Press, 2016), 20.

142 Bandes, "Share Your Grief but Not Your Anger," 20.

143 Mary Lay Schuster and Amy D. Propen, *Victim Advocacy in the Courtroom: Persuasive Practices in Domestic Violence and Child Protection Cases* (Boston: Northeastern University Press, 2011), 83.

144 Lindsey Bever, "'Dear Dzokhar Tsarnaev': A Survivor's Letter to Accused Boston Bomber," *Washington Post*, March 5, 2015, www.washingtonpost.com.

145 Bever, "'Dear Dzokhar Tsarnaev.'"

146 See Bandes, "Victims, 'Closure,' and the Sociology of Emotion," 13 (postulating that some survivors may benefit from the ability to participate).

147 Cassell, "In Defense of Victim Impact Statements," 622.

148 Tobolowsky, *Crime Victim Rights and Remedies*, 53 ("Researchers [in a study during the late 1970s] found that court attendance itself appeared to improve victims' perceptions of sentencing outcomes generally but had no impact on their perceptions of their offenders").

149 See Bandes, "Victims, 'Closure,' and the Sociology of Emotion," 112 (summarizing research findings from a study focusing on how victims' family members used the term "closure").

150 Laura Santhanam, "Does the Death Penalty Bring Closure to a Victim's Family?," *PBS Newshour*, April 25, 2017, www.pbs.org.

151 Robert T. Muller, "Death Penalty May Not Bring Peace to Victims' Families," *Psychology Today*, October 19, 2016, www.psychologytoday.com.

152 See Marilyn Peterson Armour and Mark S. Umbreit, "Assessing the Impact of the Ultimate Penal Sanction on Homicide Survivors: A Two State Comparison," *Marquette Law Review* 96, no. 1 (Fall 2012): 91–95, https://scholarship.law.marquette.edu; see also Scott Vollum and Dennis R. Longmire, "Covictims of Capital Murder: Statements of Victims' Family Members and Friends Made at the Time of Execution," *Violence and Victims* 22, no. 5 (2007): 601–19, www.ojp.gov.

153 Lisa Murtha, "These Families Lost Loved Ones to Violence. Now They Are Fighting the Death Penalty," *America Jesuit Review*, December 28, 2017, www.americamagazine.org.

154 Jason Marsh, "Does Death Penalty Bring Closure?," *CNN*, May 20, 2015, www.cnn.com ("By contrast, in 20% of cases [in a 2007 study], [victims' loved ones] explicitly said the execution did not bring them healing or closure").

155 Robert C. Davis and Lucy N. Friedman, "The Emotional Aftermath of Crime and Violence," in *Trauma and Its Wake*, ed. Charles R. Figley (Levittown, NY: Brunner/Mazel, 1986), 91 ("Evidence has begun to accumulate among researchers and practitioners that serious violent crimes also produce a major, and sometimes lasting, psychological impact on victims").

156 See Ian Freckelton, "Post-traumatic Stress Disorder and the Law," *Psychiatry, Psychology, and Law* 2, no. 1 (April 1995): 1; see also Stéphane Guay, Dominic Beaulieu-Prévost, Josette Sader, and André Marchand, "A Systematic Literature Review of Early Posttraumatic Interventions for Victims of Violent Crime," *Aggression and Violent Behavior* 46 (May–June 2019): 15–16 (listing various factors that influence a crime victim's likelihood of developing posttraumatic stress disorder); see also Myeongju Kim, Gahae Hong, Rye Young Kim, Yumi Song, Hwangwon Lee, Yoonji Joo, Jungyoon Kim, and Sujung Yoon, "Severity of Post-traumatic Stress Disorder and Childhood Abuse in Adult Crime Victims as Mediated by Low Resilience and Dysfunction Coping Strategies," *Child Abuse & Neglect* 118 (August 2021): 2 ("Exposure to violence crime is the most common traumatic event in the general population and is related to high rates (17.8% to 38.5%) of subsequent PTSD development").

157 American Psychological Association, "How Long Will It Take for Treatment to Work?" (Clinical Practice Guideline for the Treatment of Posttraumatic Stress Disorder, July 2017), www.apa.org.

158 American Psychological Association, "PTSD Treatments" (Clinical Practice Guideline for the Treatment of Posttraumatic Stress Disorder, updated June 2020), www.apa.org.

159 Marris Adlikwu, "What Is CPT Therapy and How Does It Help PTSD?," *Talk Space*, October 17, 2020, www.talkspace.com.

160 E.g., American Psychological Association, "Cognitive Behavioral Therapy (CBT)" (Clinical Practice Guideline for the Treatment of Posttraumatic Stress Disorder, updated July 31, 2017), www.apa.org; see also, e.g., American Psychological Association, "Prolonged Exposure (PE)" (Clinical Practice Guidelines for the Treatment of Posttraumatic Stress Disorder, updated June 2020), www.apa.org (ranging from eight to fifteen sessions for prolonged exposure therapy).

161 Office of Justice Programs, "The Victim as a Witness" (Office for Victims of Crime Training and Technical Assistance Center, n.d.), www.ovcttac.gov ("Victims are usually fearful about facing their traffickers (and/or turning on them) and testifying against them, and they will require a great deal of support through the process"); see Kim M. E. Lens, Antony Pemberton, Karen Brans, Johan Braeken, Stefan Bogaerts, and Esmah Lahlah, "Delivering a Victim Impact Statement: Emotionally Effective or Counter-productive," *European Journal of Criminology* 12, no. 1 (January 2015): 30 ("victims who decide to deliver a written or oral VIS display significantly higher levels of anxiety than victims who do not").

162 See Lens et al., "Delivering a Victim Impact Statement," 30.

163 Bandes, "Victims, 'Closure,' and the Sociology of Emotion," 19. A few scholars have pointed out that some liberals argue in favor of restorative justice by asserting that victims can experience closure and that their position is inconsistent with their opposition to victim impact evidence in death penalty cases. While restorative justice programs are largely beyond the scope of this book, the methods used in encounters between victims and their victimizers are much closer to a therapeutic model than is the typical confrontation in open court in non-restorative-justice settings.

164 Alex Lloyd and Jo Borrill, "Examining the Effectiveness of Restorative Justice in Reducing Victims' Post-traumatic Stress," *Psychological Injury and Law* 13, no. 4 (March 2020): 78.

165 Danielle Sered, "Across the River of Fire," in *Until We Reckon: Violence, Mass Incarceration, and a Road to Repair* (New York: New Press, 2019), 32.

166 Sered, "Across the River of Fire," 37.

167 Tobolowsky, *Crime Victim Rights and Remedies*, 86–93, 99–103 (discussing different sentencing outcomes from various state courts of appeal).

168 Waller, *Less Law, More Order*, 87 (acknowledging that some prosecutors have set up offices to support victims when they need to testify in court but highlighting that this support is not available to every victim).

169 Julie Cart, "Killer of Gay Student Is Spared Death Penalty," *Los Angeles Times*, December 31, 1999, www.latimes.com.

170 "Boston Bombing Trial: Martin Richard's Parents Urge Against Death Penalty," *NBC News*, April 17, 2015, www.nbcnews.com.

171 Deborah P. Kelly, "Have Victim Reforms Gone Too Far—or Not Far Enough," *Criminal Justice* 6, no. 3 (Fall 1991): 26, https://m.heinonline.org ("In fact, the mere existence of so many statutes may be misleading; in practice, most victims never benefit from these reforms").

172 For an additional discussion of this point, see chapter 8, which discusses how Americans might unite behind a series of proposals aimed at providing adequate health care to victims and their abusers.

173 Of course, not all VRM supporters favor the death penalty. But many of the prime movers in the VRM, including Frank Carrington and Paul Cassell, voiced or voice strong support for the death penalty.

174 Sered, "Across the River of Fire," 32.

175 Tatjana Hornle, "Distribution of Punishment: The Role of a Victim's Perspective," *Buffalo Criminal Law Review* 3, no. 1 (1999): 175 ("Generally speaking, discussions of victim's rights in the field of criminal policy are connected with demands for more punitiveness").

176 Cassell, "In Defense of Victim Impact Statements," 624–25.

177 See Frank Carrington, *The Victims* (New York: Arlington House, 1975), 8 (arguing that criminal defendants are afforded human dignity through constitutional protections at the expense of denying human dignity to crime victims).

178 *Gideon v. Wainwright*, 372 U.S. 335 (1963).

179 See chapter 4 (referencing John Blume and Rebecca Helm's article on the use of the controversial Alford plea bargain against innocent defendants).

180 Cassell, "In Defense of Victim Impact Statements," 635–36.

181 Cassell, "In Defense of Victim Impact Statements," 636–37.

182 Cassell, "In Defense of Victim Impact Statements," 636.

183 Irvin Waller, "Outlaw Violence, Not Men," in *Less Law, More Order* (proposing various reforms to prevent victimization to produce the net effect of leaving room to provide better support to existing victims).

184 James L. Buckley, foreword to *The Victims*, by Frank Carrington (New Rochelle, NY: Arlington House, 1975).

185 Raphael Ginsberg, "Victims Deserve the Best: Victims' Rights and the Decline of the Liberal Consensus" (PhD diss., University of North Carolina at Chapel Hill, 2013), 10.

186 Ginsberg, "Victims Deserve the Best," 11.

187 Ginsberg, "Victims Deserve the Best," 12.

188 See Katherine L. Hanna, comment, "Old Laws, New Tricks: Drunk Driving and Autonomous Vehicles," *Jurimetrics* 55, no. 2 (Winter 2015): 277.

189 See Erik G. Luna, "Foreword: Three Strikes in a Nutshell," *Thomas Jefferson Law Review* 20, no. 1 (Spring 1998): 7, www.ojp.gov; see also Carrington, *Victims*, 266–67 (premising the goal of increased sentences as striking the balance between the extreme leniency afforded to criminals and recognizing forgotten crime victims, especially as a deterrent for repeat offenders).

190 Tobolowsky, *Crime Victim Rights and Remedies*, 99.

191 Julian V. Roberts, "Listening to the Crime Victim: Evaluating Victim Input at Sentencing and Parole," *Crime and Justice: A Review of Research* 38 (2009): 362 (summarizing research findings for various studies on crime victim participation in criminal proceedings).

192 See generally Hugh M. Mundy, "Forgiven, Forgotten? Rethinking Victim Impact Statements for an Era of Decarceration," *UCLA Law Review Discourse* 68, no. 1 (2020), www.uclalawreview.org.

193 Susan Brandes, "Empathy, Narrative, and Victim Impact Statements," *University of Chicago Law Review* 63, no. 2 (1996): 399, https://chicagounbound.uchicago.edu.

194 See Samuel R. Sommers, "What We Do (and Don't) Know about Race and Jurors," *Jury Expert* 22, no. 4 (July 2010): 6, www.thejuryexpert.com.

195 Tobolowsky, *Crime Victim Rights and Remedies*, 100.

196 Tobolowsky, *Crime Victim Rights and Remedies*, 100–101.

197 See Clark Neily, "Prisons Are Packed Because Prosecutors Are Coercing Plea Deals. And, Yes, It's Totally Legal," *NBC News*, August 8, 2019, www.nbcnews.com (referencing a Pew Research poll from 2018).

198 21 U.S.C. § 841(b)(1) (2018) (requiring an offender convicted of trafficking twenty-eight grams or more of a mixture or substance containing cocaine base [crack cocaine] to be subject to a mandatory minimum penalty of not less than five years); 18 U.S.C. § 924(c) (2018) (requiring a mandatory consecutive term of imprisonment for the possession or use of a firearm in connection with certain underlying offenses); Armed Career Criminal Act, 18 U.S.C. § 924(e) (2018) (requiring a mandatory minimum penalty of fifteen years of imprisonment if a person commits a firearms offense and has previously been convicted of three or more "violent felonies" or "serious drug offenses").

199 See Wayne A. Logan, "Victim Impact Evidence in Federal Capital Trials," *Federal Sentencing Reporter* 19, no. 1 (October 2006): 6, https://ir.law.fsu.edu (demonstrating the use of typically highly emotional victim impact evidence by pointing to the provision of victim impact evidence use in the Federal Death Penalty Act of 1994, despite the *Payne* holding).

200 See Ray Paternoster and Jerome Deise, "A Heavy Thumb on the Scale: The Effect of Victim Impact Evidence on Capitol Decision Making," *Criminology* 49, no. 1 (February 2011): 129–62.

201 See Jerome Deise and Raymond Paternoster, "More Than a 'Quick Glimpse of the Life': The Relationship between Victim Impact Evidence and Death Sentencing," *Hastings Constitutional Law Quarterly* 40, no. 3 (Spring 2013): 611–52, https://digitalcommons.law.umaryland.edu.

202 Beloof et al., *Victims in Criminal Procedure*, 600–604.

203 Earlier I gave examples where prosecutors do not call the families of victims when the family members oppose the death penalty. See, e.g., "Boston Bombing Trial: Martin Richard's Parents Urge Against Death Penalty," *NBC News*, April 17, 2015, www.nbcnews.com.

204 See generally Christine A. Trueblood, "Victim Impact Statements: A Balance between Victim and Defendant Rights," *Phoenix Law Review* 3, no. 2 (2010), https://heinonline.org.

205 Pamela Colloff, "Does Napoleon Beazley Deserve to Die?," *Texas Monthly*, April 2002, www.texasmonthly.com.

206 Compare *Stanford v. Kentucky*, 492 U.S. 361 (1989) (affirming the death penalty for a seventeen-year-old capital defendant); see *Roper v. Simmons*, 543 U.S. 551 (2005) (overruling *Stanford v. Kentucky*).

207 See American Law Institute, Model Penal Code § 210.6 (1962).

208 See Alison Powers, "Cruel and Unusual Punishment: Mandatory Sentencing of Juveniles Tried as Adults without the Possibility of Youth as a Mitigating Factor," *Rutgers Law Review* 62, no. 1 (Fall 2009): 260–61.

209 Jim Yardley, "Execution Approaches in a Most Rare Murder Case," *New York Times*, August 10, 2001, www.nytimes.com.

210 Tobolowsky, *Crime Victim Rights and Remedies*, 100.

211 See Rachel King and Katherine Norgard, "What about Our Families—Using the Impact on Death Row Defendants' Family Members as a Mitigating Factor in Death Penalty Sentencing Hearings," *Florida State University Law Review* 26, no. 4 (Summer 1999): 1165, https://ir.law.fsu.edu (providing an example of a victim's family member who was threatened to be thrown in jail after arguing against the death penalty).

212 See generally Roland Chilton and Jim Galvin, "Race, Crime, and Criminal Justice," *Crime and Delinquency* 31, no. 1 (January 1985); see also Paul Butler, "Racially Based Jury Nullification: Black Power in the Criminal Justice System," *Yale Law Journal* 105, no. 3 (December 1995): 690 ("Imagine a country in which more than half of the young male citizens are under the supervision of the criminal justice system, either awaiting trial, in prison, or on probation or parole").

213 Ojmarrh Mitchell and Doris L. MacKenzie, "The Relationship between Race, Ethnicity, and Sentencing Outcomes: A Meta-Analysis of Sentencing Research" (U.S. Department of Justice, December 2004), 1, www.ojp.gov.

214 See generally David C. Baldus, Charles Pulaski, and George Woodworth, "Comparative Review of Death Sentences: An Empirical Study of the Georgia Experience," *Journal of Criminal Law and Criminology* 74, no. 3 (Fall 1983), https://scholarlycommons.law.northwestern.edu; see also *McCleskey v. Kemp*, 753 F.2d 877, 907 (11th Cir. 1985) (citing the Baldus Study as "far and away the most complete and thorough analysis of sentencing" ever carried out); see also Gail B. Agrawal, "David Baldus: Scholar, Teacher, Mentor and Friend," *Iowa Law Review* 97 (Special Issue; October 2012): 1868, https://iro.uiowa.edu.

215 But see Samuel R. Gross and Robert Mauro, "Patterns of Death: An Analysis of Racial Disparities in Capital Sentencing and Homicide Victimization," *Stanford Law Review* 37, no. 1 (November 1984): 120 (criticizing the validity of the Baldus study results based on the statistical models used).

216 See also Sheri Lynn Johnson, "Litigating for Racial Fairness after *McCleskey v. Kemp*," *Columbia Human Rights Law Review* 39, no. 1 (Fall 2007): 181–82, https://heinonline.org (noting a post-*Furman* death penalty study showing that during Solicitor Holman Gossett's prosecutorial career, he sought death in 50 percent of the fifty-two death-eligible white victim cases but in 0 percent of the nineteen death-eligible Black victim cases).

217 See Katherine Beckett and Heather Evans, "Race, Death, and Justice: Capital Sentencing in Washington State, 1981–2014," *Columbia Journal of Race and Law* 6 (2016): 105, https://journals.library.columbia.edu ("The finding that Washington State juries are more than four times more likely to impose death when the defendant is Black").

218 *McCleskey v. Kemp*, 481 U.S. 279, 279–82 (1987).

219 *McCleskey v. Zant*, 580 F. Supp. 338, 356 (N.D. Ga. 1985).

220 *Zant*, 363.

221 *Zant*, 365 (attributing the three most important reasons for concluding that the petitioned failed to make a prima facie case of discrimination are "that the data base is substantially flawed, that even the largest models are not sufficiently predictive, and that the analyses do not compare like cases").

222 Scott Phillips and Justin Marceau, "Whom the State Kills," *Harvard Civil Rights–Civil Liberties Law Review* 55, no. 2 (Summer 2020): 616, https://papers.ssrn.com ("In order to assess whether race impacted the actual selection of who was executed, we updated the [Charging and Sentencing Study] with new data regarding executions").

223 Philips and Marceau, "Whom the State Kills," 621.

224 Philips and Marceau, "Whom the State Kills," 632–36.

225 *McCleskey*, 753 F.2d at 907.

226 Samuel R. Gross, "David Baldus and the Legacy of *McCleskey v. Kemp*," *Iowa Law Review* 97, no. 6 (2012): 1914–15, https://repository.law.umich.edu.

227 Gross and Mauro, "Patterns of Death."

228 Criminal Justice Legal Foundation, "Kent Scheidegger" (n.d.), www.cjlf.org.

229 Criminal Justice Legal Foundation, "Kent Scheidegger."

230 See Mirko Bagaric, "Rich Offender, Poor Offender: Why It (Sometimes) Matters in Sentencing," *Minnesota Journal of Law and Inequality* 33, no. 1 (2015): 7.

231 Jill Lepore, "The Rise of the Victims'-Rights Movement," *New Yorker*, May 14, 2018, www.newyorker.com.

232 American Society for Horticultural Science, "Student Confidence Correlated with Academic Performance, Horticultural Science Class Study Finds," *Science Daily*, April 4, 2011, www.sciencedaily.com.

233 See Tobolowsky, *Crime Victim Rights and Remedies*, 84.

234 Brandon L. Garrett, *End of Its Rope: How Killing the Death Penalty Can Revive Criminal Justice* (Cambridge, MA: Harvard University Press, 2017), 53.

235 Brandes, "Empathy, Narrative, and Victim Impact Statements."

236 Amnesty International, "Harmful Errors: Texas Approaches Its 500th Execution" (June 26, 2013), www.amnestyusa.org.

237 Cassell, "Barbarians at the Gates?," 536 ("Today the criminal justice system too often treats victims as second-class citizens, almost as barbarians at the gates that must be repelled at all costs").

238 See Ginsberg, "Victims Deserve the Best," 24.

239 Institute of Governmental Studies, University of California, Berkeley, "Limitation on 'Three Strikes' Law" (November 2, 2004), https://igs.berkeley.edu.

240 See Michael Vitiello, "Brock Turner: Sorting through the Noise," *University of the Pacific Law Review* 49, no. 3 (2018): 634–38, https://scholarlycommons.pacific.edu.

241 See Vitiello, "Brock Turner," 639; "Sexual Assault Law—Judicial Recall—California Judge Recalled for Sentence in Sexual Assault Case," *Harvard Law Review* 132 (2019): 1369, https://harvardlawreview.org.

242 See Vitiello, "Brock Turner," 637; Report of Prob. Officer, *People v. Brock Allen Turner*, No. B1577162 (Cal. Super. Ct. June 2, 2016); Bridgette Dunlap, "How California's New Rape Law Could Be a Step Backward," *Rolling Stone*, September 1, 2016, www.rollingstone.com; Paul Elias, "Judge in Stanford Rape Case Often Follows Sentencing Reports," *AP News*, June 17, 2016, https://apnews.com (stating Judge Persky followed the sentencing recommendation of the Santa Clara County Probation Department).

243 Richard Gonzales and Camila Domonoske, "Voters Recall Aaron Persky, Judge Who Sentenced Brock Turner," *NPR*, June 5, 2018, www.npr.org.

244 Guyora Binder, "Punishment Theory: Moral or Political," *Buffalo Criminal Law Review* 5, no. 2 (2002): 338–48, https://digitalcommons.law.buffalo.edu; see also Kent Greenawalt, "Punishment," in *Encyclopedia of Crime and Justice*, 2nd ed., vol. 3, ed. Joshua Dressler (New York: Macmillan, 2002), 1286–87.

245 See generally Franklin E. Zimring, Gordon Hawkins, and Sam Kamin, *Punishment and Democracy: Three Strikes and You're Out in California* (New York: Oxford University Press, 2001) (discussing the California legislature's enactment of the Three Strikes Law and its implications on criminal sentencing).

246 Zimring, Hawkins, and Kamin, *Punishment and Democracy*.

247 Zimring, Hawkins, and Kamin, *Punishment and Democracy*, 94–105.

248 See Zimring, Hawkins, and Kamin, *Punishment and Democracy*, 56.

249 See Zimring, Hawkins, and Kamin, *Punishment and Democracy*, 4–7.

250 Zimring, Hawkins, and Kamin, *Punishment and Democracy*, 44.

251 See Zimring, Hawkins, and Kamin, *Punishment and Democracy*, 56; see also, e.g., U.S. Department of Justice, "Age-Specific Arrest Rates and Race-Specific Arrest Rates for Selected Offenses 1993–2001" (Federal Bureau of Investigation, 2003), www.ojp.gov.

252 Zimring, Hawkins, and Kamin, *Punishment and Democracy*, 56.

253 Zimring, Hawkins, and Kamin, *Punishment and Democracy*, 60 ("The offense charged at the current arrest is less likely to be a crime of violence for a third-strike defendant than for a defendant with no strikes at all").

254 See Tracey Kaplan, "Recall Aftermath: Will the Removal of Judge Aaron Persky Prompt a New Legal Battle?," *Mercury News*, June 6, 2018, www.mercurynews.com.

255 Kaplan, "Recall Aftermath" ("Opponents [to the recall] said . . . independence from popular opinion is what has allowed judges to rule on civil rights, integrated

schools, free speech, access to birth control and marriage equality"); see Vitiello, "Brock Turner," 652–59.

256 See Julian V. Roberts, "Public Opinion and Mandatory Sentencing: A Review of International Findings," *Criminal Justice and Behavior* 30, no. 4 (2003): 505 (concluding that the public is "sensitive to the principle of proportionality and recognize the threat to this principle created by laws that mandate the same sentence for all offenders regardless of their levels of culpability").

257 Kate Berry, "How Judicial Elections Impact Criminal Cases" (Brennan Center for Justice, 2015), www.brennancenter.org.

258 See Berry, "How Judicial Elections Impact Criminal Cases," 1.

259 See Berry, "How Judicial Elections Impact Criminal Cases," 8.

260 See Berry, "How Judicial Elections Impact Criminal Cases," 3.

261 See Berry, "How Judicial Elections Impact Criminal Cases," 9.

262 Alicia Bannon, Cathleen Lisk, and Peter Hardin, "Who Pays for Judicial Races? The Politics of Judicial Elections 2015–2016" (Brennan Center for Justice, 2017), 29, www.brennancenter.org.

263 Sagar Jethani, "Union of the Snake: How California's Prison Guards Subvert Democracy," *Mic*, February 5, 2019, https://mic.com (stating that the California Correctional Peace Officers Association "has been one of the leading backers of tough sentencing laws," spending $100,000 in support of the Three Strikes Law and $1 million on beating Prop. 66).

264 Berry, "How Judicial Elections Impact Criminal Cases," 7.

265 See, e.g., Lauren-Brooke Eisen and Inimai Chettiar, "39% of Prisoners Should Not Be in Prison," *Time*, December 9, 2016, https://time.com; ACLU Northern California, "91 Percent of Americans Support Criminal Justice Reform, ACLU Polling Finds" (November 16, 2017), www.aclunc.org; see also Peter K. Ennis, "The Public's Increasing Punitiveness and Its Influence on Mass Incarceration in the United States," *American Journal of Political Science* 58, no. 4 (2014) (examining punitive tendencies of the U.S. public since 1953 and revealing a significant decrease in public support for "tough on crime" policies since the mid-1990s).

266 See generally Berry, "How Judicial Elections Impact Criminal Cases"; see Lauren-Brooke Eisen, James Austin, James Cullen, Jonathan Frank, and Inimai M. Chettiar, "How Many Americans Are Unnecessarily Incarcerated" (Brennan Center for Justice, 2016), www.brennancenter.org (suggesting that mass incarceration will continue to rise unless bold solutions are provided, including reducing minimum and maximum required sentencing and eliminating prison terms for lower level crimes).

267 Elias, "Judge in Stanford Rape Case Often Follows Sentencing Reports"; see also "Brock Turner Sentencing Packet," *New York Times*, June 12, 2016, www.nytimes.com.

268 See "Brock Turner Sentencing Packet"; see also Cal. Penal Code § 1170; cf. Nicole Knight, "Brock Turner Sentencing Prompts California Legislators to Expand Rape Definition," *Rewire*, September 2, 2016, https://rewirenewsgroup.com; Matt Ford,

"How Brock Turner Changed California's Rape Laws," *Atlantic*, October 1, 2016, www.theatlantic.com; Mollie Reilly, "California Closes Loophole That Allowed Brock Turner's Light Sentence," *HuffPost*, September 30, 2016, www.huffpost.com.

269 See Cal. Penal Code § 1170.

270 See "Brock Turner Sentencing Packet."

271 Elias, "Judge in Stanford Rape Case Often Follows Sentencing Reports."

272 Vitiello, "Brock Turner," 631.

273 Marina Koren, "Why the Stanford Judge Gave Brock Turner Six Months," *Atlantic*, June 17, 2016, www.theatlantic.com (noting that Persky stated, "I mean, I take him at his word that, subjectively, that's his version of events").

274 See generally Michael Vitiello, "Reconsidering Rehabilitation," *Tulane Law Review* 65, no. 5 (1990–91), https://scholarlycommons.pacific.edu; Vitiello, "Defining the Reasonable Person in the Criminal Law," 1439–41; see generally Michael Vitiello, "Three Strikes: Can We Return to Rationality?," *Journal of Criminal Law and Criminology* 87, no. 2 (Winter 1997), https://scholarlycommons.law.northwestern.edu.

275 Vitiello, "Brock Turner," 637–38; Kendall Fisher, comment, "No Time Like the Present, Except the Past Fifty Years: Why California Should Finally Adopt the Model Penal Code Sentencing Provisions," *University of the Pacific Law Review* 49, no. 3 (2018): 662–64, https://scholarlycommons.pacific.edu; Wiemond Wu, comment, "Crocodiles in the Judge's Bathtub? Why California Should End 'Unregulated' Judicial Recall," *University of the Pacific Law Review* 49, no. 3 (2018): 719–21, https://scholarlycommons.pacific.edu; Justine McGrath, "Stanford Rapist Brock Turner Lost His Sexual Assault Conviction Appeal," *Teen Vogue*, August 9, 2018, www.teenvogue.com; Will Garbe, "Attorney Tells Judges Brock Turner Practiced 'Sexual Outercourse,'" *Atlanta Journal-Constitution*, July 25, 2018, www.ajc.com (changing the headline of the article and concluding in an editor's note that the article headline previously misstated the facts and alleged that Turner was convicted of rape).

276 See Elspeth Farmer and Ellen Kreitzberg, "Guest Opinion: We Need Reform, Not a Recall," *Palo Alto Online*, May 11, 2018, www.paloaltoonline.com (listing the website https://norecall2018.org/get-the-facts/ that claims to "debunk the distortions and false narrative of the recall campaign).

277 James S. Kunen, *"How Can You Defend Those People?" The Making of a Criminal Lawyer* (New York: Random House, 1983), 7 ("Criminals are uneducated and unskilled. Society has no use for them, nor they for it").

7. CALIFORNIA'S THREE STRIKES AND YOU'RE OUT LEGISLATION

1 By way of clarification, California's bloated prison and jail populations were not solely the result of the adoption of its Three Strikes Law. Other factors included the abandonment of parole, indeterminate sentencing, and sentence enhancements routinely adopted whenever a new crime made headlines.

2 See Franklin E. Zimring, Gordon Hawkins, and Sam Kamin, *Punishment and Democracy: Three Strikes and You're Out in California* (New York: Oxford Univer-

sity Press, 2001), 13 (explaining that the public seemed to be uninterested in what criminal justice experts had to say about criminal justice legislation partly due to deference to those in the executive and judicial branches of government who possessed special expertise in their jobs).

3 See Michael Vitiello, "Three Strikes: Can We Return to Rationality?," *Journal of Criminal Law and Criminology* 87, no. 2 (Winter 1997): 441–48, https://scholarlycommons.law.northwestern.edu (questioning the deterrent effect of Three Strikes).

4 Zimring, Hawkins, and Kamin, *Punishment and Democracy*, 189–90 (". . . one can decide that the punishment imposed does not conform to the hierarchy of greater punishments for greater offenses, which should inform the scale of penalties in a just penal code").

5 See Michael Vitiello, "Alternatives to Incarceration: Why Is California Lagging Behind?," *Georgia State University Law Review* 28, no. 4 (2012): 1287–94, https://core.ac.uk (citing reform efforts from Washington, Mississippi, and Texas).

6 See generally Michael Vitiello, "Brock Turner: Sorting through the Noise," *University of the Pacific Law Review* 49, no. 3 (2018): 631–60, https://scholarlycommons.pacific.edu.

7 The NRA benefitted by focusing attention on criminals rather than on reducing access to weapons when perpetrators used firearms to commit violent crimes. Joe Domanick, *Cruel Justice: Three Strikes and the Politics of Crime in America's Golden State* (Berkeley: University of California Press, 2004), 108.

8 For years, the CCPOA could boast one legislative victory after another, leading to longer sentences and more lucrative jobs for its members. Domanick, *Cruel Justice*, 114; see Vitiello, "Alternatives to Incarceration," 1304–5.

9 Vitiello, "Three Strikes," 413; Zimring, Hawkins, and Kamin, *Punishment and Democracy*, 6 (explaining how Democrats deferred in advance of Governor Pete Wilson's choice among five different iterations of the Three Strikes initiative to avoid a divide among the major political parties).

10 Zimring, Hawkins, and Kamin, "The Largest Penal Experiment in American History," in *Punishment and Democracy*, 17–28.

11 Zimring, Hawkins, and Kamin, *Punishment and Democracy*, 86 (citing the California attorney general's report titled "'Three Strikes' Era Drop in California's Crime Rate" to show crime statistics that Three Strikes proponents use to claim that this legislation has actually caused a decrease in crime).

12 E.g., Zimring, Hawkins, and Kamin, *Punishment and Democracy*, 124 (referencing the life sentence a man received for stealing a slice of pizza); Vitiello, "Three Strikes," 457n358 (quoting Senate leader Bill Lockyer as saying, "This bill is unnecessary. . . . We need more thoughtful analysis, not a rushed, panicky reaction designed to grab tough-guy headlines").

13 "Proposed Initiative Would Repeal Three Strikes Sentencing Law," *Lassen News*, December 30, 2021, www.lassennews.com (explaining the creation of the commission).

14 Vitiello, "Alternatives to Incarceration," 1295.

15 See California Law Review Commission, "Committee on Revision of the Penal Code" (Annual Report and Recommendations, December 2021), www.clrc.ca.gov.

16 See AB 3105, 2017–2018 Reg. Sess., Cal. Stat. (increasing criminal penalties for distributing fentanyl). See also S. Bill 180, 2017–2018 Reg. Sess., chap. 677 Cal. Stat. (repealing drug enhancements for certain drug convictions) and S. Bill 620, 2017–2018 Reg. Sess., chap. 682 Cal. Stat. (allowing broader judicial discretion when an offender used a firearm).

17 Domanick, *Cruel Justice*, 16–17.

18 Domanick, *Cruel Justice*, 22–23.

19 Domanick, *Cruel Justice*, 25 ("For Mike Reynolds, Davis's bloody execution represented a kind of 'justice seldom seen in America'").

20 Dominick, *Cruel Justice*, 37–38.

21 At least some commentators raised questions whether a state judge should be involved in drafting legislation that may then come before the court. Vitiello, "Three Strikes," 410–11n84; see Joshua M. Dickey, comment, "Judges as Legislators: The Propriety of Judges Drafting Legislation," *McGeorge Law Review* 29, no. 1 (1997): 124, https://scholarlycommons.pacific.edu (explaining how judges need to prevent inappropriately diverting legislative power to the judiciary when drafting legislation).

22 Vitiello, "Three Strikes," 411.

23 Domanick, *Cruel Justice*, 57.

24 Vitiello, "Three Strikes," 411.

25 See Zimring, Hawkins, and Kamin, *Punishment and Democracy*, 19; see also Vitiello, "Three Strikes," 430.

26 Zimring, Hawkins, and Kamin, *Punishment and Democracy*, 7.

27 Domanick, *Cruel Justice*, 86.

28 Domanick, *Cruel Justice*, 89–90.

29 Domanick, *Cruel Justice*, 94.

30 Lori A. Carter, "Tearful Petaluma Remembers Polly Klaas," *Press Democrat*, October 5, 2013, www.petaluma360.com (explaining the nationwide search efforts, including Polly's images being shared two billion times worldwide and the police receiving more than sixty thousand tips regarding Polly's abduction).

31 Christine Spolar and Barbara Vobejda, "Grass-Roots Crusaders Embrace a Mission to Find the Missing," *Washington Post*, March 10, 1994, www.washingtonpost.com.

32 Zimring, Hawkins, and Kamin, *Punishment and Democracy*, 5.

33 Vitiello, "Three Strikes," 412n94 (quoting Richard Kelly Heft, "Legislating with a Vengeance," *Independent*, April 25, 1995, www.independent.co.uk).

34 Domanick, *Cruel Justice*, 109.

35 Domanick, *Cruel Justice*, 108. The NRA donated $90,000 to Washington Citizens for Justice—a critical contribution that allowed the group to gather the required signatures to place the "Three Strikes, You're Out" law on Washington's ballot in 1992.

36 Domanick, *Cruel Justice*, 108.

37 Jewelle Taylor Gibbs and Teiahsha Bankhead, *Preserving Privilege: California's Politics, Propositions, and People of Color* (Westport, CT: Praeger, 2001), 57.

38 Gibbs and Bankhead, *Preserving Privilege*, 57.

39 Wayne R. LaPierre, "NRA and '3 Strikes,'" *Los Angeles Times*, March 23, 1994, www.latimes.com.

40 Domanick, *Cruel Justice*, 109. "[A] like-minded agenda and an infusion of cash can make for strange bedfellows, or in the case of Mike Reynolds, some convoluted logic. 'Look,' he said, 'my daughter was murdered with a .357 Magnum. They placed it in her ear. What I want is that kind of conduct stopped.'"

41 Dana Wilkie, "Prop 184: 3 Strikes Already on Books, Foes Say Its Passage Only Bolsters a Bad Law," *San Diego Union-Tribune*, October 12, 1994, A1; see also Tim Kowal, "The Role of the Prison Guards Union in California's Troubled Prison System" (California Policy Center, June 15, 2011), https://californiapolicycenter.org.

42 Gibbs and Bankhead, *Preserving Privilege*, 54. "In the "Three Strikes" arena, CCPOA was the second largest contributor at $101,000, after Congressman Huffington who cosponsored the bill and contributed $300,000."

43 Domanick, *Cruel Justice*, 114.

44 Domanick, *Cruel Justice*, 114.

45 Joshua Page, *The Toughest Beat: Politics, Punishment, and the Prison Officers Union in California* (Oxford: Oxford University Press, 2013), 112.

46 Laura Sullivan, "Folsom Embodies California's Prison Blues," *NPR*, August 13, 2009, www.npr.org.

47 Gibbs and Bankhead, *Preserving Privilege*, 54.

48 Domanick, *Cruel Justice*, 115.

49 Dan Pens and Paul Wright, "The California Prison Guards' Union: A Potent Political Interest Group," in *The Celling of America: An Inside Look at the U.S. Prison Industry*, ed. Daniel Burton-Rose (Monroe, ME: Common Courage Press, 1998), 137.

50 Kowal, "Role of the Prison Guards Union."

51 Page, *Toughest Beat*, 121.

52 Alexander Volokh, "Privatization and the Law and Economics of Political Advocacy," *Stanford Law Review* 60, no. 4 (2008): 1222.

53 See Zimring, Hawkins, and Kamin, "The Jurisprudence of Imprisonment in California," in *Punishment and Democracy*, 109–24.

54 Domanick, *Cruel Justice*, 128.

55 Vitiello, "Three Strikes," 418.

56 Vitiello, "Three Strikes," 413.

57 Vitiello, "Three Strikes," 415.

58 Wilson claimed to rebut the economic concerns about the cost of Three Strikes by relying on a report by his chief economic advisor, Philip Romero, which projected large savings to the public in reduced crime rates. As developed later in this chapter, such claims were, at best, wildly optimistic. See Vitiello, "Three Strikes," 418.

59 Domanick, *Cruel Justice*, 141. Even more contemptuous and racist was his comment after meeting Assembly Speaker Willie Brown in an elevator in the Sacramento Capitol: "'I pretended I didn't know him. There's one thing worse than knowing who he is, and that's not knowing who he is. . . . You know something? For two cents, I would have given him a fifty-cent tip'" (171).

60 Domanick, *Cruel Justice*, 140–141.

61 See Jerry Gilliam, "Legislators Fear Public on '3 Strikes,' Brown Says," *Los Angeles Times*, March 2, 1994, A3; see also Dan Morain, "Assembly Panel Oks Five '3 Strikes' Bills," *Los Angeles Times*, January 27, 1994, A3.

62 Assembly Bill 971 passed the Assembly by a 63–9 margin on January 31, 1994. See 1 Assembly Final History, 712 (Cal. 1993–1994 Reg. Sess.). The Senate passed it by a 29–7 margin on March 3, 1994. See 1 Assembly Final History, 712.

63 Vitiello, "Three Strikes," 451.

64 Zimring, Hawkins, and Kamin, *Punishment and Democracy*, 3 ("No outside proposal would be likely to march through the legislative process untouched by human hands again").

65 Zimring, Hawkins, and Kamin, *Punishment and Democracy*, 13–15.

66 Zimring, Hawkins, and Kamin, *Punishment and Democracy*, 14.

67 See Frank Carrington and George Nicholson, "Victims' Rights: An Idea Whose Time Has Come—Five Years Later: The Maturing of an Idea," *Pepperdine Law Review* 17, no. 1 (1989): 4; see also President's Task Force on Victims of Crime, "Final Report" (1982), www.ojp.gov.

68 Zimring, Hawkins, and Kamin, *Punishment and Democracy*, 15 (theorizing that part of the reason why Three Strikes was not simply an isolated incident is the lack of "antioffender sentiments").

69 Zimring, Hawkins, and Kamin, *Punishment and Democracy*, 167.

70 Zimring, Hawkins, and Kamin, *Punishment and Democracy*, 23.

71 Zimring, Hawkins, and Kamin, *Punishment and Democracy*, 169 (contrasting the federal law's "loud bark, small bite" approach with Mike Reynolds's "three strikes and you're out" approach).

72 Vitiello, "Three Strikes," 421.

73 Michael Vitiello, "Punishment and Democracy: A Hard Look at Three Strikes' Overblown Promises," review of *Punishment and Democracy: Three Strikes and You're Out in California*, by Franklin E. Zimring, Gordon Hawkins, and Sam Kamin, *California Law Review* 90, no. 1 (2002): 261.

74 For a comparison among three strikes laws on the books as of 1997, see Vitiello, "Three Strikes," 463–80.

75 See Zimring, Hawkins, and Kamin, *Punishment and Democracy*, 65.

76 See Zimring, Hawkins, and Kamin, *Punishment and Democracy*, 36.

77 See Cal. Penal Code § 666 (2014).

78 See *Lockyer v. Andrade*, 538 U.S. 63 (2003); see also "Pizza Thief Off to Prison until 2020," *Tampa Bay Times*, updated October 3, 2005, www.tampabay.com.

79 See *People v. Superior Court (Romero)*, 37 Cal.Rptr.2d 364, 371 (Cal. App. 1995) (quoting Judge Mudd's comments about the then-newly enacted "three strikes" law); see also Michael Vitiello, "Three Strikes and the Romero Case: The Supreme Court Restores Democracy," *Loyola of Los Angeles Law Review* 30, no. 4 (June 1997): 1606, https://digitalcommons.lmu.edu.

80 See generally Zimring, Hawkins, and Kamin, "The Largest Penal Experiment in American History," in *Punishment and Democracy*, 17–28.

81 See *Brown v. Plata*, 563 U.S. 493, 502 (2011) (referencing the findings of the Corrections Independent Review Panel).

82 See Vitiello, "Three Strikes," 423.

83 See Vitiello, "Three Strikes," 451n327.

84 E.g., Zimring, Hawkins, and Kamin, *Punishment and Democracy*, 17–18 ("A 25-year-to-life mandatory sentence is the response to conviction for *any* felony under the California scheme for defendants with two prior convictions for strike offenses") (emphasis added); see also Senate Committee on the Judiciary, "Committee Analysis of AB 971" (February 17, 1994) ("[AB 971] appears to be constitutionally infirm in that it would require cruel and unusual punishment in some cases, with no option for a lesser sentence in the interest of justice").

85 Vitiello, "Three Strikes," 429–30. The law also lacked coherence as based on retribution. An offender's current sentence seemed to be based on *past* conduct for which the offenders had already paid their dues. No doubt to avoid that criticism, proponents argued that the law worked because of incapacitation and deterrence; that is, the current sentence was based on predictions about future criminality, not the offender's past conduct.

86 E.g., Vitiello, "Three Strikes," 454 ("a defendant who has committed two residential burglaries and is currently charged with possession of narcotics will be imprisoned for a minimum term of twenty years while an offender who commits first-degree robbery will face a maximum term of nine years").

87 See Vitiello, "Three Strikes," 437n248 (quoting *United States v. Jackson*, 835 F.2d 1195, 1199 [7th Cir. 1988] [Posner, J., concurring]).

88 E.g., Eric Slater, "Pizza Thief Receives Sentence of 25 Years to Life in Prison: Crime: Judge Cites Five Prior Felony Convictions in Sentencing Jerry DeWayne Williams under 'Three Strikes' Law," *Los Angeles Times*, March 3, 1995, www.latimes.com.

89 *Lockyer*, 538 U.S. at 68 (2003).

90 Vitiello, "Three Strikes," 441; Zimring, Hawkins, and Kamin, *Punishment and Democracy*, 11.

91 Vitiello, "Three Strikes," 458 ("Identifying and incapacitating [habitual] offenders should result in meaningful reductions in crime").

92 See Zimring, Hawkins, and Kamin, *Punishment and Democracy*, 9.

93 Zimring, Hawkins, and Kamin, *Punishment and Democracy*, 91 (questioning whether the Three Strikes long imprisonment terms explain declines in crime in the first few years of the new legislation).

94 Vitiello, "Three Strikes," 443.

95 See generally Zimring, Hawkins, and Kamin, *Punishment and Democracy*. For a more detailed description of their study, see generally Vitiello, "Punishment and Democracy."

96 Zimring, Hawkins, and Kamin, *Punishment and Democracy*, 98; see Vitiello, "Punishment and Democracy," 278.

97 Zimring, Hawkins, and Kamin, *Punishment and Democracy*, 86.

98 See Zimring, Hawkins, and Kamin, *Punishment and Democracy*, 86–87.

99 See Zimring, Hawkins, and Kamin, *Punishment and Democracy*, 86.

100 See Zimring, Hawkins, and Kamin, *Punishment and Democracy*, 104.

101 Vitiello, "Punishment and Democracy," 270 (quoting Jon Hill, "Crime Stats Capture Both Arguments," *Contra Costa Times*, February 27, 2000).

102 Vitiello, "Punishment and Democracy," 269 (citing Bill Jones, "Why the Three Strikes Law Is Working in California," *Stanford Law & Policy Review* 11, no. 1 [Winter 1999]: 24).

103 See Franklin E. Zimring, *The City That Became Safe: New York's Lessons for Urban Crime and its Control* (New York: Oxford University Press, 2011).

104 Vitiello, "Punishment and Democracy," 270n71.

105 Vitiello, "Three Strikes," 419.

106 Vitiello, "Three Strikes," 435.

107 Vitiello, "Three Strikes," 436; see also 440–41 (explaining how warehousing older prisoners is especially costly).

108 Vitiello, "Three Strikes," 440–41.

109 Vitiello, "Three Strikes," 435.

110 Vitiello, "Three Strikes," 437n248.

111 Vitiello, "Three Strikes," 438–40 (explaining how Three Strikes would unfairly impact older offenders who no longer pose a serious threat to society but will be stuck in long prison terms after a nonviolent third strike offense).

112 For more information on the unique medical issues that face older prisoners, see Rachael Bedard, Lia Metzger, and Brie Williams, "Ageing Prisoners: An Introduction to Geriatric Health-Care Challenges in Correctional Facilities," *International Review of the Red Cross* 98, no. 3 (December 2016): 917–40, https://international-review.icrc.org.

113 See Vitiello, "Three Strikes," 459.

114 Vitiello, "Punishment and Democracy," 274.

115 See Zimring, Hawkins, and Kamin, *Punishment and Democracy*, 61 (highlighting further the impracticability of justifying long imprisonment sentences for older prisoners).

116 Cal. Penal Code § 12022.53 (1997).

117 Michael Vitiello and Clark Kelso, "A Proposal for a Wholesale Reform of California's Sentencing Practice and Policy," *Loyola of Los Angeles Law Review* 38, no. 2 (Winter 2004): 923, https://digitalcommons.lmu.edu (referencing the Placer Group's computer program, which guides judges and criminal law attorneys on appropriate sentencing enhancements).

118 Walter L. Gordon II, "California's Three Strikes Law: Tyranny of the Majority," *Whittier Law Review* 20, no. 3 (Spring 1999): 606 ("Prior to the passage of the three strikes bill, California planned to build twelve additional prisons by the year 2000 at the cost of $3 to $4 billion dollars. However, the new law changed these plans"); see also Prison Policy Initiative, "'Three Strikes' Laws: Five Years Later" (1999), 16, https://static.prisonpolicy.org ("The Justice Policy Institute reports that state bond expenditures in prison construction surpassed that for higher education in 1995, noting that from 1984–1992 spending per $1000 of personal income increased less than 1% for higher education while the increase for prisons was 47%").

119 "California: Trendsetter . . . as Always," *Prison Legal News*, August 24, 2016, www. prisonlegalnews.org.

120 Vitiello, "Three Strikes," 399 (citing Christopher Davis et al., "'Three Strikes': The New Apartheid 2" [Center on Juvenile and Criminal Justice, 1996]); Brian Brown and Greg Jolivette, "A Primer: Three Strikes—The Impact after More Than a Decade" (Legislative Analyst's Office, October 2005), https://lao.ca.gov; see Prison Policy Initiative, "'Three Strikes' Laws," 14.

121 Charlie Savage, "Trend to Lighten Harsh Sentences Catches on in Conservative States," *New York Times*, August 12, 2011, www.nytimes.com; e.g., Right on Crime, https://rightoncrime.com.

122 "California Guard Union Doles Out Millions to Politicians," *Prison Legal News*, August 15, 1999, 23, www.prisonlegalnews.org ("The CCPOA gave Davis more than $2 million in financial support through advertising, phone banks, and polling done on his behalf in the 1998 governor's campaign"). Davis would repay that support when he backed a 34 percent pay increase for prison guards in 2002. See "California: Trendsetter . . . as Always."

123 Vitiello, "Punishment and Democracy," 271.

124 Associated Press, "25 Years for a Slice of Pizza," *New York Times*, March 5, 1995, www.nytimes.com.

125 E.g., Vitiello, "Three Strikes and the Romero Case," 1648 ("Defendant Jesus Romero's third strike was the charge of possession of 0.13 grams of cocaine base"); e.g., Ina Jaffe, "A Mother's Fight Against 3 Strikes Law 'A Way of Life,'" *NPR*, April 10, 2013, www.npr.org ("[Shane Reams] got his third strike for being involved in the sale of a $20 rock of cocaine").

126 David Kohn, "Three Strikes," *CBS News*, October 28, 2002, www.cbsnews.com.

127 See Vitiello, "Three Strikes," 457.

128 See "Why '3 Strikes' Needs Reform," editorial, *SF Gate*, September 19, 2004, www. sfgate.com; see also Carla Bare, "Proposition 66: Fixing the Flaw" (paper, n.d.), 5, https://paperzz.com; see also Page, *Toughest Beat*, 123.

129 Marsy's Law, "About Marsy's Law" (2022), www.marsyslaw.us.

130 Bare, "Proposition 66," 7; see also Page, *Toughest Beat*, 131.

131 Staff, "Romero, Cooley Heading for Another Try on Three Strikes," *Capitol Weekly*, July 27, 2006, https://capitolweekly.net.

132 Michael Vitiello, "California's Three Strikes and We're Out: Was Judicial Activism California's Best Hope," *U.C. Davis Law Review* 37, no. 4 (April 2004): 1029, https://scholarlycommons.pacific.edu.

133 *Andrade v. Att'y Gen. of Cal.*, 270 F.3d 743 (2001); *Ewing v. California*, 538 U.S. 11 (2003).

134 *In re Cervera*, 16 P.3d 176 (Cal. 2001).

135 *People v. Superior Court (Romero)*, 917 P.3d 628, 635 (Cal. 1996) (". . . to require the prosecutor's consent to the disposition of a criminal charge pending before the court unacceptably compromises judicial independence"). See also Vitiello, "Three Strikes and the Romero Case," 1651.

136 See Legislative Analyst's Office, "Proposition 36" (2000), https://lao.ca.gov.

137 See Ballotpedia, "California Proposition 47, Reduced Penalties for Some Crimes Initiative (2014)" (n.d.), https://ballotpedia.org.

138 E.g., Ballotpedia, "California Proposition 36, Changes to Three Strikes Sentencing Initiative (2012)" (n.d.), https://ballotpedia.org.

139 Ballotpedia, "California Proposition 36."

140 Chris Micheli, "The California Law Review Commission," *California Globe*, July 11, 2020, https://californiaglobe.com.

141 Michael Romano, LinkedIn profile, www.linkedin.com/in/michael-romano-2773301/.

142 Public Safety: Omnibus, SB 94, 2019–2020 Reg. Sess., chap. 25, Cal. Stat.

143 See Don Thompson, "California Panel Urges Changes to Reduce Criminal Sentences," *AP News*, February 9, 2021, https://apnews.com.

144 Thompson, "California Panel Urges Changes."

145 California Law Review Commission, "Committee on Revision of the Penal Code: Annual Report and Recommendations" (February 2021), www.clrc.ca.gov; California State Association of Counties, "Administration of Justice Policy Committee Meeting Minutes" (November 16, 2020), www.counties.org.

146 See California Law Review Commission, "Committee on Revision of the Penal Code," 44 ("Over 98% of people sentenced to prison for a gang enhancement in Los Angeles are people of color").

147 Byrhonda Lyons, "Criminal Justice Reform Panel Scores Legislative Wins," *CalMatters*, updated October 9, 2021, https://calmatters.org.

148 See generally California Law Review Commission, "Committee on Revision of the Penal Code," 3.

149 California Law Review Commission, "Committee on Revision of the Penal Code," 47 ("Eliminating or substantially limiting the use of the Three Strikes law would recognize the law's failure to make California safer and would be a significant step towards reducing racial disparities in our criminal legal system").

150 "Proposed Initiative Would Repeal Three Strikes Sentencing Law."

151 Death Penalty Information Center, "California Penal Code Committee Recommends Repealing State's Death Penalty" (November 23, 2021), https://deathpenaltyinfo.org.

152 See California Law Review Commission, "Committee on Revision of the Penal Code," 3.

153 E.g., California Law Review Commission, "Committee on Revision of the Penal Code" (relying on data collected by the California Policy Lab to substantiate the committee's recommendations).

154 As is evident in the discussion of Three Strikes, the democratic process does not work well when public passions override sound policy choices. Without restraints, legislators have little accountability for the long-term costs of incarceration but may gain short-term public support. For a fuller discussion of this point, see Zimring, Hawkins, and Kamin, *Punishment and Democracy*. In addition, as Professor David Ball has demonstrated, at least in California, county prosecutors could appeal to local voters on get-tough-on-crime policies without much effect on local government. As long as the state paid for the prison system, local politicians, in effect, received a subsidy that allowed overreliance on incarceration in prison as a first option to deal with crime. See W. David Ball, "Tough on Crime (on the State's Dime): How Violent Crime Does Not Drive California Counties' Incarceration Rates—And Why it Should," *Georgia State University Law Review* 28, no. 4 (Summer 2012): 994.

155 SB 180.

156 SB 620.

157 AB 3105.

158 Vitiello and Kelso, "Proposal for a Wholesale Reform," 923 (citing Judicial Council of California, "1983 Annual Report" [1983], 7, www.ojp.gov).

159 E.g., Julian Glover, "Santa Clara Co. Sees Spike in Fentanyl Overdose Deaths during Pandemic," *ABC News*, September 1, 2021, https://abc7news.com; Ema Sasic, "Fentanyl Overdoses, Deaths Are Up in Riverside County. Many Don't Know They've Taken It," *Desert Sun*, July 30, 2021, www.desertsun.com; Tony Botti, "Beware of Potentially Fatal Fentanyl Pills Disguised as Xanax" (Fresno County Sheriff's Office, May 13, 2020), www.fresnosheriff.org.

160 The Drug Policy Alliance raised similar concerns in its report. Michael Collins and Sheila P. Vakhari, "Criminal Justice Reform in the Fentanyl Era: One Step Forward, Two Steps Back" (Drug Policy Alliance, January 2020), https://drug-policy.org.

161 E.g., Kaitlin S. Phillips, "From Overdose to Crime Scene: The Incompatibility of Drug-Induced Homicide Statutes with Due Process," *Duke Law Journal* 70, no. 3 (December 2020): 661 (convicting the defendant, Jarret McCasland, under a Louisiana drug-induced homicide statute rather than a traditional homicide crime).

162 The bill simply states that "every person who transports, imports into this state, sells, furnishes, administers, or gives away, or offers to transport, import into this state, sell, furnish, administer, or give away, or attempts to import into this state or transport (1) any controlled substance . . . , or (2) any controlled substance classified in Schedule III, IV, or V which is a narcotic drug, . . . shall be punished by imprisonment . . . for three, four, or five years." AB 3105. The language of the bill

does not expressly indicate that the offender must know that the drug contains fentanyl. Furthermore, the state legislature has emphasized that fentanyl trafficking cases are notoriously difficult to prosecute partly due to fentanyl manufacturers deliberately manipulating the chemical structures of the synthetic drug to avoid detection. This could suggest that the bill does not require prosecutors to prove that the defendant knew that the drug contained fentanyl in light of these difficulties. Moreover, the bill only touches on the event of death or great bodily injury triggering the punishment, not on whether the offender knew that there was a risk of death when using the drug. AB 3105.

163 Vitiello, "Three Strikes," 462 (citing Bill Ainsworth, "A Marriage of Convenience; Powerful Victims' Rights Groups Have Found a Financial Backer That Also Wants More People Behind Bars—Prison Guards," *Recorder*, November 30, 1994).

164 E.g., "Public Safety United in Opposition to Prop 57," *911 Media*, n.d., https://911media.com; see Walker Bragman and Andrew Perez, "A Prison Guard Union Is Trying to Unseat a California Criminal Justice Reformer," *Jacobin*, October 15, 2020, https://jacobinmag.com.

165 See Jerry Iannelli, "California Prosecutors' Association Reveals More Public Money May Have Been Misspent," *The Appeal*, March 5, 2021, https://theappeal.org (explaining the CDAA's deterioration from former CDAA leaders, such as George Gascón, forming the Prosecutors Alliance of California (PAC) and its opposition to PAC's efforts, including submitting an amicus brief supporting a lawsuit against Gascón's proposed justice reforms in Los Angeles County).

166 See Tana Ganeva, "Conservative District Attorney Slams Progressive DAs—Even as Her Own City Drowns in Crime," *Substance: Drugs and Crime*, January 17, 2022, https://tanag.substack.com.

167 As I complete this chapter during the spring of 2022, shootings in Sacramento, including one mass shooting downtown, are making headlines. E.g., Vicki Gonzalez, "Interview: Police Chief Kathy Lester Discusses Gun Violence, Downtown Sacramento Shooting," *Cap Radio*, April 13, 2022, www.capradio.org. Predictably, some politicians, especially Republicans in the California legislature, are questioning recent progressive reforms.

8. WHAT SHOULD WE DO IF WE REALLY WANT TO HELP VICTIMS?

1 Prominent victims' rights advocate and professor Paul Cassell captured this idea in the title of one of his articles on victims' rights: Paul G. Cassell, "Barbarians at the Gates? A Reply to the Critics of the Victims' Rights Amendment," *Utah Law Review* 479, no. 2 (1999): 479–543, https://papers.ssrn.com. At least in his mind, many VRM critics see members of the VRM as unworthy adversaries. One can easily find more extreme examples, including instances when Judge Aaron Persky, of the Brock Turner sexual assault case, received death threats after imposing what was believed to be a woefully inadequate sentence on Turner. Dan Whitcomb, "Judge in Stanford Rape Case Receives Death Threats Amid Recall Efforts," Reuters, June 8, 2016, www.reuters.com.

2 Many critics of the VRM, including me, have empathy for victims and, as developed in this chapter, believe that more effective remedies are available to help victims (and victims defined broadly).

3 Even if this chapter's recommendations were followed universally, some individuals would still become victims.

4 A recent example is the GOP's response to the Buffalo shooting: "In the days since the shooting, some Republicans opposing calls for gun reform have voiced support for measures focused on mental health." Aris Folley, "Senate GOP Resist Calls for Gun Control after Buffalo Shooting," *Hill*, May 18, 2022, https://thehill.com.

5 Cathy S. Widom and Michael G. Maxfield, "An Update on the 'Cycle of Violence'" (National Institute of Justice: Research in Brief, February 2001), www.ojp.gov.

6 Patient Protection and Affordable Care Act, Pub. L. No. 111–148 (2010). Selena Simmons-Duffin, "12 Holdout States Haven't Expanded Medicaid, Leaving 2 Million People in Limbo," *NPR*, July 1, 2021, www.npr.org.

7 RAND Corporation, "The Relationship between Firearm Availability and Suicide" (Gun Policy in America, March 2, 2018), www.rand.org.

8 Pew Research Center, "Key Facts about Americans and Guns" (September 13, 2021), www.pewresearch.org; John Bowden, "2 in 3 Support Stricter Gun Control Laws," *Hill*, April 14, 2021, https://thehill.com.

9 At one time, Remington was operated as a limited liability company. It filed for Chapter 11 bankruptcy protection in 2018 and again in 2020. In the latter proceeding, its assets were sold to various purchasers. Currently, two companies use the Remington name. Brakkton Booker, "Remington Gun-Maker Files for Bankruptcy Protection for 2nd Time since 2018," *NPR*, July 28, 2020, www.npr.org.

10 Andrew Solomon, "The Reckoning: The Father of the Sandy Hook Killer Searches for Answers," *New Yorker*, March 10, 2014, www.newyorker.com.

11 Solomon, "Reckoning."

12 Office of Governor Ned Lamont, "Governor Lamont Directs Flag to Half-Staff Tuesday for the Anniversary of the Tragedy in Newtown" (press release, December 13, 2021), https://portal.ct.gov.

13 Liz Goodwin, "Sandy Hook Report: Shooter's Mom Wanted to Buy Him Gun for Christmas," *Yahoo! News*, November 25, 2013, https://sports.yahoo.com.

14 Doug Stanglin, "Adam Lanza's Mom Was Alarmed by His Gruesome Images," *USA Today*, April 8, 2013, www.usatoday.com.

15 Solomon, "Reckoning."

16 Solomon, "Reckoning."

17 Douglas E. Beloof, Paul G. Cassell, Meg Garvin, and Steven J. Twist, "Defining the 'Victim,'" in *Victims in Criminal Procedure* (Durham, NC: Carolina Academic Press, 2018), 45–107.

18 Widom and Maxfield, "Update on the 'Cycle of Violence.'"

19 Treatment Advocacy Center, "Serious Mental Illness and Mass Homicide" (June 2018), www.treatmentadvocacycenter.org.

20 Brandon L. Garrett, "Mercy v. Justice," in *End of Its Rope: How Killing the Death Penalty Can Revive Criminal Justice* (Cambridge, MA: Harvard University Press, 2017), 49–78.

21 Kurt Freund, Robin Batson, and Robert Dickey, "Does Sexual Abuse in Childhood Cause Pedophilia: An Exploratory Study," *Archives of Sexual Behavior* 19, no. 6 (December 1990): 557–68.

22 Pew Research Center, "Key Facts about Americans and Guns"; Victor Agbafe, "The Vast Majority of Americans Support Universal Background Checks. Why Doesn't Congress?" (Harvard Kennedy School Institute of Politics, n.d.), https://iop.harvard.edu.

23 For example, the NRA's Institute for Legislative Action's website contends that the NRA's long-standing position has been for an improved mental health care system. National Rifle Association, Institute for Legislative Action, "Mental Health and Firearms" (January 24, 2013), www.nraila.org.

24 A. J. Willingham, "At Its First Meeting after Parkland, the NRA Draws Attention to Mass Shootings," *CNN*, May 2018, www.cnn.com.

25 Willingham, "At Its First Meeting after Parkland, the NRA Draws Attention to Mass Shootings."

26 Hefei Wen, Jason M. Hockenberry, and Janet R. Cummings, "The Effect of Substance Use Disorder Treatment Use on Crime: Evidence from Public Insurance Expansions and Health Insurance Parity Mandates" (National Bureau of Economic Research, Working Paper 20537, 2014).

27 Erkmen G. Aslim, Murat C. Mungan, Carlos I. Navarro, and Han Yu, "The Effect of Public Health Insurance on Criminal Recidivism" (George Mason University Law & Economics Research Paper Series, 2019).

28 Franklin E. Zimring and Gordon Hawkins, *Incapacitation: Penal Confinement and the Restraint of Crime* (New York: Oxford University Press, 1995), 85–86.

29 Wen, Hockenberry, and Cummings, "Effect of Substance Use Disorder," 9.

30 Jennifer L. Doleac, "New Evidence That Access to Health Care Reduces Crime" (Brookings Institute, January 3, 2018), www.brookings.edu.

31 Monica Deza, Johanna Catherine Maclean, and Keisha T. Solomon, "Local Access to Mental Healthcare and Crime" (National Bureau of Economic Research, Working Paper 27619, 2020), 19, www.nber.org.

32 Hefei Wen, Jason M. Hockenberry, and Janet R. Cummings, "The Effect of Medicaid Expansion on Crime Reduction: Evidence from HIFA-Waiver Expansions," *Journal of Public Economics* 154 (2017): 79.

33 Jacob Vogler, "Access to Healthcare and Criminal Behavior: Evidence from the ACA Medicaid Expansions," *Journal of Policy Analysis and Management* 39, no. 4 (Fall 2020): 1184.

34 Vogler, "Access to Healthcare and Criminal Behavior," 1188.

35 Elisa Jácome, "How Better Access to Mental Health Care Can Reduce Care" (Stanford Institute for Economic Policy Research, July 2021), https://siepr.stanford.edu.

36 John Gramlich, "What We Know about the Increase in U.S. Murders in 2020" (Pew Research Center, October 27, 2021), www.pewresearch.org.

37 World Health Organization, "COVID-19 Disrupting Mental Health Services in Most Countries, WHO Survey" (October 5, 2020), www.who.int.

38 Azza Altiraifi and Nicole Rapfogel, "Mental Health Case Was Severely Inequitable, Then Came the Coronavirus" (Center for American Progress, September 10, 2020), www.americanprogress.org.

39 Kristina Lugo and Roger Przybylski, "Estimating the Financial Costs of Crime Victimization" (Justice Research and Statistics Association, December 2018), www.ojp.gov.

40 A victim in California, for example, can receive help in the form of mental health services, safety net services, and assistance through the California Victim Compensation Board for crime-related expenses. State of California Department of Justice, "Victims' Services Unit" (2022), https://oag.ca.gov. California provides financial help to victims of over twenty different categories of crime. North Carolina, on the other hand, provides compensation only to victims of rape, assault, child sexual assault, domestic violence, drunk driving, and homicide. North Carolina Department of Public Safety, "Victim Services" (2022), www.ncdps.gov.

41 Chapter 2 discussed the VRM's success in getting the federal government and many states to provide funds for victims beyond health. For example, states often provide for funding for pecuniary losses, beyond medical care. As with health care provided by such funds, coverage varies and may not be provided for many individuals in need. Some injured Americans already receive coverage under federal Social Security Disability Insurance. Social Security Administration, "Part I—General Information" (2022), www.ssa.gov. Those benefits are limited not only to whom they apply to but also to the kinds and duration of injuries sustained. Social Security Administration, "How We Decide if You Have a Qualifying Disability" (2022), www.ssa.gov. Many states also have such insurance programs. Society for Human Resource Management, "Which States Require Employers to Have a Short-Term Disability Plan?" (February 11, 2022), https://sts.shrm.org. Unifying and expanding such coverage would also provide more victims the help that they need.

42 National Rifle Association, Institute for Legislative Action, "Mental Health and Firearms."

43 National Rifle Association, Institute for Legislative Action, "What Is the Second Amendment and How Is It Defined" (2022), www.nraila.org (describing that the Second Amendment's reference to "a well-regulated militia" is in reference to the populace as a whole, thereby entitling every citizen to a gun and the ensuing rights to use that gun in certain circumstances).

44 National Rifle Association, Institute for Legislative Action, "Mental Health and Firearms."

45 National Alliance on Mental Illness, "The NRA's Rhetoric Is No Commitment to Mental Health (October 2, 2013), www.nami.org.

46 National Alliance on Mental Illness, "NRA's Rhetoric Is No Commitment to Mental Health."

47 National Alliance on Mental Health, "Crisis Response for Mental Health" (2022), www.nami.org.

48 National Alliance on Mental Illness, "NRA's Rhetoric Is No Commitment to Mental Health."

49 Kaiser Family Foundation, "Status of State Medicaid Expansion Decisions: Interactive Map" (April 26, 2022), www.kff.org; Jennifer Liberto, "NRA Power and Money Goes a Long Way in States," *CNN Business*, December 20, 2012, https:// money.cnn.com.

50 Jennifer Rubin, "Opinion: Living in Red America Can Be Life-Threatening," *Washington Post*, March 17, 2020, www.washingtonpost.com.

51 Alan Judd, "NRA Push on Mental Health: Solution or Diversion?," *Atlanta Journal-Constitution*, November 28, 2014, www.ajc.com.

52 Solomon, "Reckoning."

53 Anthony A. Braga and Philip J. Cook, "Guns Do Kill People," *Regulatory Review*, November 5, 2018, www.theregreview.org.

54 Willingham, "At Its First Meeting after Parkland, the NRA Draws Attention to Mass Shootings."

55 Angela Stroud, "Guns Don't Kill People . . . : Good Guys and the Legitimization of Gun Violence," *Humanities and Social Sciences Communications* 7, no. 169 (December 2020), www.nature.com. That such dogma is almost messianic is not hyperbole. See Peter Manseau, "The Myth of 'Good Guy with a Gun' Has Religious Roots," *New York Times*, June 23, 2022, www.nytimes.com.

56 "US Gun Control: What Is the NRA and Why Is It So Powerful?," *BBC News*, August 6, 2020, www.bbc.com. A measure of that outsized influence can be seen in polling data after a spate of mass shootings during 2022. Even some gun control measures opposed by the NRA have support from a majority of Republicans. Rani Molla, "Polling Is Clear: Americans Want Gun Control," *Vox*, June 1, 2022, www. vox.com. Despite broad public support, legislative reforms are hard-fought and seldom won.

57 Bipartisan Safer Communities Act of 2022, Pub. L. No. 117–159, 136 Stat. 1313 (2022); Chip Brownlee and Tom Kutsch, "What You Need to Know about the Senate Gun Reform Bill," *Trace*, June 24, 2022, www.thetrace.org.

58 John R. Lott Jr., "Background and History" (2022), www.johnrlott.com.

59 John R. Lott Jr., *More Guns Less Crime: Understanding Crime and Gun Control Laws* (Chicago: University of Chicago Press, 1998); John R. Lott Jr., *Gun Control Myths: How Politicians, the Media, and Botched "Studies" Have Twisted the Facts on Gun Control* (Independently published, 2020); John R. Lott Jr., *The War on Guns: Arming Yourself Against Gun Control Lies* (Washington, DC: Regnery, 2016).

60 Lott, *More Guns Less Crime*, 190.

61 National Research Council of the National Academies, *Firearms and Violence: A Critical Review* (Washington, DC: National Academies Press, 2005), 269.

62 David Hemenway, review of *The Bias Against Guns: Why Almost Everything You've Heard about Gun Control Is Wrong,* by John Lott Jr. (Harvard School of Public Health, 2003), www.hsph.harvard.edu.

63 Ian Ayres and John J. Donohue III, "Shooting Down the 'More Guns, Less Crime' Hypothesis," *Stanford Law Review* 55, no. 4 (April 2003): 1193.

64 Evan DeFilippis and Devin Hughes, "The Bogus Claims of the NRA's Favorite Social Scientist, Debunked," *Vox,* August 30, 2016, www.vox.com.

65 Samantha Raphelson, "How Often Do People Use Guns in Self Defense?," *NPR,* April 13, 2018, www.npr.org.

66 Rand Corporation, "Effects of Concealed-Carry Laws on Violent Crime" (updated April 22, 2020), www.rand.org.

67 Sripal Bangalore and Franz H. Messerli, "Gun Ownership and Firearm-Related Deaths," *American Journal of Medicine* 126, no. 10 (October 2013): 873–76, www.amjmed.com.

68 Flemish Peace Institute, "Firearms and Deaths by Firearms" (June 2015), https://vlaamsvredesinstituut.eu.

69 Susan Gluss, "'It's No Secret.' Prof. Zimring on How Weapons Fuel America's Mass Shootings," *Berkeley Law,* August 13, 2019, www.law.berkeley.edu.

70 Franklin E. Zimring and Gordon Hawkins, *Crime Is Not the Problem: Lethal Violence in America* (Oxford: Oxford University Press, 1997).

71 Gluss, "'It's No Secret.'"

72 John Gramlich, "What the Data Says about Gun Deaths in the U.S." (Pew Research Center, February 3, 2022), www.pewresearch.org.

73 Gramlich, "What the Data Says about Gun Deaths in the U.S."

74 Giffords Law Center, "Domestic Violence & Firearms" (2022), https://giffords.org.

75 David M. Studdert et al., "Homicide Deaths among Adult Cohabitants of Handgun Owners in California, 2004 to 2016," *Annals of Internal Medicine,* April 5, 2022.

76 Studdert et al., "Homicide Deaths among Adult Cohabitants."

77 Studdert et al., "Homicide Deaths among Adult Cohabitants."

78 Gramlich, "What the Data Says about Gun Deaths in the U.S."

79 Gramlich, "What the Data Says about Gun Deaths in the U.S."

80 Brady: United Against Gun Violence, "Uncovering the Truth about Pennsylvania Crime Guns" (2022), www.bradyunited.org.

81 Brady Handgun Violence Protection Act, Pub. L. No. 103–159, 107 Stat. 1536 (1993).

82 National Rifle Association, "An Award-Winning Crime Prevention Program," *NRAExplore: Discover the Possibilities* (2022), https://rtbav.nra.org; National Rifle Association, Institute for Legislative Action, "About the NRA Institute for Legislative Action" (2022), www.nraila.org.

83 Sheryl Gay Stolberg, "Why the N.R.A. Opposes New Domestic Abuse Legislation," *New York Times,* April 1, 2019, www.nytimes.com.

84 Studdert et al., "Homicide Deaths among Adult Cohabitants."

85 For example, an organization like Brady: United Against Gun Violence, formed after John Hinckley Jr.'s failed assassination of President Reagan, is a victims'

rights organization, which is obviously at odds with the NRA. But major VRM organizations like the NRA and, in California, the California Correctional Peace Officers Association are strong gun rights supporters. Connor D. Wolf, "Largest California Police Union Joins Opposition to Gun Restriction Bill," *Daily Caller*, May 9, 2016, https://dailycaller.com.

86 Aaron Blake, "Manchin-Toomey Gun Amendment Fails," *Washington Post*, April 17, 2013, www.washingtonpost.com.

87 Jonathan Weisman, "Senate Blocks Drive for Gun Control," *New York Times*, April 17, 2013, www.nytimes.com.

88 Patricia Zengerle, Dan Burns, and Edith Honan, "NRA Calls for Armed School Guards as U.S. Mourns Massacre," Reuters, December 21, 2012, www.reuters.com.

89 Meghan Keneally, "How Gun Laws Have Changed in the 5 Years since Sandy Hook," *ABC News*, December 12, 2017, https://abcnews.go.com.

90 Libby Cathey, "Why the Second Amendment May Be Losing Relevance in Gun Debate," *ABC News*, October 28, 2013, https://abcnews.go.com.

91 As this book was nearing print in 2022, Congress did enact a modest gun control bill. The new law received tepid support from gun control advocates. For example, it did little to address access to automatic weapons. See Brownlee and Kutsch, "What You Need to Know about the Senate Gun Reform Bill."

92 Alex Putterman, "Connecticut Gun Control Advocates Cheer $73 Million Settlement between Remington and Sandy Hook Families," *Hartford Courant*, February 15, 2022, www.courant.com.

93 Champe Barton, "The Sandy Hook Lawsuit Against Remington Is Over," *The Trace*, February 15, 2022, www.thetrace.org.

94 Protection of Lawful Commerce in Arms Act, Pub. L. Law No. 109-92 (2005).

95 Protection of Lawful Commerce in Arms Act.

96 Barton, "Sandy Hook Lawsuit Against Remington is Over"; *Britannica*, s.v. "The Aftermath of Sandy Hook and the Legislative Response" (December 14, 2012), www.britannica.com.

97 Brian Doherty, "Gun-Maker Remington Settles with Sandy Hook Families over Alleged Liability for Misuse of Weapon They Made," *Reason*, February 15, 2022, https://reason.com.

98 Michael Marshall, "The Second Amendment Is about an Individual Right, Not a Collective One" (University of Virginia, School of Law, February 8, 2002), www.law.virginia.edu; German Lopez, "How the NRA Resurrected the Second Amendment," *Vox*, May 4, 2018, www.vox.com.

99 For a discussion of the NRA's role in pushing for an expanded reading of the Second Amendment, see Lopez, "How the NRA Resurrected the Second Amendment."

100 *United States v. Miller*, 307 U.S. 174 (1939); Brian L. Frye, "The Peculiar Story of United States v. Miller," *NYU Journal of Law & Liberty* 3, no. 1 (2008): 48–82.

101 Eric Posner, "The Tragedy of Antonin Scalia," *Slate*, February 15, 2016, https://slate.com.

102 Saul Cornell, "Originalism on Trial: The Use and Abuse of History in District of Columbia v. Heller," *Ohio State Law Journal* 69, no. 4 (2008): 625–40.

103 *District of Columbia v. Heller*, 554 U.S. 570, 626 (2008).

104 *Heller*, 626–27.

105 Nina Totenberg, "From 'Fraud' to Individual Right, Where Does the Supreme Court Stand on Guns?," *NPR*, March 5, 2018, www.npr.org; Eric Ruben, "What the Supreme Court's Latest Second Amendment Ruling Means for Future Cases" (Brennan Center for Justice, May 1, 2020), www.brennancenter.org.

106 *McDonald v. Chicago*, 561 U.S. 742 (2010).

107 Darrel A. H. Miller, "The Second Amendment and Second-Class Rights," *Harvard Law Review Blog*, March 5, 2018, https://blog.harvardlawreview.org.

108 See, e.g., *Silvester v. Becerra*, 138 S. Ct. 945 (2018). There, Thomas argued that the Court was treating the Second Amendment as a second-class constitutional right. Some commentators have rebutted the claim that gun rights are treated as second-class rights. Eric Ruben and Joseph Blocher, "No, Courts Don't Treat the Second Amendment as a 'Second Class' Right" (Brennan Center for Justice, November 18, 2021), www.brennancenter.org.

109 *New York State Rifle & Pistol Association, Inc. v. Bruen*, No. 20–843, slip opinion (S. Ct., June 23, 2022).

110 *Bruen*, slip opinion at 62.

111 *Bruen*, slip opinion at 30.

112 *Bruen*, slip opinion at 21.

113 *Bruen*, slip opinion, Kavanaugh, J.'s concurrence at 2.

114 *National Rifle Association of America, Inc. v. ATF*, 700 F.3d 185 (5th Cir. 2012) (holding that a federal law banning the sale of handguns to those under the age of twenty-one did not violate the Second Amendment because Congress demonstrated that handguns in the hands of those under twenty-one led to an increase in violence and because the burden placed on those under twenty-one was not significant since they could be given a gun in the home by a responsible family member); *United States v. Staten*, 666 F.3d 154 (4th Cir. 2011) (holding that a law preventing those convicted of domestic violence from possessing firearms was constitutional because the government had a strong interest in reducing domestic gun violence). Such balancing of state versus individual interest involving other constitutional rights is hardly unique.

115 *Bruen*, slip opinion at 10.

116 *Bruen*, slip opinion, Breyer, J.'s dissent at 5.

117 "Brief of the States of Louisiana, Arizona, Montana, and Eighteen Other States as *Amici Curiae* in Support of Certiorari," *Young v. Hawaii*, No. 20–1639, www.texasattorneygeneral.gov.

118 Center for American Progress, "Frequently Asked Questions about Gun Industry Immunity" (May 4, 2021), www.americanprogress.org.

INDEX

AB 971. *See* Three Strikes Law, California
ACA (Affordable Care Act), 150–51, 153
Adam Walsh Child Protection and Safety
    Act, 2006, 15
Affordable Care Act (ACA), 150–51, 153
Agnew, Spiro, 12, 35, 180n21
Alaska, statute of limitations in, 67
Alford plea bargain, 193n85
ALI (American Law Institute), 2–3, 28
American Beverage Institute, 21
American Law Institute (ALI), 2–3, 28
Americans for Effective Law Enforce-
    ment, 11, 51
America's Most Wanted, 171n35
Anger and Forgiveness (Nussbaum), 47
Anti-Sexual Assault Movement, 28
Appleton, Ray, 125
Aquilina, Rosemarie, 91, 102, 104
Ardaiz, James, 125
Arizona, 38
Armaly, Miles, 35–36
Armed Career Criminal Act, 214n198
Armour, Marilyn, 103–4
Atlanta Journal-Constitution, 153–54
attempt liability, 100
Ayres, Ian, 155

background check expansion legislation, 159
bail reform, 13
Baker, Katherine, 74
Baldus, David, 113–15
Ball, David, 228n154
Bandes, Susan, 73, 101–2, 168n12
Bankhead, Teiahsha, 172n51
basic fairness: victim impact statements
    and, 92–93, 107; VRM and, 24–26
Bazelon, Lara, 42
Bean v. Thomas, 207n99

Beazley, Napoleon, 89, 111–12, 116
Bentham, Jeremy, 117
Berk, Richard, 115
Betts v. Brady, 60
Biden, Joe, 1
Black, Hugo, 60
Blackmun, Harry, 52
blameworthiness: criminal law and, 94;
    sentencing and, 86; victim impact
    statements and, 86, 93
bodily injury, sentencing and, 96–97
Booth v. Maryland, 84–87, 90, 99, 203n16
Boston Globe, 68–69
Boston Marathon attack, 103, 105
Boy Scouts of America, 65, 69
Brady Bill, 23, 158
Brady: United Against Gun Violence, 158,
    234n85
Brennan, William, 86
Brennan Center for Justice, 118, 218n266
Brewer v. Williams, 54
Breyer, Stephen, 162
Brown, Jerry, 139
Brown, Michael, 62
Brown, Willie, 167n9, 223n59
Buchhandler-Raphael, Michal, 184n104
Buffalo shooting, 2022, 230n4
Burger, Warren, 12, 52, 57
burglary, as qualifying felony under Three
    Strikes Law, 131–32, 137, 224n86
Bush, George H. W., 1, 167n5
Bush, George W., 15, 159

California, 3; Committee on Revision
    of the Penal Code in, 140–42, 144,
    178n41; on felony murder, 98; fentanyl
    abuse in, 143–44, 228n162; intoxication
    and sexual assault in, 184n104;

California (*cont.*)
  mass incarceration in, 128, 219n1;
  prison construction plans in, 226n118;
  Proposition 9, 16; Proposition 36 in, 140;
  Proposition 47 in, 140; Proposition 66
  in, 128; sentencing in, 119, 141–44; statute
  of limitations in, 67; victim compensation funds in, 29, 232n40; victimhood
  definition in, 37; Victims' Bill of Rights
  in, 25–26. *See also* Three Strikes Law
California Correctional Peace Officers
  Association (CCPOA), 10, 17–18, 123,
  127–28, 144, 170n13, 218n263, 226n122
California District Attorneys Association,
  129
California Victim Compensation Board
  (CalVCB), 29, 232n40
capital punishment. *See* death penalty
"carceral state," 3
Carrington, Frank, 1, 5, 10, 25, 35, 123;
  Americans for Effective Law Enforcement formed by, 11, 51; Crime Victims'
  Legal Advocacy Institute, Inc. founded
  by, 13; on death penalty, 109, 186n4;
  on expertise, 128–29; on *Miranda v.*
  Arizona, 51; Silent Majority and, 12, 35,
  129; VRM's early days and, 11–13, 51; on
  Warren Court, 49, 60, 64, 107
Cassell, Paul, 4, 16, 54–55, 101, 170n27; on
  basic fairness, 107; on sentencing, 108–9;
  on victim impact statements, 88–91, 93,
  103, 107, 108–9, 204n49; on VRM critics,
  229n1
Catholic priests, 65, 68–69
CCPOA (California Correctional Peace Officers Association), 10, 17–18, 123, 127–28,
  144, 170n13, 218n263, 226n122
central details, memory and, 75
Chiampou, Ken, 129
child sex abuse, 18; Boy Scouts of America
  and claims of, 69; by Catholic priests,
  68–69; feminists and panic on, 174n77;
  statute of limitations in cases on, 66–67
Civil Rights Movement, 34
Clinton, Bill, 2, 21, 35, 171n47
"closure": anecdotal support for, 102–3;
  meaning of, 102; myth of, 5, 103–4; objections to concept of, 101–2; restorative
  justice and, 212n163; statute of limitations and re-evaluation of, 72–73; statute
  of limitations expansion for, 70; victimhood and, 48; victim impact statements
  for, 90–92, 101–6, 205n59
Cochran, Johnnie, 139
Collateral Damage (Humane Justice), 46
colonial America, criminal justice system
  in, 24
Committee on Revision of the Penal Code,
  California, 140–42, 144, 178n41
common law, in England, 94
Commonwealth v. Berkowitz, 77
Confrontation Clause, victim impact statements and, 88
Connecticut, statute of limitations in, 67
consent: burden of proving, 19; by jurisdiction, 199n72; mens rea and, 78; "self-
  deception" and, 199n64; signaling lack
  of, 206n75
Conservative Movement, victimhood and,
  32–36. *See also* law-and-order conservatives
constitutional amendment, VRM's aim of,
  4, 9, 82
The Contradictions of American Capital
  Punishment (Zimring), 102
Cooley, Steve, 139
Cooper v. Brown, 79
correlations, multicollinearity and, 114
Cosby, Bill, 5, 65–66, 195n3; lawyers
  retained by, 195n9; sexual assault cases
  against, 70
counsel, right to, 61–63, 107, 192n82
COVID-19 pandemic, 69, 151
crime, societal costs of, 29
Crime Is Not the Problem (Zimring and
  Hawkins), 156
crime rates: gun rights advocates and, 155,
  157; mental health and, 149–52; right-to-
  carry laws and, 155; Three Strikes Law
  and, 134–36
Crime Victim Rights and Remedies, 84, 110
Crime Victims' Legal Advocacy Institute,
  Inc., 13
Crime Victims' Rights Act, 2004, 26

Criminal Justice Legal Foundation, 115
criminal justice system: bail reform and, 13; basic fairness in, 24–26; blameworthiness and, 94; in colonial America, 24; evolution of, 50; forgiveness and, 47–48; guilty pleas by innocent defendants in, 62; healing and, 41–42; politics of, 130; racial bias in, 3–4; rape victims ignored by, 2; right to counsel in, 61–63, 107, 192n82; VRM on rebalancing, 13
criminal law: ALI professionalizing, 2–3; attempt liability and, 100; blameworthiness and, 94; common law and, 94; culpability and punishment in, 95–96, 98, 100–101; guilt beyond reasonable doubt in, 96, 185n110, 200n78, 202n103; liberty and, 96; modern, 97–99; principle of lenity and, 96; principles of, 95; social harm and, 96–97; tort law and, 94
criminal procedure revolution, of Warren Court, 49, 51, 60
critical race theory, 33
cruel and unusual punishment, 111–12
Cruel Justice (Domanick), 222n40, 223n59
culpability: felony murder and, 98, 207n107, 208n120; MPC and, 97–98; punishment and, 95–96, 98, 100–101; statute of limitations and, 70, 73–75; Supreme Court on, 97
Cuomo, Andrew, 35

Dauber, Michele, 44, 46
Davis, Gray, 138, 139, 226n122
Davis, Joe, 125
Davis, Richard Allen, 126
death penalty: Carrington on, 109, 186n4; cruel and unusual punishment and, 111–12; distinction of, 205n64; family members opposing, 105; healing and, 104; mock jury research on victim impact statements and, 111; racial bias and, 113–16; Supreme Court on, 84–87; victim impact statements and, 108–12
Deise, Jerome, 111
democracy, punishment and, 117–20, 228n154

Democrat Party, 1–2; Three Strikes Law supported by, 130; victimhood and, 35
deterrence, Three Strikes Law and claims of, 134
Dickerson v. United States, 54–55
dignity, from victim impact statements, 103
District of Columbia v. Heller, 160–62
DNA evidence, statute of limitations and, 71, 200n89
Dockterman, Eliana, 197n29
Domanick, Joe, 222n40, 223n59
domestic violence, 18
Donohue, John, 155
Doyle, Charles, 196n10
D'Souza, Dinesh, 34
Dubber, Marcus, 92, 168n12
Dukakis, Michael, 1, 167n5, 167n6
Dweck, Carol, 41
Dworkin, Andrea, 173n60

egocentric victimhood, 35
egoism, of victimhood, 40
Eighteenth Amendment, 9–10, 18
Eighth Amendment, 84, 86, 101, 140, 143
emotion: in victim impact statements, 89, 110, 168n12; VRM's appeal to, 3
encoding, memory, 75
Enders, Adam, 35–36
End of Its Rope (Garrett), 63–64, 148
Enez, Edna, 108
England, common law in, 94
Epstein, Jeffrey, 65, 70
Estrich, Susan, 24, 26–27
Europe, gun violence in, 155–56
evidence: feminists and rules on, 19; statute of limitations and DNA, 71. See also victim impact statements and evidence
exclusionary rule, 57–59, 189n43, 190n50, 190n56

Family and Friends of Missing Persons, 14
faulty memory, statute of limitations, innocent defendants and, 75–80
Federal Bureau of Investigation (FBI), 151
felony murder, culpability and, 98, 207n107, 208n120

feminists: child sex abuse panic and, 174n77; evidentiary rules and, 19; law-and-order conservatives and, 18–20; pornography and, 173n60; racial bias and, 173n57; rape and sexual assault redefined by, 18–19, 177n32; sentencing complications and, 20–21; stand-your-ground laws and, 174n69; VRM and, 11, 18–21, 36

The Feminist War on Crime (Gruber), 11, 20, 39

fentanyl, sentencing and, 143–44, 228n162

Fifth Amendment, 54, 185n110

First Amendment, *Mapp v. Ohio* and, 56

Florida, 16

Floyd, George, 99

"forcible compulsion," 77

forgiveness, victimhood and, 47–48

Fortas, Abe, 52, 61

Fourth Amendment, 11, 13, 50; *Mapp v. Ohio* and, 56–57; *United States v. Calandra* and, 58

Frankfurter, Felix, 56

Frankl, Viktor, 41, 45

Furman v. Georgia, 12, 85

Garrett, Brandon, 63–64, 148

Garvin, Meg, 4, 16

Gascón, George, 229n165

Georgia, 114, 153–54

Gibbs, Jewelle Taylor, 172n51

Gideon v. Wainwright, 50, 107; failed promise of, 60–64; law-and-order conservatives on, 61; Sixth Amendment and, 60; unanimous ruling in, 61

Giffords Law Center to Prevent Gun Violence, 156

Gilbert v. California, 191n68

Ginsberg, Raphael, 109

Gossett, Holman, 215n216

Graham v. Florida, 198n54

Green, Bruce, 42

Greene, Marjorie Taylor, 33

Gross, Samuel, 115

Gruber, Aya, 22, 41, 44, 174n71, 174n74; on feminists uniting with VRM, 11, 20–21, 36; on spousal abuse victim cooperation at trial, 39; on Willie Horton ad, 1

guilt beyond reasonable doubt, 96, 185n110, 200n78, 202n103

guilty pleas, innocent defendants and, 62

gun control, 7; age limits and, 236n114; background check expansion legislation for, 159; Brady Bill for, 23, 158; in Europe, 155–56; lawsuits and, 146, 159–60; legislation, 6; Supreme Court on, 160–62; unreality of, 158–63; VRM and, 162–63

gun rights advocates: crime rates and, 155, 157; mental health care focus of, 145, 149, 230n4; political influence of, 146, 149, 154, 233n56; right-to-carry laws and, 155; stand-your-ground laws and, 174n69; Supreme Court and, 160–62. *See also* National Rifle Association

gun violence: in Buffalo shooting of 2022, 230n4; in Europe compared to United States, 155–56; firearm access causing, 156–57, 164; in Sandy Hook shooting, 145–48, 159; in suicide, 157, 164; against women, 156–57

harm, victim impact statements and evidence on, 89–90

Harvard Civil Rights-Civil Liberties Law Review, 41–42

Hawkins, Gordon, 117, 130, 137, 149, 156, 164

Hawley, Josh, 33

headline cases: misrepresented facts in, 119; politics driven by, 20, 80; Three Strikes Law and, 133, 138, 144; VRM utilizing, 9, 22

healing: criminal justice system and, 41–42; death penalty and, 104. *See also* "closure"

health care, 30–31, 145; ACA and Medicaid expansion of, 150–51, 153; HIFA waivers and, 150; mass incarceration and, 132; substance abuse treatment, 150. *See also* mental health care

Health Insurance Flexibility and Accountability (HIFA) waivers, 150

Hemenway, David, 155

Heritage Foundation, 12

Herring v. United States, 58–59

HIFA (Health Insurance Flexibility and Accountability) waivers, 150

Hill, Anita, 34
Hinckley, John, Jr., 158
Holder, Eric, 61
Holmes, James, 63–64, 148
Hopper, Jim, 75–76
Horton, Willie, 1, 167n5, 167n6
Horwitz, Robert B., 34–36, 179n11, 180n17
Hullinger, Charlotte and Bob, 14
Humane Justice, 46
Human Rights Watch, 17, 198n52

identity, trauma and, 182n56
Incapacitation (Zimring and Hawkins), 149
incarceration. See mass incarceration; sentencing
innocent defendants: guilty pleas and, 62; post-indictment lineups and, 191n68; statute of limitations, faulty memory and, 75–80
In re Cooper, 181n43
In re McNulty, 181n45
In re Roser, 181n43
interviewing techniques, in law enforcement, 80
intoxication, sexual assault and, 184n104

Jacobellis v. Ohio, 180n33
Jacob Wetterling Crimes Against Children and Sexually Violent Offender Registration Act, 1994, 15, 21, 171n47
Jácome, Elisa, 151
Jessica's Law, 15
John and Ken Show, 129
Johnson, Lyndon B., 52
Jones, Bill, 125
judicial elections, sentencing practices and, 118
juveniles, sentencing of, 198n54

Kamin, Sam, 117, 130, 137
Kanka, Megan, 15, 20
Kaplan, Margo, 27–28
Kaufman, Scott Barry, 40, 182n56
Kavanaugh, Brett, 162
Keegan v. Minneapolis & St. Louis R.R. Co., 207n99
Klaas, Joe, 139

Klaas, Polly, 123, 126–27, 139, 144
Kobylt, John, 129
Ku Klux Klan, 10

Lamont, Ned, 147
"Landmarks in Victims' Rights and Services," 14
Lanza, Adam, 145–48, 154, 159
Lanza, Nancy, 147
Last Call (Okrent), 18
law-and-order conservatives, 11–12; feminists and, 18–20; on Gideon v. Wainwright, 61; on Mapp v. Ohio, 57; on Miranda v. Arizona, 50; Nixon and, 52; power of, 170n27
law enforcement: interviewing techniques in, 80; Miranda v. Arizona work-arounds of, 55; post-indictment lineups and, 191n68; rape response of, 27; sexual assault training programs for, 27; urbanization and development of, 94; victimhood and cooperation with, 39
lawsuits, gun control and, 146, 159–60
legal victimhood, 180n24
legislation: Armed Career Criminal Act, 214n198; for background check expansion, 159; Brady Bill, 23, 158; Crime Victims' Rights Act of 2004, 26; gun control, 6; Jessica's Law, 15; Marsy's Law, 15–17, 26; Megan's Law, 15; Omnibus Crime Control Act of 1968, 53–54; PLCAA, 159, 162; "rape shield," 19; sex offender registration, 15, 17, 20–21, 171n47, 172n48, 174n74; on sexual assault, 19; stand-your-ground, 174n69; Victim and Witness Protect Act of 1982, 13, 83–84; Violence Against Women Act of 1994, 2, 23, 158; VOCA, 29; VRM, 2, 9. See also Three Strikes Law
lenity, principle of, 96
Lewis, Buck, 125
liberty, criminal law and, 96
Lightner, Candace, 14, 21, 26, 171n33, 172n50, 175n1
Linkletter v. Walker, 57
Loftus, Elizabeth, 76, 78–79
Los Angeles Times, 127
Lott, John, Jr., 155

Lungren, Dan, 125, 134, 138
Luttig, Michael, 89, 111–12, 116

MacKenzie, Doris L., 113
MacKinnon, Catharine, 173n60
MADD. *See* Mothers Against Drunk Driving
Malloy, Dannel, 147
Manchin, Joe, 159
Man's Search for Meaning (Frankl), 41, 45
Mapp v. Ohio, 11, 50; erosion of, 55–59; exclusionary rule and, 57–59, 190n50, 190n56; First Amendment and, 56; Fourth Amendment and, 56–57; law-and-order conservatives on, 57
Marceau, Justin, 114–15
Marsy's Law, 15–17, 26
Maryland Crime Victims' Resource Center, 14
Massachusetts, victimhood definition in, 37–38
mass incarceration, 3–4, 6; in California, 128, 219n1; cost of, 80–81; health care and, 132; sentencing reform to reverse, 218n266; Three Strikes Law and, 122, 138–42, 226n118; war on drugs and, 149–50
McCleskey v. Kemp, 113–14
McCulloch v. Maryland, 189n44
McDonald v. Chicago, 161
Medicaid expansion, 150–51, 153
Megan's Law, 15
memory: as malleable, 78–79; statute of limitations, innocent defendants and faulty, 75–80; trauma and processes of, 75, 79
mens rea: felony murder and, 98, 208n120; sexual assault and, 78
mental health: crime rates and, 149–52; extreme violence and, 148; of Landa, A., 147–48; psychological well-being and, 45–46; PTSD and, 104; in suicide, 157. *See also* psychological well-being
mental health care: access for, 149–52; gun rights advocates focusing on, 145, 149, 230n4; NRA and reform for, 152–54

#MeToo Movement, 3, 68
Michigan, victimhood definition in, 38
midlevel offenders, Three Strikes Law and, 118
Miller, Chanel, 43–47
Miller, Terrence, 193n95
Mindset (Dweck), 41
Minow, Martha, 41
Miranda v. Arizona, 11; *Brewer v. Williams* and, 54; Carrington on, 51; erosion of, 53–55; law-and-order conservative anger over, 50; law enforcement working around, 55; Nixon and, 55; Warren's statements on, 53–54
Missing Children's Assistance Act, 14–15
Mitchell, Ojmarrh, 113
mock jury research, on victim impact statements and death penalty, 111
Model Penal Code (MPC), 2, 97–98, 100, 207n100, 207n107
Morris, Herbert, 185n115
Mothers Against Drunk Driving (MADD), 1, 10; formation of, 14, 21; mission statement of, 26; sentencing goals of, 109–10
MPC (Model Penal Code), 2, 97–98, 100, 207n100, 207n107
multicollinearity, correlations and, 114
murder rates, COVID-19 pandemic and, 151
Murder Victims' Families for Reconciliation, 104

NAMI (National Alliance on Mental Illness), 153
Nassar, Larry, 91, 102, 104
National Alliance on Mental Illness (NAMI), 153
National Center for Missing and Exploited Children, 15
National Organization for Victim Assistance (NOVA), 14, 109
National Rifle Association (NRA), 6, 10, 123; mental health care reform and, 152–54; political influence of, 146, 149, 233n56; Second Amendment and, 152; stand-your-ground laws and, 174n69;

Three Strikes Law and, 17, 127, 172n51; VRM and, 158

Newsom, Gavin, 124

New York, 135, 161

New Yorker, 146, 154

New York State Rifle & Pistol Association, Inc. v. Bruen, 161–62

New York Times, 195n3

Nicholas, Henry, 15–16

Nicholas, Marsy, 15–16, 20

Nixon, Richard, 1, 11, 51; law-and-order conservatives and, 52; *Miranda v. Arizona* and, 55; Silent Majority and, 12, 129; Supreme Court appointments of, 52, 55; Warren Court and, 49–50

NOVA (National Organization for Victim Assistance), 14, 109

Novey, Don, 127–28

NRA. *See* National Rifle Association

NRA's Institute for Legislative Action (NRA-ILA), 152, 232n43

Nussbaum, Martha, 47

NYU Annual Survey of American Law, 94–95

Obama, Barack, 146

Ocasio-Cortez, Alexandria, 33

Ohio State Criminal Law Journal, 115

Okrent, Daniel, 18

Omnibus Crime Control Act, 1968, 53–54

PAC (Prosecutors Alliance of California), 229n165

Parents of Murdered Children, 14

parole, abandoning, 109

Paternoster, Raymond, 111

Payne v. Tennessee, 86–87, 90, 101, 116, 120

Pennsylvania, 69, 95

People v. Dillon, 208n121

peripheral details, memory and, 75

Persky, Aaron, 44–45, 117–19

Peters, Kevin, 128

Phillips, Scott, 114–15

PLCAA (Protection of Lawful Commerce in Arms Act), 159, 162

plea bargaining, 110, 193n85

politics: of criminal justice system, 130; gun rights advocates' influence in, 146, 149, 154, 233n56; headline cases driving, 20, 80; victimhood and, 32–36, 180n17; VRM history in, 1–2

Pope, Alexander, 47, 48

pornography, 18, 173n60

Posner, Richard, 136

post-indictment lineups, 191n68

posttraumatic stress disorder (PTSD), 73, 104

Powell, Lewis, 12, 52, 93, 99

Powell v. Alabama, 60

President's Task Force on Victims of Crime, 1982, 83–84, 92, 105–6, 117

principle of lenity, 96

procedural rights, 2

progressive reforms, 124, 142–44

Prohibition, 9–10, 18

Proposition 9, California, 16

Proposition 36, California, 140

Proposition 47, California, 140

Proposition 66, California, 128

Prosecutors Alliance of California (PAC), 229n165

Protection of Lawful Commerce in Arms Act (PLCAA), 159, 162

"protective retribution," 185n115

psychological well-being: "closure" and, 48; forgiveness and, 47–48; mental health and, 45–46; Seligman on, 45; victimhood and, 40–43. *See also* mental health

PTSD (posttraumatic stress disorder), 73, 104

public defenders, 61, 107, 193n95

punishment: certainty of, 198n53; cruel and unusual, 111–12; culpability and, 95–96, 98, 100–101; democracy and, 117–20, 228n154; victim impact statements and purposes of, 93–101; VRM contributing to excessive, 130. *See also* death penalty; sentencing

Punishment and Democracy (Zimring, Hawkins, Kamin), 117, 130, 137

purposes of punishment, victim impact statements and, 93–101 racial bias: in criminal justice system, 3–4; death penalty and, 113–16; feminists and, 173n57; inadequate counsel and, 63–64; in sentencing, 5, 113–16, 121; statistical damages tables and, 209n126; tort law considering, 99; victim compensation funds and, 29–30; victim impact statements and, 110, 113–16, 121

RAINN (Rape, Abuse, and Incest National Network), 70, 74

RAND Corporation, 136, 155

rape: criminal justice system ignoring victims of, 2; feminists redefining, 18–19, 177n32; "forcible compulsion" and, 77; law enforcement response to, 27; "self-deception" and, 199n64; serial, statute of limitations and, 70, 73–75; Turner case study on, 43–48

Rape, Abuse, and Incest National Network (RAINN), 70, 74

rape reform, VRM and, 26–28

"rape shield" laws, 19

Reagan, Ronald, 1, 11, 51, 158

Real Rape (Estrich), 27

reasonable doubt, guilt beyond, 96, 185n110, 200n78, 202n103

Rebutting the Myths about Race and the Death Penalty (Scheidegger), 115

Reeves, Tate, 33

Regina v. Cunningham, 97

rehabilitating offenders, victim impact statements for, 92, 106

Rehnquist, William, 50, 52, 55, 86, 90, 99–100, 116

Remington, 146, 159–60, 230n9

Republican Party, 1–2; on Buffalo shooting of 2022, 230n4; Three Strikes Law supported by, 130; victimhood and, 32–36. *See also* law-and-order conservatives

residential burglary, as qualifying felony under Three Strikes Law, 131–32, 137, 224n86

resources, for restitution, 30

restitution, VRM and, 29–31, 39

restorative justice: aim of, 183n71; "closure" and, 212n163; components of, 105; need

for, 182n66; responsibility taken in, 185n110; victimhood and, 42

retributive proportionality, Three Strikes Law and, 133, 224n85

Reynolds, Kimber, 124–25, 144

Reynolds, Mike, 123, 125–29, 139, 172n50, 222n40

Richard, Martin, 105

right-to-carry laws, 155

right to counsel, 61–63, 107, 192n82

risk-assessment measures, for sentencing, 43

Roberts, John, 58–59, 162

Romano, Michael, 140

Romero, Philip, 136, 222n58

Roper, Roberta, 14, 109

Roper, Stephanie, 14

Rotunno, Donna, 195n9

Ryder, Winona, 126

Salarno, Nina, 141

Sanders, Bernie, 2

Sandy Hook shooting, 145–48, 159

Scalia, Antonin, 55, 87, 100, 160–61

Scheidegger, Kent, 115

Schumer, Chuck, 1

Schwarzenegger, Arnold, 139

Second Amendment, 7, 152, 159–62, 236n108, 236n114

second-strike provision, in Three Strikes Law, 125–26, 132, 224n84

"self-deception," rape and, 199n64

self-defined victimhood, 180n24

self-rehabilitation, statute of limitations and, 198n52

Seligman, Martin, 41, 45–46

sentencing: blameworthiness and, 86; bodily injury and, 96–97; in California, 119, 141–44; culpability and, 95–96; democracy and, 117–20, 228n154; feminists and complications over, 20–21; fentanyl and, 143–44, 228n162; Jessica's Law on, 15; judicial elections and practices in, 118; of juveniles, 198n54; MADD's goals for, 109–10; mass incarceration and reform of, 218n266; racial bias in, 5, 113–16, 121; risk-assessment measures for, 43; of Turner, 43–44; victim impact statements in, 84, 108–16, 120–21; VRM on minimum, 61–62. *See also* death penalty; Three Strikes Law

Sered, Danielle, 106

serial rapists, statute of limitations and, 70, 73–75

sex offender registration legislation, 15, 17, 20–21, 171n47, 172n48, 174n74

sexual assault: Boy Scouts of America and claims of, 69; by Catholic priests, 68–69; Cosby and, 70; Epstein and, 70; feminists redefining, 18–19, 177n32; "forcible compulsion" and, 77; intoxication and, 184n104; law enforcement training programs on, 27; legislation on, 19; mens rea and, 78; statute of limitations in cases of, 28, 68–71; Turner case study on, 43–48; Weinstein and, 69. *See also* rape

Shepard, Matthew, 105

Silent Majority, 12, 35, 129

Sixth Amendment, 28, 38, 50, 177n33; *Gideon v. Wainwright* and, 60; post-indictment lineups and, 191n68; right to counsel and, 63

social harm, criminal law and, 96–97

social media, factual distortions on, 119

Social Security Disability Insurance, 232n41

Society for Human Resource Management, 232n41

sociocultural victimhood, 180n24

Solomon, Andrew, 147

South Carolina v. Gathers, 85–86

spousal abuse victims, cooperation at trial of, 39

Stailey, Glen, 141

Stanford Law Review, 155

Staples v. United States, 97

statistical damages tables, racial bias and, 209n126

statute of limitations: Boy Scouts of America, sexual assault and, 69; Catholic priest sexual assault and, 68–69; in child sex abuse cases, 66–67; "closure" opportunities by expanding, 70; "closure" re-evaluation and, 72–73; Cosby sexual assault cases and, 70; counterargu-

ments against eliminating or extending, 72–80; culpability and, 70, 73–75; DNA evidence and, 71, 200n89; Epstein sexual assault cases and, 70; faulty memory, convicting innocent defendants and, 75–80; federal law on, 66; overview of, 66–68; self-rehabilitation and, 198n52; serial rapists and, 70, 73–75; in sexual assault cases, 28, 68–71; state law on, 67; support for eliminating or extending, 65–66, 70–71; Weinstein sexual assault cases and, 69

Stephanie Roper Family Assistance Committee, 14

Stewart, James Potter, 37, 39, 54

Stone, Geoffrey, 60

storage, memory, 75

Strauss, David, 60

substance abuse treatment, 150

suicide, gun violence in, 157, 164

Supreme Court: on culpability, 97; on death penalty, 84–87; Nixon's appointments to, 52, 55; on Second Amendment, 7, 160–62, 236n108; on victim impact statements and evidence, 84–87, 90. *See also* Warren Court; *specific cases*

survivorship, victimhood compared to, 45–48

systemic victimhood, 35–36

Take Back the Night, 18

Taslitz, Andrew E., 199n64

Tennessee, 87

Thomas, Clarence, 34, 161–62, 236n108

Thompson v. Oklahoma, 198n54

Thornberry, Homer, 52

Three Strikes Law, California, 6; alternative bills to, 129; CCPOA and, 17–18, 218n263; city-by-city comparisons with, 135–36; Committee on Revision of the Penal Code and, 140–42; crime rates and, 134–36; Democrats and Republicans voting for, 130; deterrence claims with, 134; excesses of, 117–18, 130, 136–38, 142; goal with, 109–10; grieving fathers and origins of, 124–30; headline cases and, 133, 138, 144;

Three Strikes Law (*cont.*)
impact of, 130–38; judicial challenges to, 139–40; mass incarceration and, 122, 138–42, 226n118; midlevel offenders and, 118; misleading literature supporting, 131; NRA and, 17, 127, 172n51; overview of, 122–24; passage of, 117; Proposition 66 for reform of, 128; public regret for supporting, 138–39; reforming, 142–44; residential burglary as qualifying felony under, 131–32, 137, 224n86; retributive proportionality and, 133, 224n85; savings claims with, 136, 222n58; second-strike provision in, 125–26, 132, 224n84; voter initiatives for reforming, 140; Washington state influencing, 125, 127

Toomey, Pat, 159

tort law, 94, 99

trauma: identity and, 182n56; memory processes and, 75, 79; victimhood and, 40, 73

Trump, Donald, 32, 33, 42

Turner, Brock, 32, 43–48, 78–80, 117–19, 201nn92–93

unhealthy victimhood, 41

Uniform Crime Reports, FBI, 151

United States v. Calandra, 58

United States v. Hunter, 181n45

United States v. Leon, 58, 59

United States v. Miller, 160–61

United States v. Wade, 191n68

urbanization, law enforcement development and, 94

Victim and Witness Protection Act, 1982, 13, 83–84

victim compensation funds, 29–31, 39, 232n40

victimhood, 4–5; "closure" and, 48; Conservative Movement and, 32–36; counting, 146–48; defining, 37–39, 146, 174n71; egocentric, 35; egoism of, 40; forgiveness and, 47–48; forms of, 180n24; law enforcement cooperation and, 39; politics and, 32–37, 180n17; prevention of, 145; psychological well-being and, 40–43; restorative justice and, 42; survivorship compared to, 45–48; systemic, 35–36; tendency for interpersonal, 40; trauma and, 40, 73; Trump on, 32, 33, 42; Turner case study on, 43–48; unhealthy, 41; victims of, 179n11

victim impact statements and evidence, 5, 13, 82, 204n49; arguments against, 93–107; basic fairness and, 92–93, 107; blameworthiness and, 86, 93; for "closure," 90–92, 101–6, 205n59; Confrontation Clause and, 88; death penalty and, 108–12; dignity from, 103; early days of, 83–88; emotion in, 89, 110, 168n12; on harm, 89–90; of Miller, C., in Turner case, 44, 46; mock jury research on death penalty and, 111; *Payne v. Tennessee* and, 101, 120; purposes of punishment and, 93–101; racial bias and, 110, 113–16, 121; for rehabilitating offenders, 92, 106; in sentencing, 84, 108–16, 120–21; in states, 84; support for, 88–93; Supreme Court on, 84–87, 90; therapeutic benefits to, 103; victimhood definition and, 38; voluntary participation for, 91

victim programs, 14

The Victims (Carrington), 12, 51, 109

Victims' Bill of Rights, California, 25–26

Victims of Crime Act (VOCA), 1984, 29

Victims' Rights Movement (VRM): basic fairness and, 24–26; Cassell on critics of, 229n1; coalition around, 10; constitutional amendment aim of, 4, 9, 82; on criminal justice system rebalancing, 13; early days of, 11–13, 51; emotional appeal of, 3; excessive punishment contributions of, 130; feminists and, 11, 18–21, 36; gun control and, 162–63; headline cases utilized by, 9, 22; history of, 9–22; legislation, 2, 9; members abandoning, 21–22; on minimum sentences, 61–62; NRA and, 158; organizations joining, 14–18; *Payne v. Tennessee* advancing, 87; political history of, 1–2; rape reform and, 26–28; staying power of, 22; success of, 1, 4, 23–31; victim compensation funds, restitution and, 29–31, 39; Warren Court and evolution of, 51–53

Violence Against Women Act, 1994, 2, 23, 158

Virginia, 38

VOCA (Victims of Crime Act), 1984, 29

Vogler, Jacob, 150–51

"The Voodoo Economics of California Crime" (Zimring), 136

VRM. *See* Victims' Rights Movement

Vulture, 195n3

Wallace, George, 52

Walsh, Adam, 14–15, 20, 172n50, 175n1

Walsh, John, 171n35

war on drugs, 3, 149–50

Warren, Earl, 50; *Miranda v. Arizona* statements of, 53–54; retirement of, 52

Warren Court, 2–3; basic fairness issues with, 25; Carrington on, 49, 60, 64, 107; controversial decisions of, 50; criminal procedure revolution of, 49, 51, 60; 1968 presidential election and, 51–52; Nixon and, 49–50; VRM's early days and, 11–13; VRM's evolution and, 51–53. *See also Gideon v. Wainwright; Mapp v. Ohio; Miranda v. Arizona*

Washington, Three Strikes Law in, 125, 127

Washington Coalition of Sexual Assault Programs, 28

Waxman, Olivia, 18

Weeks v. United States, 56

Weinstein, Harvey, 5, 65–66, 195n3; lawyers retained by, 195n9; sexual assault cases against, 69

West Memphis Three, 193n85

Wetterling, Jacob, 21, 171n47

Wetterling, Patty, 21–22, 171n47, 172n50

"Whom the State Kills" (Phillips and Marceau), 114–15

Wilson, Genarlow, 174n74

Wilson, James Q., 155

Wilson, Pete, 129

Wolf v. Colorado, 56

women, gun violence against, 156–57

Women's Movement, 9–10, 18–21, 173n57

Woodworth, George, 113

Zimring, Frank, 117; on access to firearms and gun violence, 156, 164; on "closure," 102; on Three Strikes Law, 130, 132–34, 136–37; on war on drugs, 149

ABOUT THE AUTHOR

MICHAEL VITIELLO is Distinguished Professor of Law at McGeorge School of Law. He is a nationally recognized expert on criminal law, sentencing policy, and marijuana law. The U.S. Supreme Court cited his first article on California's Three Strikes Law. He is a member of the American Law Institute and has worked on projects reforming the Model Penal Code.